Early Debates about Industry

Early Debates about Industry

Voltaire and His Contemporaries

Florian Schui

palgrave
macmillan

First published in 2005 by
PALGRAVE MACMILLAN
Houndmills, Basingstoke, Hampshire RG21 6XS and
175 Fifth Avenue, New York, N.Y. 10010
Companies and representatives throughout the world.

PALGRAVE MACMILLAN is the global academic imprint of the Palgrave Macmillan division of St. Martin's Press, LLC and of Palgrave Macmillan Ltd. Macmillan® is a registered trademark in the United States, United Kingdom and other countries. Palgrave is a registered trademark in the European Union and other countries.

ISBN-13: 978–1–4039–4799–4 hardback
ISBN-10: 1–4039–4799–6 hardback

This book is printed on paper suitable for recycling and made from fully managed and sustained forest sources.

A catalogue record for this book is available from the British Library.

Library of Congress Cataloging-in-Publication Data

Schui, Florian, 1973–
Early debates about industry : Voltaire and his contemporaries / Florian Schui.
p. cm.
Includes bibliographical references and index.
ISBN 1–4039–4799–6 (cloth)
1. Industries – France – Philosophy. 2. Industrialization – Philosophy. 3. Industrialization – Europe – History – 18th century. 4. Voltaire, 1694–1778 – Political and social views. I. Title.

HC275.S366 2005
338.94′009′033—dc22 2005049294

10 9 8 7 6 5 4 3 2 1
14 13 12 11 10 09 08 07 06 05

Printed and bound in Great Britain by
Antony Rowe Ltd, Chippenham and Eastbourne

For my parents

Contents

Acknowledgements

My interest in the subject of this book dates back to a seminar paper which I wrote in a class on the history of economic thought of the late Professor Robert Heilbroner at the New School for Social Research. I am indebted to Professor Heilbroner for inspiring my interest in the history of eighteenth-century economic thought.

The book in its current form is based on my doctoral dissertation which I completed at St Edmund's College, University of Cambridge, in 2004. The manuscript was written during the first year of my post-doctoral Junior Research Fellowship at St Edmund's College. I am grateful for the support from the college and from Hans-Böckler Foundation. During the work on the dissertation, I have received advice and encouragement from many sides. In particular I would like to thank my supervisor Ms Emma Rothschild for reading the long drafts of the dissertation. I am indebted to her for her insightful comments and her support. I also owe a great deal to the discussion with my examiners Professor Colin Jones and Professor Gareth Stedman Jones. Their comments on the dissertation were crucial for the preparation of the manuscript. Among those who have read and commented on the dissertation or parts of it, I am particularly grateful to Jennifer Fronc, Sunil Amrith, William O'Reilly, Gabriel Paquette, Gemma Simmonds and David Todd. I would also like to thank Professor Stephen Frowen for his support and Nikolay Belkov, who translated a Russian article for me. I am grateful to Amanda Hamilton, Economics Publisher at Palgrave-Macmillan for commissioning this book and supporting me throughout the production process. I also am indebted to Katie Button and everybody at Palgrave Macmillan who was involved with the production of the book for their support and advice.

During the archival research the support of Dr Ingeborg Schelling-Reinicke and her colleagues at Geheimes Staatsarchiv Preußischer Kulturbesitz in Berlin-Dahlem was invaluable. The staff of Leibniz Archiv in Hannover and Musée et Institut Voltaire in Geneva have also helped me greatly in my research. I would like to thank the director of Leibniz Archiv, Prof. Dr Herbert Berger, and the Curator of the Musée et Institut Voltaire, Charles Wirz, for their kind support. I am indebted to the staff at the following libraries and archives: National Archives, Kew, New York Public Library, University Library, Cambridge and

Staatsbibliothek, Berlin. The cover image is used by kind permission of the Syndics of Cambridge University Library. I would also like to express my gratitude to Inga Huld Markan and her colleagues at the Centre for History and Economics, King's College, for their friendliness and their help.

The Hans-Böckler Foundation, Düsseldorf, has provided me with generous financial support throughout my PhD. I am grateful for the commitment of Prof. Dr Dietmar Petzina, who has followed my work on behalf of the Foundation. I am equally thankful for grants from the Cambridge European Trust, St Edmund's College and the Centre for History and Economics.

I would also like to thank my family and friends for their unfailing support. And last but certainly not least: thank you, Rita, for being wonderful and for supporting my work.

Introduction

> At that time a revolution began in commerce, in the power of nations, in customs, in industry, and in the government of all nations.
>
> Abbé Raynal, *Histoire philosophique et politique des établissements et du commerce des Européens dans les deux Indes* (7 vols, Amsterdam, 1770), I, p. 1

> Reason and industry will always make new steps forward.
>
> Voltaire, 'Conclusion et examen de ce tableau historique' (1763), *M*, XXIV, p. 475

Industry has been at the centre of some of the most formidable political and economic debates of the nineteenth, twentieth, and twenty-first centuries. This book is concerned with the pivotal decades of the eighteenth century in which industry became, for the first time, the focus of heated debates in France and in many other European countries. Voltaire and other prominent thinkers of the enlightenment[1] were involved in these controversies in which the modern concept of industry developed. However, the concept of industry and the great accounts of the rise of industry are not normally associated with the authors of the enlightenment. Many historians have even questioned whether the contemporaries were at all aware of the great economic changes that began to happen under their eyes. In a way this book is an attempt to rehabilitate the thinkers of the enlightenment who stand accused of ignoring the beginnings of one of the greatest transformations in the history of humanity. This study aims to contribute to a more complete picture of the debates of the enlightenment by concentrating on an extensive public controversy about industry that occurred in the second and third quarters of the eighteenth century: many contemporary observers were keenly aware of the rise of industry and tried to understand, predict, and shape its development. In order to conceptualise this new economic development, the term 'industry' started to be used to mean the rapidly growing manufacturing sector. In this period the older qualitative meaning of the term 'industry' (in the sense of 'industrious') began to take second rank and the modern meaning, denoting the economic sector of manufacturing (in the sense of 'industrial'), started to appear in contemporary debates. In a more general sense this book is an enquiry into the way in which a new economic concept emerged in the context of the interaction of rapidly changing ideas, policies and economic reality in the eighteenth century. For it seems that the real problem is not the lack of contemporary awareness of the rise of industry, but an incomplete understanding of the concepts that eighteenth-century authors used in order to discuss the economic transformation that they saw. The development of the concept of industry in the debates of the enlightenment is therefore at the centre of this study.[2]

The modern concept of industry developed in an extraordinarily dynamic century. Ideas, policies and economic reality changed quickly in the eighteenth century. It was truly an 'age of revolutions': it saw the rise of the enlightenment which forever changed the world of ideas, profound economic transformations that led to the 'industrial revolution', political changes that culminated in revolutions in France and North America and an unprecedented cosmopolitan exchange of goods and ideas. Not least, the century also saw the first globally fought conflict: the Seven Years War. In what follows I will mainly be concerned with the interaction of the progress of the enlightenment and the rise of industry. These two processes changed the world of the contemporaries more profoundly than any other transformation process of the period and they also formed the specific context in which the modern concept of industry emerged. This enquiry will focus mainly on the interaction of the two processes in France and to a lesser extent in Prussia and Russia. The enlightenment and the rise of industry were European phenoma, but France was in many ways at the centre of the development: the salons of Paris were the hotbeds of enlightenment thought. French debates influenced the thought and language of contemporaries across Europe. At the same time, France was the largest industrial nation in the eighteenth century. Its industrial growth was equal to that of England or perhaps even faster. Products, technologies and fashions were exported from France to the rest of Europe and other parts of the world. However, before going on to illuminate the evolution of the concept of industry in French and European debates of the period it will be useful to briefly discuss the understanding of 'the enlightenment' and 'the rise of industry' on which this study is based.

The enlightenment

The term 'enlightenment', referring to the great transformation that changed the intellectual landscape of the eighteenth century, was coined by the contemporaries themselves. While France was a centre of the turbulent debates of the enlightenment, the changes reached even some of the most remote regions. In provincial Königsberg, Immanuel Kant reflected on the question 'What is enlightenment?' His answer – famous to this day – was not humble. 'Enlightenment', he wrote, 'is man's release from his self-incurred tutelage'. He was well placed to give this answer. After all, he was one of the most important exponents of enlightenment thought. Writing in 1784, Kant had been concerned with the lack of self-determination that man left behind. Roughly 150 years later, Theodor Adorno and Max Horkheimer focused on the state of self-determination which man had entered: the principal aim of the enlightenment, they found, had been to install human beings as 'masters'. The different attempts to disenchant the world and to 'control praxis' gave rise to a new intellectual paradigm which became dominant in the eighteenth century.[3]

And a powerful new paradigm it was. 'Pure insight', Hegel wrote about the period of the enlightenment, spread like 'a perfume in unresisting atmosphere'. Movement was in fact an integral part of the new intellectual paradigm: ideas, individuals and goods travelled on an unprecedented scale. Voltaire's works, Herder marvelled, were read from Lisbon to Kamchatka and from Zembla to the Indian colonies. One may add that this diffusion was not always easy: Voltaire was also censored from Berlin to Transylvania. And while Herder was celebrating the success of Voltaire's works, Voltaire himself expressed his amazement at the fact that he was following the latest events in India from his home in the Swiss mountains. No region of the world and no aspect of life were safe from the critical scrutiny of the enlightenment. Superstitions collapsed with a 'Bautz! Baradautz!', as Hegel pointed out onomatopoeically. Under the assault of the *philosophes*, natural phenomena found new explanations, religious beliefs were scrapped, and social institutions crumbled. Even activities as prosaic as the production and consumption of goods were not safe from the hunger for knowledge and critical enquiry that defined this age. As Condorcet noted when he edited Voltaire's works towards the end of the century, it was around the middle of the century that Voltaire and others began to debate the matters of political economy with great passion. The concept of industry was central to these debates and must therefore be central to the history of thought of the eighteenth century.[4]

The unfamiliar views and language of these early debates about industry make it at times difficult to fully understand the contemporary comments but the historian of ideas neglects them at his own peril. 'An

Aufklärung', Franco Venturi warned, 'which does not mention the state, the land, or commerce, is clipped in at least one of its wings.' The present enquiry would like to add 'industry' to this list. For too long enlightenment thinkers have been portrayed as otherworldly philosophers who were mainly concerned with esoteric scientific experiments and obsessed with their fight against the Christian religion. Today this distorted picture has largely been overcome. Peter Gay and Nannerl Keohane have drawn our attention to the pragmatic political concerns of many enlightenment authors; Maxine Berg has illuminated the contemporary concern with a rich and rapidly changing material culture; and Albert Hirschmann and others have explored the enlightenment origins of political and economic concepts. Increasingly historians have studied the worldly concerns of enlightenment thinkers: specific political and economic questions were at the centre of many controversies of the period. However, the contemporary controversies about the prosaic activities of manufacturing have not received much attention from intellectual and cultural historians. Noteworthy exceptions are the works of Emma Rothschild and Michael Sonenscher who have illuminated the debates about the guilds and trades in eighteenth-century France. But while economic historians have written extensively about the rise of industry in the period, the contemporary debates about industry have hardly been illuminated by intellectual historians. This book examines a heretofore unexplored sphere of enlightenment concerns which was central to many contemporary debates: the fascination of many enlightenment thinkers with the new and rapidly expanding phenomenon of industry.[5]

The rise of industry

The rapid increase of manufacturing output was the second great transformation process of the eighteenth century besides the progress of the enlightenment. The eighteenth century was clearly a century of new ways of producing and consuming. Above all it was a century of producing and consuming more manufactured goods. The sector of manufacturing grew rapidly and much faster than other parts of the economy. The production of textiles, glass wares, iron tools, furniture, carts, carriages and innumerable other manufactured goods multiplied. Eventually industry irreversibly supplanted the traditional economy in the 'industrial revolution' and became the dominating economic sector. This development made itself felt already throughout the eighteenth century. In France, for example, manufacturing output quadrupled between 1700 and the 1780s. The strong growth and the fact that France was western Europe's most populous country made France the principal industrial nation of eighteenth-century Europe.[6] The transformation did not go unnoticed by the contemporaries in France and elsewhere. In 1770 Raynal wrote of a 'revolution' in commerce and industry. This change, he was convinced, had started since trade and conquest had linked the European nations to many distant territories. The description of economic change as 'revolutionary' was not unique to Raynal. Six years later Condillac predicted a 'revolution in commerce, arts, and agriculture' if international and domestic trade continued to grow. In a similar vein Voltaire wrote about the way in which industry had begun to join together all parts of the globe. And while these authors were praising the rise of industry, Rousseau complained in his *Reveries of a solitary walker* that even in the most remote parts of Switzerland his lakeside walks were now disturbed by the 'clickety-clack' of a factory that made stockings.[7] Raynal, Condillac, Voltaire, Rousseau and their contemporaries saw the growth of a phenomenon which has since become a defining feature of the modern world: industry. Economic historians have not been shy to put important labels on this development. The 'industrial revolution' has been called the 'the most fundamental transformation of human life in the history of the world recorded in written documents'. An event so important that it compares to the 'advent of monotheism' and the 'development of written language'. While economic historians agree about the impact of the rise of industry they differ greatly about the reasons, the trajectory and the timing of the economic change. As one prominent economic historian points out in a survey of the literature, 'little agreement has emerged about fundamental questions'.[8]

A close reading of contemporary observations may help to answer some of the open questions about the rise of industry or at least help to ask the right questions. Many historians voice deep reservations about the observations of contemporary commentators: 'How can we be certain that they actually saw what they thought they saw?', is a frequently asked question.[9] Clearly, contemporary comments can not be taken at face value. However, no historical source material can, and the number of contradictory views about the rise of industry held by economic historians today does not necessarily inspire confidence in modern explanations. Today's methods are without a doubt more sophisticated, but as D. McCloskey underlines 'the evidence is thin'. Most accounts of the rise of industry therefore include to some extent contemporary observations as evidence. Accounts of travellers are among the most frequently used sources but also folk songs and other more colourful material is sometimes used. However, contemporary observations should not be treated merely as an inferior substitute of other forms of evidence. They are historical sources about the rise of industry in their own right. Patrick O'Brien and Caglar Keyder in their quantitative work on industrial growth emphasise that 'statistics must ... be placed in context' and go on to discuss a number of contemporary observations. Similarly, Gareth Stedman Jones recommends to reconsider the 'at first sight quirkish' contemporary views of Jean-Baptiste Say about the industrial revolution. Eric Hobsbawm warns in his *Industry and empire* not to neglect contemporary observations and devotes the opening chapter of his study to these sources. And even Joel Mokyr, despite his pronounced scepticism about the accuracy of contemporary observation, emphasises that the observations of pre-Adamite writers constitute a 'body of evidence' about that rise of industry 'that requires scrupulous attention'. However, even where historians have discussed contemporary observations they are mostly concerned with comments on specific aspects of industrialisation such as the development of single factories or the application of certain technologies. Hardly any attention has been paid to contemporary perceptions of industry as a whole. The principal reason for this is that historians have simply assumed that the contemporaries were unaware of the rise of industry. However, contemporaries were keenly aware, and their comments are an important source about the economic development of the period. As Joseph Schumpeter points out, one of the answers to the question 'Why do we study the history of economics?', is: 'to derive new inspiration'. Contemporary observations about the rise of industry and the language in which they were expressed sometimes seem unfamiliar and even nonsensical to the modern reader. Often they do not fit into an imaginary straight line of development of the history of economic thought. And without any doubt they need to be approached critically. However, they should not be ignored. For if they are closely read and discussed in their historical context they are an important body of historical evidence and a source of inspiration for modern interpretations and theorising about the rise of industry.[10]

In particular, eighteenth-century observations lend strong support to an explanation for the rise of industry proposed by the economic historian Jan de Vries. He argues that the key to an understanding of the 'industrial revolution' of the nineteenth century is the concept of an 'industrious revolution' which took place in the seventeenth and eighteenth centuries. His explanation focuses on the fundamental change in economic behaviour. Changes in the 'industrious disposition' of individuals, he argues, preceded large scale mechanisation and were more important in bringing about the economic transition. Strikingly, the two 'companion concepts' put forward by De Vries – 'industrial' and 'industrious' revolution – reflect the two connotations in which the term industry was used in the eighteenth century.[11] As we will see, contemporary perspectives support and illuminate de Vries's approach but also suggest new lines of inquiry. The fact that the concept of industry was coined before the advent of large scale mechanisation suggests that the key characteristics of industry are not associated to any particular type of machinery. The machinery used in industry has changed in its long history and continues to change. Rather than by specific techniques, industry is characterised by the dispositions and conditions of the individuals that participate in this sector of production and by the rules that govern their interaction. This view emerges clearly from contemporary perspectives on industry and supports de Vries's concentration on changes in economic behaviour as a driving force behind the rise of industry. However, contemporary observations also differ from the picture that de Vries paints in important ways. His approach concentrates on increased labour time as a result of widespread changes in demand patterns. Eighteenth-century concerns with industry were at the same time narrower and broader. They were narrower in the sense that contemporaries mostly associated the shift in demand patterns with the king and wealthy individuals. At the same time their concerns were broader because they also included a discussion on the increase of the quality of the labour and the creation of an adequate institutional environment: the men of industry worked not only more hours but they were also more skilled and dextrous and their work was often organised in new ways. Also, they worked in an environment free from the feudal rules and the regulations of the corporations. There was, therefore, a strong concern in the eighteenth century with conflicts of the existing institutional order of the Ancien Régime and the growth of industry. By illuminating contemporary ideas about industry, our attention is drawn to aspects which have not received sufficient attention in modern explanations of the rise of industry.

The development of the concept of industry

This study is concerned with the way in which the concept of industry developed in the context of the rise of industry and the progress of enlightenment. These processes were not merely contemporaneous. They interacted and depended on each other in many ways. Often the progress of industry and enlightenment involved the same individuals, happened in the same places, and reflected the same attitudes: since the

1760s Matthew Boulton's state of the art factory near Birmingham attracted visits from some of the most prominent princes, administrators and authors of the enlightenment. Boulton's four hundred workers initially produced a wide range of consumer products. The products included buttons, snuff boxes and candelabra. The factory became an even bigger international attraction when it began to produce James Watt's steam engine. At the same time, Watt, Boulton and many of the manufacturers and inventors who were close to them had strong ties to the intellectual life in France. They thought of themselves as members of the European family of *philosophes* and sent their sons to the continent to be educated in the spirit of the new intellectual current that flourished in France. If the inventors and early industrialists of the period saw themselves as a part of the intellectual movement of the enlightenment, many of the *philosophes* were not less accustomed to being part of the economic and political world of their time: Helvetius was not only the author of some of the most influential tracts of the enlightenment but he was also a high-ranking official in the French tax administration; Turgot was equally at home in the salons of Paris and in the government offices of Limoges and Paris where he served as *intendant* and minister; and Voltaire was not only the most famous author of the enlightenment but also one of the most successful entrepreneurs of the period. Economic, technical, scientific and intellectual change were equally at the heart of contemporary interest. The close ties are well illustrated by an anecdote from a contemporary travel diary. In June 1760 the noted playwright and collaborator of the *Encyclopaedia* Jean François Marmontel was on his way to Paris after a journey through the south of France. In his *Memoirs* he tells his readers about the difficulties in deciding on a travel itinerary for himself and his fellow traveller *Monsieur* Gaulard. Should they first go to see Lyon with its 'master-pieces of industry' or to Ferney in order to visit Voltaire, the most prominent of enlightenment thinkers? The philosopher was apparently considered to be the greater attraction. The visit to Lyon's industry was left for the return trip.[12]

The concept of industry developed in the context of manifold links between economic reality and intellectual disposition. It may be said that the new concept was one of the offsprings of the 'happy marriage' that Francis Bacon described between 'human rationality' and 'the nature of things'. The way for the progress of industry was prepared by the scientific discoveries, the technical inventions, the conception of man and the intellectual disposition of the enlightenment. However, the intrinsic link between the rise of enlightenment and industry worked both ways.

It was this joint progress that Voltaire described when he predicted that 'reason and industry will always make new steps forward'.[13] The application of the social and political vision of the enlightenment depended in many ways on the growth of industry. In particular, the concept of individual freedom was difficult to reconcile with the political, social and economic structures of the Ancien Régime. The evolution of industry and enlightenment were thus dependent on each other and linked by a constant exchange of stimuli and impulses. However, many details of this interaction, or – to use Bacon's analogy – the every day life of the happy marriage between intellectual and economic evolution remain in the dark. How did economic change and political and economic thought in the eighteenth century interact? How were the changes in manufacturing perceived and how did the way that the economic reality was conceptualised contribute to shape it? However indiscreet this undertaking may be, it is necessary to illuminate the minute details of the marriage between the enlightenment and the rise of industry in order to understand how the concept of industry was born, raised and how it eventually started a life of its own.

The development of the concept of industry is reflected in the semantic change of the term. Before the period that this enquiry is concerned with, an author who wrote of 'industry' was most likely referring to a character trait of a person. In particular, the attribute 'industry' would be used for a skilful, inventive or industrious person. Around the middle of the eighteenth century an extraordinary semantic transition took place. While the term industry continued to be used for individual qualities, it began to take on a new meaning. It started to denote the sum of individual qualities applied to the goal of manufacturing goods. It thus became an abstract term summarising the multitude of activities that are part of the production of manufactured goods. In the eighteenth century the term was sometimes also used in an even broader sense. It was then understood to include the production and exchange of all goods, thus including commerce and agriculture. This meaning was superseded by the more narrow connotation of 'activities in manufacturing'. Nevertheless, the broader meaning lingers on today in terms such as 'entertainment industry' or 'agricultural industry'. Raymond Williams points out in his *Keywords*, that the two basic connotations of the term industry are best defined by the corresponding adjectives 'industrious' and 'industrial'.[14] In what follows the former connotation will be referred to as the 'qualitative meaning' while the latter will be called the 'sectoral meaning'. One must, however, bear in mind that in the actual use of the term 'industry' the two connotations cannot always be distinguished clearly. The ambiguity of the term in the transition period of the eighteenth century reflects the struggle of those who used it to conceptualise the economic reality of their time.

The semantic shift from the qualitative to the sectoral meaning also reflects a shift of attention. Contemporaries in eighteenth-century France felt that a new abstract term for activities as prosaic and as different as the making of pottery and weaving was needed in order to conceptualise the profound transformation that many trades were undergoing. In a remarkable way the new term abstracts from the concrete process of making a piece of fabric or a pot to a level of something that would later be called 'the economy'. Individuals cannot make industry their trade or profession. They can only become weavers or potters. And yet, by adopting the trade of potter or weaver the individual becomes part of industry. The term is thus not associated with any particular tool, trade or production process. Instead, the term emphasises the common economic function of a great number of very different activities: the production of goods.

The new word did not appear quietly: it was formed in some of the most heated controversies of the eighteenth century. Prominent authors of the time such as Voltaire were suddenly concerned with the advantages and disadvantages of the phenomenon that came to be known as industry. It is with this singular shift of attention and the associated semantic development that the present enquiry will be concerned. In 1795, the newly found interest in industry resulted in the publication of a *Dictionary of industry* in six volumes. Under the common heading of 'industry' the editor of the work, Henri-Gabriel Duchesne, assembled over two thousand entries about trades and techniques as diverse as apiculture, the construction of windmills, and the production of paper. In his introduction Duchesne put particular emphasis on the fact that finally the 'human industry' received the same attention as the 'imposing spectacle of nature'. His vision was of a library of all human knowledge in which the *Dictionary of industry* would stand alongside and on an equal footing with the *Dictionary of natural history*. Together, he wrote, the two encyclopaedias would form an enchanting picture of human knowledge.[15] For Duchesne, the prospect of industry commanding the same attention as nature was the culmination of a protracted rise of interest in the matters of industry. The interest in natural phenomena was at the time already well established and was the benchmark for the degree of attention devoted to other subjects such as industry. However, the interest in the objects of nature has a long and complex history itself. It is the history of attention to objects that were initially considered banal or even repulsive. Lorraine Daston has given an account of the long and slow process in which natural objects such as bugs or plants became subjects of attention and enquiry. These living things, she points out, had existed long before attention elevated them out of the 'chaos' of every day experience and turned them into objects of enquiry and interest.[16] Similarly, in the eighteenth century matters of industry began slowly to emerge from the multitude of activities that have accompanied human existence for a long time. Just as bugs and plants had existed a long time before they started to be objects of attention, weavers and bee-keepers had done their work long before Duchesne decided to alphabetically list descriptions of their trades and call them 'human industry'.

This process by which qualitatively very different production processes became all part of the single concept of industry reflects the tendency that Adorno and Horkheimer have emphasised as the main characteristic of the enlightenment. 'The manifold affinities between existing things', the two exponents of the Frankfurt School argued, 'are supplanted by the single relationship between the subject who confers meaning and the meaningless object, between rational significance and its accidental bearer.' The reality that is recorded and categorised is nothing more than the substratum for this activity and loses all qualities that may distinguish it. In order to achieve this the rationality of the enlightenment mercilessly cuts away the 'incommensurable'. It is only interested in ends and must of necessity destroy qualities. In this way the enlightenment prepared nature for industry by imposing the 'levelling rule of abstraction, which makes everything in nature repeatable'. In the case of the concept of industry the purpose of the various production processes – the production of goods – supersedes the great number of their different qualities: the movements, the materials, and the product of the weaver, the potter and the smith could not be more different and yet they are all reduced to the one function that makes them a part of industry: the concept of industry embodies the enlightenment's tendency to make 'dissimilar things comparable' by reducing them to abstract values.[17]

However, the manufacturing activities of industry were not only a static 'substratum' for the efforts of the enlightenment to take control of reality by 'recording' and 'categorising' it. The rise of the concept of industry was not only the result of a change in the eye of the enlightened observer. The object of observation changed as well. As pointed out, the transformation of manufacturing manifested itself in an enormous increase of production in the eighteenth century. Almost inevitably this extraordinary growth of industry led to a considerable interest in the source of this increase in wealth and object of consumption. There was also a particular interest in the prosperity that the production of these objects seemed to bring even to the most sterile lands. The article 'industry' in the *Encyclopaedia* emphasised this effect: industry 'fertilises everything, & spreads everywhere abundance & life'. The continuous increase of manufacturing was all the more intriguing since it did not appear as the result of a single event or invention. An evolution was nonetheless evident in the way in which the many individuals whose activities made up the phenomenon of industry went about their trades. It is this change with which contemporary observers were concerned. They tried to understand it, to form an opinion about it but also to shape it.[18]

The contemporary attempts to shape the development of industry are particularly remarkable because they attest a high level of reflection and awareness. At the same time, these attempts were instances when concept of industry which was derived from the observation of industry was reflected back on the economic reality and changed the further economic development. A concept that was the result of the enlightenment's efforts to intellectually take control of reality now turned to shaping reality. The concern with industry was also intertwined with the other great topics of enlightenment debates. The campaign that Voltaire, Turgot and others led in the 1770s against serfdom in France and Russia is a case in point. Serfdom was condemned as an oppressive regime that enslaved the individual. But it was also condemned as an obstacle to industry and hence to the prosperity of the individual and the nation. If one adds to this that ecclesiastical institutions were among the most prominent feudal lords remaining in France it becomes apparent that it is virtually impossible to separate Voltaire's dislike for religious infamy, his concerns with industry, and his belief in the freedom of the individual. The way in which the publicist Voltaire and the minister Turgot conceptualised industry – as an economic sector in which individuals freely buy and sell their labour – informed their political campaign against institutions that embodied other economic structures. Serfdom and the guilds were their main target. Even more direct was the link between the conceptualisation of industry and specific policy decisions in the case of another interlocutor of Voltaire. Frederick II of Prussia was not only an author who lived in a largely agrarian country and contemplated the nature of industry, he also introduced many of the policies that eventually turned Prussia into one of the principal industrial nations of the world.

Eavesdropping on Voltaire and his contemporaries

In order to illuminate the details of the dialectical interaction between the development of economic reality, and political and economic thought the historian needs to chose a method that makes it possible to learn about the unfamiliar economic world of the eighteenth century and listen carefully to the conversations of the contemporaries about this world. The greatest barrier to understanding the history of thought of any given period lies in a twofold asymmetry of information. On the one hand there is a deficit of information on the part of the historian about the context in which the opinions of the contemporaries were formed. On the other hand there is an excess of information on the part of the historian because he or she knows what happened in the two and a half centuries after Voltaire, Raynal and other eighteenth-century observers debated industry. The first part of this problem can be addressed through the detailed study of the rules, institutions, events, impressions and intellectual currents that surrounded the authors who wrote about industry. The second part of the problem seems more difficult to address. Is it really possible to read eighteenth-century comments today like a reader who did not even suspect that there would be a revolution in France? Is it possible to read eighteenth-century texts about industry without thinking of nineteenth-century accounts of the 'industrial revolution'? In what follows, an attempt will be made to approach contemporary comments as much as possible from an eighteenth-century perspective. In order to illuminate the evolution of the modern concept of industry in as much detail as possible, this enquiry will focus on the most prominent writer of the enlightenment and the debates in which he was involved. Voltaire's exchanges about industry with many other prominent enlightenment authors such as Saint-Pierre, Turgot and the Physiocrats are at the centre of this enquiry. Why a concentration on one author and his interlocutors? The difficulties involved are obvious: one author and the debates in which he was involved are taken to be at least to some extent indicative for a whole period. However, any enquiry of the intellectual life of a period is necessarily selective in the use of source material. Rather than trying to be comprehensive – which is impossible – it is important to select the concentration in a way that yields meaningful results. If one traces the development of the concept of 'industry' in debates which took place at different times and which involve changing sets of authors one can merely state that a development in the use of the term occurred. The question *why* and *how* the evolution occurred can only be answered with a clear concentration on the use of the term of one author or a small group. Their use of the term has to be traced from the time when they used the term in the qualitative meaning to a period when they used it in the sectoral meaning. Voltaire's life – he was born in 1694 and died in 1778 – spans the crucial period: he began his writing career in the first decades of the eighteenth century when the dictionary of the Académie Française still defined industry solely as an individual quality. However, when Voltaire wrote his last works, the sectoral meaning had become common in his writings and with many other authors in public debate. The present enquiry sets out to illuminate in detail the transition that occurred in the meantime. The ways in which different eighteenth-century authors became acquainted with the phenomenon of industry vary of course greatly. This study examines Voltaire's development as an exemplary case and as an inroad to illuminate a larger intellectual transformation. The change can be traced in Voltaire's writings and in his participation in public debate in a uniquely detailed way. For only if one author and his interlocutors are placed at the centre of the enquiry the dynamic and continuity of the development of the concept can be illuminated. Only a clear focus of the enquiry can bring out the specific experiences, observations and influences that influenced the gradual semantic change. Just as the phenomenon of industry did not appear abruptly, the perception of it also grew slowly.

Another question that needs to be addressed is: why Voltaire? There are compelling arguments for this choice: First, Voltaire embodies the enlightenment and the spirit of his century like no other author. Historians have called the eighteenth century the century of Voltaire but even more importantly his contemporaries were also of this opinion. Goethe declared: 'Voltaire's great talent … of being able to communicate in all forms made him, for a certain time, the absolute intellectual master of his nation. Whatever he offered her she had to absorb; resistance was futile'. But Voltaire's works were not only admired. Herder describes the contemporary reaction to Voltaire's works as a trinity of learning, admiring and following. And Condorcet's biography of Voltaire starts with the sentence: 'Voltaire's life is the history … of the power that he exercised on the opinions of his century'. It is this power to form the ideas and the language of his contemporaries across Europe that makes Voltaire's views particularly relevant for the study of the contemporary perception of industry. In particular because his authority also captured some of the most prominent political economists of his time. Smith called him 'the most universal genius which France has ever produced'. Other economists showed similar reverence for Voltaire. He is among the most cited authors in Say's *Treatise on political economy* of 1828. Voltaire is cited more frequently by Say than such prominent writers on political economy as Turgot.[19]

Second, Voltaire participated in many of the crucial debates about industry of his time. He exchanged his views on industry with Turgot, Necker, Saint-Pierre the Physiocrats and other prominent contemporaries and he was one of the most ardent supporters of the rise of industry – always ready to defend the new economic sector against his more sceptical contemporaries. Not least, he also started earlier than others to use the modern concept of industry. Voltaire has been pointed out as the first user of the term in the modern connotation in the French language. While it is important that Voltaire was an early and influential user of the term, the question whether he was the first is less relevant. The present enquiry is more concerned with the dynamics of the rise of a concept than with hunting for its 'first ever use'. The author thus hopes to escape what Venturi once called the 'Germanic nostalgia for the *Ur*'.[20]

Third, Voltaire was truly a worldly philosopher. Later generations may have named him 'the French Vergil' but he was also a shrewd business man who was well acquainted with the economic reality of his time. Famously, his father who did not trust the literary ambitions of the young François Marie included a provision in his will limiting his son's access to the inheritance: the bequest should only be paid out after his son had completed his thirty-fifth birthday and grown more mature. However, by the time that Voltaire could access his inheritance he had already made a fortune of his own. With investments in everything from watch manufactures – he was personally involved in the management and sales – to the French East India trade, Voltaire accumulated a sizeable fortune. There were thus many instance where Voltaire personally observed industry, invested in industry, enjoyed the fruits of industry or tried to influence political decisions regarding industry.[21] In this sense this book is also a contribution to a more accurate picture of the most famous thinker of the enlightenment. The distorted view of Voltaire as a superficial wit has already been recorded by Flaubert in his *Dictionary of accepted ideas* as a topos of nineteenth-century bourgeois conversation. The view lingers on until today even among historians. This is despite the studies of Peter Gay and René Pomeau who have explored many of Voltaire's practical political concerns and his steady dedication to the causes he adopted. The concern with industry is among the issues which have occupied his attention in one way or another over decades. Pomeau draws our attention to the long standing interest of the philosopher for the matters of industry. In his magisterial biography *Voltaire in his time* he remarks: 'It would be interesting to research the appearance of the term industry in its modern meaning in Voltaire's works.'[22]

Finally, Voltaire is at the centre of this book about early debates about industry because he was an extremely well-travelled Frenchman. Voltaire's native France was a centre of the enlightenment and of the development of industry. At the same time, Voltaire lived for longer or shorter periods in many other parts of Europe including England, Prussia, Holland and Geneva. He was also engaged in debates and business transactions associated to industry that included locations as distant as Saint Petersburg, Cadiz and Pondicherry. His was therefore a European and international perspective on industry and his involvement in debates beyond the French borders reflects that debates about industry, just as the growth of industry itself, transcended national boundaries.

However, the international character of the debates also gives rise to a methodological difficulty. Most of the debates about industry that will be discussed here were in French and some in English and German. However, in order to make this book more readable all quotations are translated into English. The French *industrie*, the German *Industrie*, and the English 'industry' therefore uniformly appear as 'industry'. The development and meaning of the term is similar in these languages but as every linguist will confirm translations never fully fit the original meaning. This creates a difficulty when writing the history of a concept. In order to preserve the full complexity of the contemporary comments the original text of the citations is included in the endnotes. When reading this book it is crucial to bear in mind at all times the different connotations in which the term 'industry' was and still is used. *The Oxford English Dictionary* reminds us that the meaning of 'intelligent or clever working; skill, ingenuity, dexterity or cleverness in doing anything' is now dated but that the term continues to include meanings as diverse as, 'diligence or assiduity in the performance of any task', 'systematic work or labour; habitual employment in some useful work, now esp. in the productive arts or manufactures', and 'a particular form or branch of productive labour'.[23] In order to illuminate the development of the term in the early debates about industry Chapter 1 of this book gives a short overview of the 'French way to industrialisation' in Voltaire's lifetime and of the development of the concept of industry in the works of Voltaire and other contemporary authors. Chapter 2 focuses on Voltaire's first hand observations about industry during his stay in

Prussia in the 1750s. Chapter 3 discusses his subsequent dispute with Boisguilbert and Beaumelle about the right path to the growth of industry. Chapter 4 analyses the controversy over the economic and moral value of industry that pitted Voltaire and Necker against Fenélon, Saint-Pierre and the Physiocrats. The final chapter examines the political campaign against serfdom and for the progress of industry which Voltaire led in the 1760s and 1770s together with Turgot and others.

1
Industry in Voltaire's Time

Industry is like a chameleon. It constantly changes its appearance: nineteenth-century observers wrote about steam-engines, smoking chimneys, deafening noise and inhumane working conditions in Manchester's cotton mills. Visitors of today's car plants in Wolfsburg or Rüsselsheim see computerised machine tools which operate more or less silently on clean factory floors. The appearance of these concerns could hardly be more different and yet they are both industry. It is virtually impossible to understand contemporary comments about industry in any period without familiarising oneself as much as possible with the specific economic reality of the day. This is particularly true of the eighteenth century which saw the birth of many of our political, social and economic institutions but which was still a world strikingly different from ours in many ways. It already contained the seeds of modernity. 'Much of what was modern in France', Michael Sonenscher points out, 'was already there, many generations before Marx wrote the *Eighteenth Brumaire of Louis Bonaparte*'.[1] At the same time the economic world of the eighteenth century was still dominated by many traditional institutions, technologies and behaviours. It will, therefore, be useful to remind ourselves of the development of French industry at the time, before going on to examine the contemporary comments about industry.

The economic world of the eighteenth century seems unfamiliar mainly because the growth of industry was much less driven by mechanisation than in subsequent periods. Another characteristic feature of the eighteenth century was that many of its manufacturing products were not the cheap low quality wares that we have come to associate with industry. In particular in France products of industry were often sophisticated and even luxurious goods. This 'richly varied and expanding material culture' of the seventeenth and eighteenth century is at the centre of de

Vries's concept of an 'industrious revolution' which led to the 'industrial revolution'. The desire to possess the more refined products of industry changed the economic behaviour and dispositions of contemporaries across Europe. The objects of desire – 'trinkets and baubles' as Adam Smith famously called them – were readily available to anyone who could afford to pay for them. Contemporaries therefore worked more, and above all, in different ways. More people sought to work where they could earn the necessary money: in the production of marketable goods or directly for a wage. Domestic and agrarian forms of production became less attractive because they were mostly geared towards supplying goods for self-consumption. Workers moved into the workshops and factories and contributed to the significant growth of industrial output. In more theoretical terms it was the 'absorption into the market economy of the last remaining substance of the household' that was the motor to the rise of industry in the period.[2]

De Vries's interpretation with its concentration on changes in economic dispositions rather than on mechanisation is well adapted to explain the French way to industrialisation. The characteristics of the French development are particularly salient when they are compared to the British path to industrialisation. In this comparison, France has been depicted by many economic historians as the economy that developed later and less successfully. In the late 1960s, however, a re-evaluation of the relative industrial development of France and Britain was ushered in.[3] In this debate Patrick O'Brien and Caglar Keyder argued that France's way to industrialisation was not less successful than that of England but that productivity of labour employed in French industry was, on average, above British levels until the 1890s. 'Industrialisation in France', they maintained, 'simply took place in a different legal, political and cultural tradition'. In their view the French path to industrialisation was 'more humane and no less efficient' than that of England. One does not have to follow the radical judgements of Charles Kindleberger ('simply incredible') or David Landes ('figments') to agree that the findings can hardly be taken as precise measurements. However, at the end of the day it emerged clearly from the debate that France and England followed different but equally successful paths to industrialisation.[4] What exactly was the 'French way' to industrialisation in the eighteenth century? Five elements seem to be characteristic: first, a dynamic growth; second, a predominance of the textile and iron industries; third, a relative concentration on high quality products; fourth, a limited use of machinery; and, fifth, a prominent role for the state.

Industrial growth in eighteenth-century France

The growth of French industry was of an exceptional intensity and duration throughout the whole of the eighteenth century. In quantitative terms, industrial output was four times in the 1780s what it had been in the first decade of the century. During this 90-year period – it matches Voltaire's lifetime (1694–1778) almost exactly – French industry experienced an average annual growth of 1–1.9 per cent. The significant growth of French industry also corresponds to a strong growth in trade. From the first decades of the century to the Revolution French foreign trade increased from 215 million *livres tournois* to 1062 million. The increase was almost fivefold. Foreign trade in England and Wales did not even triple in the same period. This is all the more surprising since England did not only lag behind in growth rates. Throughout most of the century the absolute volume of French foreign trade was higher than that of England and Wales. Through this commerce – its centres were Bordeaux, Nantes and Rouen – French industries provided much of the manufactured goods that were bought in the French colonies, Italy, the eastern Mediterranean and in Spain and its colonies.[5] This trade was of crucial importance for French industry. The difficulties of overseas trade after the revolution had severe consequences for France's economy. It should be noted that the external commerce of France was not only important as a way of distribution for industrial products (and, of course agricultural products). Trade was in itself an important industry and source of growth. The heated debates about the French East India Company will be discussed later. They have to be seen in the context of the significant increase of trade in the period.

The principal branches of industry: textiles and iron

The strong increase of foreign trade leads to the second characteristic of the 'French way'. The branches of French industry that contributed to the impressive growth over the eighteenth century were principally the textile industry (mainly wool, silk and linen) and – to a lesser extent – the iron industry. Textile production was clearly the largest industry of France. Together the wool, silk and linen industry produced 50 per cent of France's industrial output. The output of the wool industry increased from 90 million *livres* at the beginning of the century to 225 million *livres* towards the end of the century.[6] Wool fabrics of all qualities made up the bulk of wool products. The wool industry, however, also featured a great variety of other products. Hats and tapestries played an important role. Another characteristic feature of the wool industry was its presence in practically all parts of the country. This great geographical spread corresponded with the great variety in the forms of production. From royal *manufactures* that produced some of the finest fabrics to small farmers producing coarse woollens for local consumption all forms of production were represented. In Voltaire's writings the wool industry is often associated with the Van Robais factory of Abbeville. Its product – the famous woollen cloth of Van Robais – was among the most prominent products of French industry at the time.

Another great textile industry of France was silk production. Its centres were Lyon and Tours, but there was also a significant presence in Languedoc. From 1720 to 1788, Lyon's silk industry saw a 185 per cent growth and a threefold increase in the number of looms. Even more impressive was the increase in Nîmes where the number of looms in silk manufacturing rose from 459 in 1729, to 1156 in 1761, and to 2571 in 1789. However, the silk industry was significant not only for its particularly strong growth. To fully grasp its economic weight it is helpful to take a more detailed look at the trades and businesses that were attached to this industry. In places like Lyon the silk industry made up the fortune of a whole city. Aside from being a very labour intensive production process itself, silk production was connected to a list of other industries. Velvet makers, silk dyers, silk carders, makers of passementerie, silk throwster, silk folders, makers of silk stockings, wimple makers and silk reelers were but a few of the artisans who were involved in the production of silk in Lyon and other cities. In addition to these industries, there were wood and metal workers who built and maintained the looms and other tools. If the silk industry dominated the economy of some cities it also had a great impact on the hinterland. Before the silk could undergo the long and complicated process of separating, dying, and weaving, the silkworm had to produce the raw material first. While most of the raw silk was imported, considerable efforts were made to develop a local production. Breeding of thousands of silkworms required a sufficient supply of silkworm food in the shape of mulberry leaves. Consequently, the ever increasing consumption of mulberry leaves shaped whole stretches of countryside near the silk producing centres. In the region of Nîmes alone, 500,000 mulberry trees were planted from 1752 to 1759.[7] Thus, despite the fact that the silk industry's products were only attainable for the privileged few, the growth of silk production had a broad economic impact. Not only were a number of industries in the urban centres dependent on it but it also affected the rural populations. It is thus hardly surprising that the silk industry appears repeatedly in Voltaire's observations and comments concerning France and Prussia.

In contrast to Voltaire's loquaciousness a propos of the textile industries he remains largely silent about the iron industry. Modern economic historians, however, rank it among the important French industries of the time, despite the fact that little is known about this branch of industry. François Crouzet estimates the yearly iron production before the revolution at 90–100,000 tons. At the same time, however, he does not venture any precise estimates about growth rates. Cautiously, he suggests that French growth rates in this industry were probably higher than those of England. Other authors are equally reluctant to make any precise statements about the French development in the course of the century.[8] This branch of industry was certainly much less a 'motor of growth' than other branches such as textiles. In particular, it played no significant role among the exports of France.

The French concentration on high quality products

The third characteristic of French industrialisation in the present period was a concentration on high quality products. The names of Beauvais, d'Aubusson, Gobelin and Van Robais were synonymous with woollen products of the highest quality. The silk-fabrics – often with additions of gold or silver – were similarly sought after everywhere in Europe. The average quality of wool fabrics seems to have continuously increased during the eighteenth century. One explanation for the concentration on high quality textiles – without completely neglecting the simpler qualities – was the contemporary view that this market segment was more resistant to demand fluctuation in crisis. An increased demand for textiles of better quality also corresponds to de Vries's perspective on changing demand patterns. Another explanation is a specialisation of French industry along the lines of comparative advantage. This, of course, begs the question why French comparative advantage lay in 'quality and design' while England's was 'cheapness'. The answer may lie in the supply of English coal. The readily available combustible opened the way to more energy consuming and more mechanised industries which tended to produce cheap mass market products.[9] The taste for luxury of the French court and those imitating its fashions, in turn, resulted in a big potential for highly skilled producers of luxury goods in France. One could certainly add that the regime of vigorous quality controls introduced by the minister Colbert helped to create a potential of skilled labour. In addition, there was another political decision that contributed to France's concentration on high quality products. From 1686 until 1759, the production, import and the use of cotton fabrics was illegal in France. While Colbert had attempted to foster the French cotton industry, his successors gave in to the pressure of the domestic wool industry. Most European countries restricted the growth of the cotton industry on similar grounds. Only Holland, Switzerland and Britain established a more liberal policy. The production of cheap cotton textiles in England became an important 'motor of growth'. Whether the French decision of 1686 was a wise one is certainly open to debate. It is, however, certain that this political decision shaped the nature of French industrialisation to no small extent. In a similar way, Britain's concentration on the production of cheap cotton textiles was the result of conscious political choices. From a modern perspective it is easy to underestimate the importance of the luxury trades for the development of industry. However, the sophisticated production methods, the complex division of labour and the system of credit between the different producers and for the consumers of luxury goods contributed significantly to the economic development of the period.[10] In addition to these factors, the attractiveness of the manifold products of industry for the consumers of all ranks is also central to the explanation of the 'industrious revolution'.

No mechanisation of labour

The fourth characteristic of French industrialisation derives to a large extent from the concentration on labour intensive luxury production which was difficult to mechanise. Consequently, technical progress or, as Landes phrased it, the substitution of machines for 'human skill and effort' played a comparably small role in French industry. Because mechanisation played a minor role, other changes account for the output growth in this period.[11] Aside from population growth and an increase in labour time, the principal source of growth in French industry seems to have been organisational change. The nature of eighteenth-century industrial progress can be illustrated with the case of the already familiar Van Robais textile manufactory in Abbeville. It may be noted that this particular factory is not only used as an example in modern literature about the development of France's industry. Van Robais's fabric was one of Voltaire's favourite examples for the success of Colbert's policies. In more than one place Voltaire declared: 'I could never tolerate that a man who wears cloth made from Van-Robais's fabric ... should speak badly about Jean-Baptiste Colbert'. The founder of the factory had, indeed, been lured from the Netherlands to France by Colbert in 1665. Josse Van Robais had had a textile factory in Middleburg. From there he brought with him a number of skilled workers as well as the necessary tools. With a royal privilege he installed himself in Abbeville. Soon his business flourished and the fine woollen cloth became famous all over Europe. Although initially the production sites had been spread in different parts of Abbeville, in the early eighteenth century a descendant of the founder, also named Josse Van Robais, decided to improve the production process by concentrating it on one site. Mechanisation or technical change did not play a major role in this important step on the way to industrial development. Mechanisation of production was strikingly absent before or after the reorganisation. Van Robais himself gave an insight into his motives for the reorganisation: it was the advantage of having the whole production process 'under our eyes' and 'all workers assembled behind one door'.[12] Van Robais was less concerned with mechanisation than with the supervision of his workers, with their skill, their reliability, and their industriousness. Summing up all these qualities in one word, one may say that Van Robais was concerned with the individual industry of his several hundred workers. This insight into the preoccupations of an eighteenth-century entrepreneur is not without interest for the present subject. For Van Robais, the success of his business depended on the performance or individual industry of his workers. It is in this way that the association of the two meanings of industry that co-exist in contemporary arguments have to be understood: the older meaning of industry as an individual quality and the new meaning of industry as a sector of the economy. The growth of any branch or the whole of the national industry depended to a much larger extent on the organisation of the industry of the individual worker than in later periods where technical progress became the crucial factor.

State and industry in France

The Van Robais factory in Abbeville is not only a good illustration of the nature of industrial progress in France. It also illustrates the fifth characteristic of French industry: the prominent role for the state. As Keyder points out in his *State and industry in France*: 'The continuity of the importance of the state is what sets France apart.' This fifth characteristic of French industrialisation in the eighteenth century is without any doubt the most controversial of its features. However, as Woronoff puts it: 'No matter whether one accepts the idea or whether one fights it, industry is a matter for the state'. The examples of governmental regulation, protection and intervention are, indeed, ubiquitous. It may suffice to point out some examples that are related to the industries that were discussed here: the wool factories of Van Robais and Gobelin had been established by Colbert and the quality of their products was regulated in great detail; the cotton industry had been forbidden by the government; the silk manufacturing in Lyon and Tours was revived by Colbert; the mulberry plantations around Nîmes were subsidized with twenty-five *livres* for one hundred trees planted; the manufacturers of silk-stocking in Nîmes were only allowed to produce for exportation in order not to compete with Lyon and Tours; finally, there was continued court action in Nîmes between the cap-makers and locksmiths over the question who should be allowed to build the special loom needed to produce silk caps.[13] This small sample of governmental interventions may be enough to illustrate that there can be no doubt as to the prominent role for the state in French industrial development. The importance of government interventions for the growth of industry in France should, however, not be understood as a unique case. While the French government may have been more involved in the micro-management of industrial development, government involvement in industrial growth was prominent in other countries of the period. Prussia under Frederick II is a famous example, but even in Britain the state exercised considerable influence on economic development. In the period from 1660 to 1815, for example, the British government appropriated an extraordinary and increasing share of output through taxation.[14] In the light of such findings the view of 'laissez-faire Britain' and 'interventionist France' might have to be reconsidered for the eighteenth century.

Many historians see governmental interventions as traumatic for the French economy. Terence Hutchison speaks of 'Colbertian–Stalinist "crash" programmes of industrial development' while Charles Cole likens Colbert to the, in his view, probably only marginally less monstrous Robespierre. Crouzet sees in eighteenth-century France many instances of a 'demagogic alliance' against the entrepreneurial spirit. More soberly, Jean-Pierre Rioux describes the 'state dirigism' as a brake that hampered France's eighteenth-century take off. Similarly, Landes sees in England's allegedly superior development the 'superior performance of free industry to that of state-supported enterprise'. Woronoff takes a more balanced position when he speaks of a joint progress of state and industry in France. The active role of the state, he points out, provided important support for the long-term industrial development. He sums up the successful governmental efforts to guide, protect and support France's industry when he calls today's French entrepreneurs 'Colbert's orphans'. Even more outspoken is Keyder's judgement who – after having described the success of the 'French way' in his 1978 monograph – calls on economists to 'advocate industrial policy and a state–economy relationship derived from the French experience'.[15] In the light of these discordant views on the issue it will be interesting to enquire into the perspective of contemporary observers. Voltaire found a benign connection between the development of France's industry and the intervention of the French state. However, the relationship between state and industry was not less controversial in the eighteenth century than it is today. The rapid development of France's industry sparked controversial debates and invited the contemporaries to coin a new name for the emerging economic sector: industry.

Intellectual context: the term 'industry' up to the 1750s

One of the first instances in which Voltaire used the term industry was in the year 1725. He celebrated his thirty-first birthday in that year and was not yet a poet and publicist of European fame. Nevertheless he was already considered to be a rather promising young author and his latest theatrical piece *The Eavesdropper* was staged with at least some success. His use of the term in the comedy is exemplary for the period: in the one-act play young Clitandre can be found wooing the beautiful Hortense. But as misfortune strikes, Hortense is going to attend the next ball at the side of the dreadful Damis, Clitandre's rival. In this situation Clitandre decides to enlist the help of his servant Pasquin whom he praises for his 'industry' in matters of intrigue and deceit. ('Industry' rhymes in this case with 'let us disturb this amity' – that of Hortense and Clitandre's rival.)[16] Here industry is used in the original meaning of individual skilfulness and inventiveness. Voltaire's use of the term is in no way associated with an economic activity in this period.

This use of the term was not an idiosyncrasy of Voltaire. If he had looked up the meaning of the term 'industry' while he was writing *The Eavesdropper* he would probably have reached for the latest edition of the French Academy's *Dictionary*. There, 'industry' was defined as a personal quality synonymous with 'skill'. No indication of any relation of the term to economic activity was given. Instead, the definition of the academy emphasised the pejorative connotations of 'industry'. To live off one's industry, for example, was equated with sustaining one's life by swindling. Those who lived by their 'industry' rather than by their wealth were derogatively called *chevaliers d'industrie* (literally 'knights of industry') as opposed to real knights who lived off their inherited wealth.[17] If Voltaire had written just two years later, he could have used Pierre Richelet's smaller and handier *Dictionary of the ancient and modern French language* which was published in 1732. Like the academy Richelet defined industry as the individual quality of 'address'. There is no distinction between industry applied to a trade or any other 'non-economic' task. The 'non-economic' understanding of the term in the dictionary is further underlined by the association of 'industry' with certain 'industrious' animals such as swallows, beavers and bees. In Richelet's dictionary whereas animals are praised for their industry, humans who live off their industry are looked upon with suspicion. To 'live off one's industry' is defined as finding 'good or bad' ways to survive.[18]

This understanding of the term is strikingly different from the use that became common in Voltaire's later years: in 1776, two years before his death and 51 years after he had written *The Eavesdropper* Voltaire wrote from his chateau in Ferney to the king in Paris in order to ask for political and economic reforms in his remote region of France. The aim, he wrote, was the advancement of the three sources of wealth in the region: 'agriculture, commerce and industry'.[19] Here industry is not the individual quality of a scheming servant anymore. It has become an economic sector, clearly distinct from agriculture and commerce but not less important as a source of wealth. Again, Voltaire's use is not atypical for the period. Many examples could be given. One of the most salient is Turgot's use of the term in his *Reflections on the creation and distribution of wealth*. In this work Voltaire's friend and admirer wrote about industry alongside with agriculture and commerce as economic sectors and sources of revenue. Turgot is using 'industry' in a sectoral sense. This is made clear by a passage where he substitutes the terms 'agriculture', 'industry' and 'commerce' with the synonymous 'enterprises in farming, manufacturing and commerce' in order to avoid repetition.[20] A similar understanding can be found in the works of Baron von Holbach who warned in 1776 against the danger that wars posed against the sources of happiness of a nation. Among these sources he names a trinity of economic sectors 'agriculture, commerce, industry'. These economic sectors are also sometimes also put into the framework of kinship like relations. Raynal speaks of a base of 'agriculture' on which 'commerce' develops as the child of 'industry' and the father of 'wealth'. However, the family relationship between the sectors is not always seen as peaceful. The debates of the eighteenth century are pervaded by a concern about an excessive growth of industry at the expense of the more primordial economic sector of agriculture. Diderot juxtaposes the two sectors when he warned in a dialogue with Grimm not to 'build industry on the ruins of agriculture'. Many other instances of use of the term in a sectoral meaning will be cited in what follows. The sectoral meaning had become well established and was widely used in public debate in the period. Besides the meaning also the moral judgement of many contemporaries had changed since Voltaire had used the term in 1725. During the period an increasing number of observers overcame the traditional suspicion against industry and started to regard it not only as a very profitable but also as a morally laudable way of life.[21]

The use of the term industry

The different ways in which Voltaire used the term industry in 1725 and 1776 are milestones of a semantic and intellectual development. An intriguing process in which the concept of industry changed significantly took place during this period. A useful method to capture and understand this change is to look at the evolution of the frequency in which the term 'industry' was used. An increased use of the term is a phenomenon that calls for an explanation and is thus a useful tool to guide the qualitative analysis to the crucial moments in the transition. Thanks to the electronic edition of the works of Voltaire it is possible to record precisely the frequency with which he used the word 'industry' in any period.[22] There are clearly inherent limitations in a quantitative analysis and more detailed remarks can be found in the Notes.[23]

From Voltaire's birth in 1694 until 1730 – the year in which he wrote *The Eavesdropper* – the search for the word industry in his works remains frustrating. The word only appears three times and for one of the writings in question Voltaire's authorship is uncertain.[24] In all three passages 'industry' is used in the original meaning of individual skilfulness and inventiveness. It is in this period in no way associated with an economic activity. A brief look into Frantext – one of the largest databases of francophone texts – confirms this picture: hardly any use of the term in the sectoral sense is recorded before 1694. Also in the first three decades of the eighteenth century the sectoral meaning remains extremely rare. One of the few examples for sectoral use can be found in Vauban's writings about fiscal reform where he distinguishes revenue from 'land', 'commerce' and 'industry'.[25] In the 1730s and 1740s Voltaire started to use the word slightly more often. There are respectively 27 and 22 appearances of 'industry' in these decades. That is already a more sizeable number although it has to be seen in relation to Voltaire's sustained prolific output. As in the previous period, he uses the term many times to qualify a person or an action that has nothing to do with economic activity. In the *Temple of Taste,* for example, a painter claims that he paints with the same 'industry' as Raphael, and in the *Essay on Epic Poetry* Voltaire criticises the arrangement of Homer's *Iliad* for its lack of 'industry'.[26]

Parallel to this use of the term, there are many examples of the sense of individual industry as applied to a business enterprise. Voltaire describes, for instance, the industry of the inhabitants of Altona that made them rich and was responsible for commerce to flourish on the northern bank of the Elbe.[27] While industry becomes clearly more closely associated with economic activities in this period, it still remains mainly a personal quality. It is one among the individual talents that are needed in a good and prosperous society ('courage, strength, and industry') and its absence characterises a backward society with neither 'abundance, industry, taste, or cleanliness'. Significantly, the personal quality of industry starts to be associated at this time with government and ministers: 'The people are what the kings or the ministers make them. Courage, strength, industry, all their talents remain hidden until a genius appears and brings them to life.' Equally, industry occupies an increasingly important position in Voltaire's thought. It is a leitmotiv in Voltaire's pamphlet *Observations about MM. Jean Lass, Melon, and Dutot.* The word industry concludes this small work where it is treated as a foundation of progress and prosperity.[28]

This period also sees the first instance where industry was used by Voltaire in the sectoral sense, abstractly denoting a branch of economic activities. When Voltaire distinguishes 'the cultivation of land, commerce, and industry' in a 1739 version of the *Observations,* industry appears for the first time as a branch of the nation's economy rather than as a character trait of individuals. With his use of the term industry in the sense of a sector of the economy that was distinct from the 'cultivation of land' and 'commerce' in 1739, Voltaire was ahead of his time. The 1740 edition of the dictionary of the Académie Française still defined industry mainly as an individual quality, namely as 'skill'. However, the dictionary's definition had also changed in significant ways. By now it contained a sentence that hinted at least at a sectoral meaning of the term. Industry, it was stated, could also mean 'work', 'commerce' and 'know-how'. In this definition, industry took on the sense of a sphere or a sector of activities but this sector was still not sharply defined.[29] Voltaire already clearly distinguished industry from commerce and agriculture. It was only in 1835 that the dictionary of the Académie gave a clearly defined sectoral meaning as a second meaning of the term. 'Industry', the authors added in 1835, 'also describes the mechanical arts and manufacturing in general'.[30] The dictionary of 1740 also indicates a change in the moral attitudes towards industry. The academy had found in 1694 that the term *chevalier d'industrie* was used 'as a term of mockery' while in 1740 it decided that the term was now used 'jokingly'.[31] However, despite these changes in the 1740s the term – in particular in the sectoral meaning – still remained rare in Voltaire's writings and with other authors until the 1750s.

The transformation of the 1750s

In the 1750s, the word 'industry' can be found almost five times as often in Voltaire's writings as in the preceding decade. His use in the 1750s is even more striking compared to the period between his birth and 1730: between the time when he wrote his first text in 1712 and the year 1730 – a period of 18 years – Voltaire used the term 'industry' only three times while he used the word 101 times in the ten years from 1750 to 1759. However, his overall writing output in the second period was also significantly higher than in the first. Until 1730 he wrote 184,256 words while he wrote 1,016,663 words in the 1750s. Nevertheless, even considering the differences in output the increase in the use of 'industry' remains noteworthy. The use of the term 'industry' increased almost 34 times while overall output increased less than six times. In the texts assembled in Frantext the frequency of the term multiplies almost by a factor of seven from the 1740s to the 1750s. On Frantext also the frequency of the term relative to the overall number of words increases dramatically and reaches its highest level in Voltaire's lifetime in the 1750s.[32] In the case of Voltaire the increase is almost exclusively due to two works: *The age of Louis XIV* of 1751 and the *Essay on Universal History* of 1753. Both works are histories: the *Essay* starts with the beginnings of humanity and ends with the reign of Louis XIII where, as is made clear in the title, *The Age of Louis XIV* takes over. The *Essay* has been called Voltaire's *Spirit of the Laws* and it is true that both books go far beyond ordinary historical chronicles of events.[33] Both aim at explaining the progress and development of humanity. Among these forms of progress the development of industry plays a prominent role. Voltaire concludes that France owed its industry as well as its commerce – he uses both terms in the sense of categories of economic activities – to Colbert's efforts. Voltaire devotes two entire chapters to the 'new industry' of that period: the silk factories, the Gobelin weavers, the wool fabric makers, the French East India Company, the mirror makers, the steel production and many other forms of industry receive detailed attention. That the term and the phenomenon of industry should figure so prominently in a text such as the *Age of Louis XIV* is rather significant. After all, the work undertakes to explain how the reign of Louis XIV came to be one of the four great ages of humanity. It was, as Nicole Ferrier-Caverivière pointed out, a praise to the 'modernity' of the age of Louis XIV.[34] The work opened a period in which Voltaire's use of the term industry increased significantly and in which the sectoral meaning of the term moved to the centre of attention. This position makes the *Age of Louis XIV* particularly relevant for this enquiry. Moreover, the work stands out through its genesis. Voltaire had started to collect material and 'interview' those who had personal memories of the age of Louis XIV since the 1730s. However, the actual act of writing, the period in which Voltaire chose the words for what he wanted to express, was unusually concentrated. The work was finished in 1750/1751 during his stay in Prussia.

As for the connotations of industry in the 1750s, a shift towards the sectoral use can be observed without seeing the other meanings vanish from Voltaire's vocabulary. Most significant in this period is the perspective on industry as a sector of activities that is of the utmost importance for the nation as a whole. Speaking of the rich merchant cities of Italy, Voltaire wrote: 'it is only over a period of time that commerce and industry have formed that state of prosperity that makes up the wealth of a nation'. Note again, the use of the pair 'industry' and 'commerce' which clearly describes the two terms as interrelated but distinct economic sectors and sources of the wealth of nations. In the 1750s Voltaire was not alone with this view of industry. The use of the sectoral meaning of the term was not quite as common, yet, as in the 1760s and 1970s but some other authors began to use the term as Voltaire did. Slightly more poetic than Voltaire's description of the interrelation of industry, commerce and the prosperity of the nations was that of Mirabeau the elder: 'The state', the physiocratic economist wrote in 1755, 'is a tree, whose roots are agriculture, whose trunk is the population, whose branches are industry, and whose leaves are commerce'. Literally, industry is described as a 'branch' of the economy rather than as an individual quality. In an expression like this one there is no sense of the older qualitative meaning anymore. Increasingly, Voltaire uses language in which the amount of industry is a characteristic of a nation and even a criterion of comparison between nations. Voltaire's reader encounters, for example, a comparison between the industry of different nations in which England ends up second without a clear indication as to who takes first place. If industry comes to be associated with an advanced nation, the opposite also applies. In backward Spain, for example, 'no industry built on ... the gifts of nature'. According to Voltaire, it is in general the backward and boorish nations who do not have any industry. The concern with industry was not limited to France; it was perceived as a phenomenon that transcended national borders. It was seen as a source of progress in many European nations of the period. When Voltaire looked back at several thousand years of human development he observed: 'reason and industry will always make new steps forward'. This belief in the progressive nature of industry and its close association with cultural progress pervades Voltaire's thought.[35]

While industry is increasingly seen as a specific branch of economic activities it also remains a quality of individuals or groups. When Voltaire condemned Louis XIV for the revocation of the edict of Nantes, it was for the king's intolerance but equally because the Huguenots took with them 'their industry'. This qualitative meaning is also evoked when Voltaire insists that in the development of humanity 'the spirit of commerce, of industry and of economy has been communicated from one person to another'. A similar understanding transpires from the writings of Voltaire's fellow philosopher Montesquieu who discussed in the *Spirit of the Laws* how the 'spirit of commerce and industry' developed in England. In both cases the emphasis associated to economic change is on a 'spirit of industry' that is spread and not on machinery or invention. The focus is on a change in mentalities and dispositions of those who engage in economic activity. However, despite the fundamental linguistic transformation of this period the original non-economic qualitative meaning of industry still lingered on. In the *Age of Louis XIV* Voltaire describes how Vice-admiral d'Estrée and an other officer brought honour to the 'military industry' of the French nation. Clearly, he was not referring to the Krupps of his time but to the skill of the naval officers of Louis XIV. It may be noted, though, that even the progress of this kind of 'non-economic industry' was attributed by him to 'Colbert's efforts'.[36] After the mid-century rise, Voltaire's attention to the phenomenon of industry remained at a high level. In the debates of the following decade the sectoral meaning of the term industry was widely used by Voltaire and his opponents. In particular the Physiocrats with their condemnation of industry as a sterile economic sector contributed to establish the sectoral connotation in the vocabulary of the contemporaries from the late 1750s onwards.[37] However, the sectoral meaning became important without substituting the qualitative meaning. As with Voltaire the term industry continues to be used in both connotations by many authors of the period. The parallel use of the period does not only indicate an ongoing development but also the direct link that contemporaries saw between the way in which individual industry was exercised and the growth of the industry sector.

This journey through Voltaire's writings gives a first idea of the development of the term: a word that Voltaire first used to describe a supporting character in a moderately successful play, industry started to become a key term in his interpretation of the rise and fall of regions and whole nations. The word was not only used more often, more importantly it also started to denote a new concept and moved to the centre of both Voltaire's attention and that of many other writers. For the purpose of looking at the eighteenth century's most prominent author is to observe a fundamental transformation in the mirror that his works hold up to his century. Having traced the semantic change and the shift of attention in Voltaire's work, the question remains why this shift of attention occurred from the 1750s onwards. To answer this question it is necessary to examine the concrete historical experiences and circumstances that formed the context of this transformation. In Voltaire's biography and in European history the 1750s were a time of transition and new beginnings. The War of Austrian Succession had lasted for most of the 1740s. Prussia's invasion of Silesia had triggered the war but the conflict involved France, Britain, Austria and many others of Europe's larger and smaller powers. In 1748 the treaty of Aachen finally brought peace to the regions that were ravaged by the war and the nations that had paid a high price for the conflict. The minds of administrators and commentators turned to other, more peaceful matters. Commerce and industry were among the topics that captured the attention of the contemporaries. As has been pointed out, Condorcet noted in his edition of Voltaire's works that the great philosopher and his contemporaries started to debate matters of political economy with great passion after the peace of 1748. In Voltaire's biography this was a time of loss and new beginnings. After the death of his long time lover, Madame de Châtelet in 1749, he left Paris in order to settle in Prussia. The country of Frederick II had been at the centre of the war. After the peace treaty – which confirmed the Prussian annexation of Silesia – the country now began to concentrate on economic and cultural development. Prussia was at this time still largely agrarian but the development of industry was one of the highest priorities and widely discussed in Potsdam and the Prussian provinces. It will therefore be helpful for the understanding of Voltaire's growing concern with industry and his position in the later debates in France to investigate in more detail the impressions of the Prussian stay and their influence on his writings in this period.

2
Voltaire, Prussia and Industry

The newspaper *Berliner Nachrichten* was a publication that kept the reading public of eighteenth-century Berlin well informed. In the year 1750, for instance, it ran stories about romantic picnic spots outside the Brandenburg gate and about the new privileges for the royal Prussian Asiatic trade company. In that year, the reader may have been equally interested in an article announcing the discovery of a *perpetuum mobile* in Danzig or a new edition of the *Spirit of the laws*. Or, the reader's attention may have been caught by three lines that were placed in the lower right hand corner of the paper's front page on 16 July 1750: 'On the 10th of this month the French royal chamberlain and historiographer, Mr. de Voltaire, arrived from Paris in Potsdam with his Majesty the King.'[1]

This chapter will discuss Voltaire's subsequent three-year stay in Prussia. Needless to say, not all facets of Voltaire's chosen exile will be considered here. Others have written about it in depth.[2] The chapter will focus on his travel and his exile only in so far as they form the context in which the matters of industry started increasingly to interest Voltaire. This interest is impressively documented in *The Age of Louis XIV* which he finished in Prussia and other writings of the time. Voltaire's intellectual development in this period, it will be argued, is to be seen in the context of his observations about the development of Prussia and the progress of its industry. It is therefore helpful to remind the modern reader of the experiences, events and intellectual currents that influenced Voltaire in this period.

Voltaire's departure from Paris

Voltaire decided to leave Paris for a number of reasons. Frederick II had invited him many times to come to Berlin where he had already been for brief visits in 1740 and 1743. That Voltaire finally followed the monarch's invitation for a longer stay in 1750 was the result of the hostile atmosphere that he and his works encountered in France. Moreover, Voltaire's journey to Berlin was also the consequence of a personal loss that weighed heavily on him: seven months before his arrival in Berlin the 'divine Émilie' – Voltaire's great philosophical lover of twenty-four years – had died.[3] All these motives played a role in Voltaire's decision to leave Paris and to embark on the thousand-kilometre journey to Berlin. The circumstances of the journey also explain why Voltaire took more interest in the details of the economic and cultural development of Prussia than during previous travels: at least initially it seemed possible that he would settle in Prussia for a longer period. In order to understand how the Prussian journey influenced Voltaire's state of mind it is necessary to examine the environment that he left behind in Paris. The street in which he lived in Paris, Rue Traversière, is today near the Gare de Lyon. In the 1750s, however, the street was called Rue Traversine and there was no railway station. Instead the area was characterised by the nearby gardens of the Palais Royal and the Tuileries.[4] The house in Rue Traversine had already been the Paris *pied-à-terre* of the 'divine Émilie' – Gabrielle-Émilie Le Tonnelier de Breteuil, marquise du Châtelet-Lomont – and Voltaire. After her death Voltaire made it his permanent residence. A document that was drawn up after the death of Madame du Châtelet makes it possible to take a closer look at Voltaire's life in Paris. The document in question is an inventory of all furniture and other movable objects in his house. The detailed list offers a glimpse of the kind of objects that surrounded Voltaire in his daily life before his departure to Prussia.[5]

In itself the fact that it took seven men several days to draw up the inventory gives an initial impression of the house's size. Even though the dimensions of the 'halls', 'rooms' and 'antechambers' are not specified, the house must have been sizeable since the inventory mentions fourteen different rooms, a basement and stables. These fourteen rooms were well filled with everything from an 'old umbrella' to an 'enamel chandelier with six arms'. In between one could find objects like 'seven different pagoda figures from China', 'eight armchairs of gilded wood ... covered with damask', 'two glass parrots covered with gilded copper', a cupboard filled with silver ware, several pieces of furniture 'varnished in the Chinese fashion', and finally a number of paintings among them a depiction of 'Venus scourging love'. In the stores, finally, were two four-wheeled carriages, both with green velvet interiors, one fitted with suspension.[6]

These carriages are of particular interest. First of all they remind the reader of the document of Voltaire's imminent departure. However, the coaches in Voltaire's household need also to be perceived in the way that eighteenth-century observers saw them: new, comfortable, even elegant and certainly fashionable inventions. Denis Diderot's article 'Carriage' in the *Encyclopaedia* gives a sense of the way in which coaches were surrounded by an aura of luxury and novelty in the eighteenth century: Diderot speaks of carriages as a 'new invention' which has become more common but is still mainly available to 'masters' and 'rich citizens'. Two paragraphs of the article are devoted to the futile sumptuary laws that had been made in the past against what was seen as an excessively comfortable and luxurious way of transportation. True to the spirit of the *Encyclopaedia*, Diderot does not omit to inform the reader about the production process that provides 'masters' and 'rich citizens' with this new commodity: all the skill and know-how of the lock maker, the saddler, and a number of other craftsmen goes into the making of a carriage.[7] It was, however, not only Diderot who commented on this product of the lock maker and the saddler. Presumably the user of the two carriages of Rue Traversine, Voltaire himself wrote down his thoughts about them. In his 1751 pamphlet *Dialogue between a philosopher and a comptroller general of finances* Voltaire reflected on the progress of France since the times of Hugh Capet. As it happens, the most prominent example of progress given in this opuscule is Voltaire's own carriage. Comparing his way of living with that of Hugh Capet he wrote: 'If he had to be taken anywhere ... it was in a cart, whereas I travel in a comfortable and pleasant carriage'. The phenomenon that Voltaire identifies as the source of this amenity is of particular interest. Diderot had already mentioned the know-how of the craftsmen. Voltaire, however, used a different term. He used a term that aggregates all the work, the skill and the know-how that the saddler, the smith and the other craftsmen put into his carriage: 'It was not more money that was needed in the kingdom to suspend a painted wooden box on leather straps, it was only industry that was needed.' The concept of industry is used here to explain the invention of new products and, more generally, an increase in the quality of life.[8]

The carriages were not the only fruits of industry that made Voltaire's life in Paris enjoyable. The death of Madame du Châtelet provides the historian with another document about the consumption habits of 'the Voltaires'. The document results from certain financial troubles on the part of Madame du Châtelet. While Voltaire could write in 1750, 'I am rich, even very rich for a man of letters', his partner had run up the prodigal sum of 165,229 *livres* in debts when she died.[9] The list of creditors reads like an inventory of the best that French industry had to offer in the eighteenth century. First of all, there are the potential makers of the carriages of Rue Traversine: a coach builder Richter, the saddlers Carboudin and Dossier, a cartwright Bereche, and the locksmiths Gabriel and Bettancourt. They are accompanied by a long list of other businesses: the jeweller Girost (or, for that matter, the jewellers L'Empereur, Hebert, Fayolles, Spote, La Vigne, Le Brun, Le Roy, Gillet), the lace maker Beauvin, the grocer Trudon, the silk maker Gaucherelle, the fashion merchant Alexandre, the enamel-worker Ecosse, the cabinet-maker Migeon, the lapidary Cheron, an anonymous maker of mathematical instruments, the perfume maker Du Lac, the watch maker Waltrain, the bird-organ-maker Richard, a maker of fancy inlaid ware such as chess boards and articles of ebony by the name of Auxerre and the sculptor Pithouin.[10] One may be misled by this list to see in Madame du Châtelet a rather shallow person, devoted to the superficial and glamorous. She was, however, quite the opposite. Not only did she conduct research on the 'propagation of fire' and on the 'institutions of physics' but she also took a closer look at the kind of consumption that is documented in the above list.[11]

Her unpublished translation of the *Fable of the bees* has survived as a fragment in Voltaire's library. It is entitled 'translation' but it is in reality a treatise in its own right on the same subject as Mandeville's poem. In the preface Madame du Châtelet complains about the members of the privileged classes who only got up at midday and who were ignorant of the many different forms of work and effort that were necessary to prepare and serve them their dinner in the evening. For her taste, too few observers realised the moral and economic implications of the amenities of daily life which she refers to as 'a comfort which has become too common to be noticed'. It is only the philosopher, she concludes, who is able to see in this 'comfort' the fruit of 'the industry ... of a whole people'.[12] One philosopher who was certainly able to see this point was her beloved M. de Voltaire. In well-known verses from *The Worldling,* Voltaire described the house of an 'honest man' and the source of that man's comfort: the ornaments of his house, 'multitude of fine arts', and all the other 'children of taste' that can be found in the house were the product of the 'thousand hands' of a 'brilliant industry'. Industry is the source of the beautiful objects surrounding the honest man in his house. The pair 'industry' and 'comfort' also appears in Voltaire's poem. For him the frugal life of Adam and Eve was best described by the absence of these inseparable phenomena that characterised his own times: 'They were lacking in industry and comfort'.[13]

A tour of the beaux-arts and fruits of industry that made up Voltaire's Paris world must not omit the art of theatre. In the months before Voltaire's departure he had established in his house a home to one of his greatest passions: he arranged private theatre performances for his circle. Before his departure to Prussia, Voltaire's latest work *Rome Saved* was staged in his house.[14] Condorcet, in his introduction to *Rome saved* in the Kehl edition of Voltaire's works, mentions that Voltaire himself played Cicero in the play. Without stating his sources, Condorcet reports that Voltaire-Cicero recited the line 'Romans, I love glory' with such verve that the audience was not quite sure whether Cicero or Voltaire was speaking.[15] This perception of Voltaire by the audience of Rue Traversine is illustrative of his appreciation of the arts and amenities that Paris offered.

The Voltaire who was about to leave Paris was quite similar to the 'honest man' in *The Worldling* who enjoyed a comfortable life; a life filled with the fine arts, amenities and latest inventions of his period. In more reflective moments, however, when he put his own enjoyment into perspective and thought about its sources and future, the word 'industry' started to make an appearance. There was no thought yet of the kind of industry that decided the rise and fall of nations and people. However, the considerations of Madame du Châtelet make clear, that there was a distinct appreciation of industry as the phenomenon that made the life of Voltaire and his affluent contemporaries comfortable. It is an understanding of industry as the source of beautiful and useful objects for the well to do that is the point of departure of Voltaire's journey. Industry as a source of prosperity for the whole nation was yet to become a prominent concept in Voltaire's thought.

This contemporary perception of industry as a source of values for individual consumption must also be seen in the light of de Vries argument about a contemporary fascination with an 'ever multiplying world of goods' which was the driving force behind the 'industrious revolution'. Household-level changes in demand habits, he argues, brought about the fundamental economic transformation before the 'industrial revolution'.[16] However, in the light of contemporary observations, it remains open to debate how large the section of the population was that contributed to the economic transformation through changes in patterns of demand. The comfortable household of Voltaire and Madame du Châtelet can certainly be seen as an example of the contemporary fascination with luxury goods. These commodities were used, Sonenscher points out, 'to denote luxury and, by extension, to pass judgement upon the tenor of public life; they were used to to evoke the international division of labour ... ; they were used finally to define the difference between the past and the present, and illustrate the principles of social organisation that distinguished commercial from landed societies'.[17] The extent to which social and economic commentary was associated to the refined products of the eighteenth century emerges from the reflections of Voltaire and Madame du Châtelet. Their curiosity in the concept of industry was associated to their own consumption habits. As we will see, the abundance of products of industry in Paris, the lack thereof in Prussia and the experiences of travelling between the two situations inspired reflection on the wider ramifications of industry and its precise nature.

The journey through industry-less Westphalia

As Madame du Châtelet had pointed out, the fruits of industry had become too common to be noticed. While this observation may have been true in Paris, the situation was different on the muddy roads of Westphalia where Voltaire found himself soon after his departure. Already while playing Cicero in Paris, preparations for his departure were taking concrete shape. He had written to arrange for his arrival at Kleve, the westernmost outpost of the Prussian monarchy, situated between the lower Rhine and the city of Nijmwegen.[18] Then, on 25 June 1750 at five o'clock in the morning, he left his house in Rue Traversine to embark on his journey to Berlin.[19] He was to return to Paris only to die there twenty-seven years later. From Paris, Voltaire took the road north and stopped in Compiègne, the French 'summer capital', to ask Louis XV for permission to leave.[20] He was, after all, still France's official historiographer of his 'most christian' majesty Louis XV. Voltaire's biographer, René Pomeau, speaks of a cold and short audience in which Louis happily granted him permission to quit France. The king considered Voltaire a dangerous and subversive author. To the monarch the writer's departure was certainly not a loss for France.[21] From Compiègne, Voltaire continued northward where the plains of Picardy and Flanders inspired a couple of verses: 'Frenchmen, Englishmen, Germans, today so calm/was it necessary to kill each other in order to be such good friends'.[22] He was, of course, referring to the wars of Louis XIV.

On 2 July he arrived in Kleve where he had to wait for several days before he could continue his journey. While he was impressed with the baroque gardens of this spa he did not quite enjoy his stay in a town which had 'hardly any affluence'. The town even inspired him to pen a passage about the decline of the Holy Roman Empire.[23] While his impressions of Kleve led him to these moderate considerations the next territories that he saw triggered an almost violent reaction. From Halberstadt he wrote with total indignation to his future host: 'Sire what a dog of a country Westphalia is.'[24] In a letter to his niece he seemed to be struggling for the most fitting insult for the province with its 'desolate and sterile and detestable' countryside. It will be necessary to dwell for a moment on Voltaire's tirades about Westphalia. His Westphalia is inhabited by 'animals that are called humans' who live in 'big huts that are called houses' and whose bread resembles 'a certain hard, black and glutinous stone'.[25] It is impossible not to think of the first chapter of *Candide* with its descriptions of Westphalia and the castle of 'Baron Thunder-ten-tronckh'. In Voltaire's novel, the baron was the most powerful aristocrat of Westphalia because his castle had a door and windows.[26] Just as in the description of young Candide in 1759, the inhabitants of Westphalia in Voltaire's observations of 1750 are a kind of 'noble savages'. To his niece he wrote that these prehistorical-seeming men were 'healthy, vigorous, and happy'.[27] Stuck in this 'desolate countryside', Voltaire thought back to the comfort of his home in Paris as he wrote about the Westphalians: 'It is not that I envy them, / I very much love our gilded wainscots, / I bless the happy industry, / That procures us the hundred pleasures, / That I loved to praise.'[28] There was Voltaire travelling in his carriage which he regarded as one of the most exquisite products of French industry and as an example for the progress that industry could procure. But when he looked out from his carriage he saw the 'desolate countryside' and the primitive men of Westphalia. The fundamental importance of the fruits of industry and of industry itself on everyday life could hardly have been impressed on him more forcefully. In his desperation in the midst of Westphalia, lacking all the comfort that he was used to, Voltaire even started to revert to religious formulas and blessed a phenomenon as worldly as industry. He even praises it as 'happy industry'. Under the impression of the backwardness of Westphalia, Voltaire repeated what he had already said when he considered the abundance that existed in Paris: he reiterated the association between industry and what might today be called 'standard of living'. There are, however, not only the hundred pleasures procured by industry that are lacking in Westphalia; there are also the words 'that I loved to praise' in the poem. It is not farfetched to see this as a reference to Voltaire's *The Worldling* and thus as a reiteration of the link between the comfortable life and industry as its source. In *The Worldling*, Voltaire had mocked the 'golden age' of Adam and Eve because they lacked 'industry and comfort'. By analogy, he calls Westphalia a replica of that 'golden age' which has elsewhere – notably in Paris – been superseded by the 'iron age' with its 'industry' and 'comfort'.[29]

Industry in Westphalia

Voltaire who was stuck in Halberstadt for several days ('waiting to be fortunate enough to leave') was not the only observer of the matters of industry in Westphalia.[30] Already in 1729 Montesquieu had travelled in Westphalia. He wrote about the misery in the region. In particular, he described the tax burden in the Prussian parts of Westphalia as excessive. Commerce was submitted to heavy and above all arbitrary tariffs that prevented economic development. Montesquieu's views thus confirm Voltaire's negative judgement about the region. However, he also disagreed in one noteworthy respect with his fellow philosopher. About the same Westphalian bread that Voltaire had dismissed as a 'hard, black and glutinous stone', Montesquieu wrote that it was 'excellent with butter'.[31]

Voltaire's host Frederick II also had thoughts about the development of Westphalia. Already as a young crown prince, in 1738, he had visited the Prussian territories in Westphalia and wrote to Voltaire about the rural simplicity of the region.[32] Despite the fact that the western Provinces of Prussia generally received less attention from the Prussian government than the eastern parts of the country, Frederick was resolved to change the situation in Westphalia.[33] Soon after he became king, he ordered the local administration, the Kriegs- und Domänen Kammer of Minden and Ravensberg, to give annual reports about the lack of manufactures and craftsmen in the province.[34] The Kammern were an important institution in the Prussian administration. They had been introduced in 1723 in order to ensure a prompt and efficient execution of the orders of the Prussian government. The older forms of local administration that contained corporative elements made it difficult to implement decisions that were in conflict with local interests. The Kammern thus became one of the principal tools of governmental policies for the encouragement of industry. At the same time, they were also reporting to Berlin about local conditions.[35] In the year of Voltaire's travel, for instance, the 25 page report was entitled 'Most humble report of the chamber of Minden about the lack of manufactures and tradesmen.'[36] The 1750 report was one of the most extensive. It detailed the possibilities that the local administration saw for a further development especially of the linen manufactures; incentives suggested by the local administration were tax breaks and subsidies. In the report, detailed statistical tables registering the number of craftsmen and manufactures as well as tax revenues and other data were promised for the future. Indeed, for the next years steadily improving tables can be found. It would, however, not be until 1765 that a comprehensive set of tables was compiled. The brochure contained for each town in the province the name of the manufacturers and notes about the quality and quantity of output. In addition to that, it also featured a column that noted the kind of subsidies that entrepreneurs had received and whether they had stuck to the promises that they had made in return.[37] Even more detailed tables were compiled for other Prussian provinces as early as in 1749.[38]

Frederick's goal was, however, not only to survey and administer the lack of manufactures and craftsmen. The remedies employed hold no surprises. Already after the first report about the lack of manufactures in 1749, a new excise tariff was declared for the province of Minden and Ravensberg. The new tariffs for foreign goods entering the cities were in some cases ten times higher than for the local produce. In particular the local textile production was shielded from foreign competition.[39] Other local trades were apparently considered less worthy of tariff protection: under the common subject heading 'comedians' – a category that was listed alongside with 'livestock trade' and 'timber' – it can be seen that puppeteers, dentists and oculists were all subject to the same tariff, no matter whether they were foreigners or locals.[40] At the same time the local newspapers were used to announce premiums for whoever was willing to set up a new manufacture or trade. In Frederick's cabinet orders the subsidies were referred to as 'encouragement' or 'enlivening' ('Aufmunterung') for factories and manufactures.[41] It may be added that the perception of Westphalia as a backward region seems to have been a common sentiment among the Prussian public. In 1751, the already familiar *Berliner Nachrichten* reviewed an anthology of poems by a Westphalian writer, a certain E.C. Franckfurt. The critic could not but express his surprise that a Westphalian was brave enough to publish poetry. The province was after all one, he wrote, 'where the Muses do not normally like to dwell'.[42] A prominent French visitor who travelled to Prussia some years later, made more favourable comments on the industry of Westphalia than the philosopher king. More than thirty years after Voltaire, the Count de Mirabeau – not to be confused with his father, the already mentioned Marquis de Mirabeau – made the same journey from Paris to Berlin. But while Voltaire reached Potsdam as a travelling poet, the count's visit had an ulterior motive. As the death of Frederick II was imminent, Mirabeau's charge was to report to the French government about the monarch's health and the court's intrigues. After Frederick had died – as a consequence of an excessively large lobster for dinner, as Mirabeau maintained – the informant stayed on and tried to promote his Physiocratic views with the new king. His stay did not only result in brief secret reports, some of which could only be smuggled out with carrier pigeons,[43] Mirabeau also composed an opus far too heavy for any carrier pigeon: the four-volume work *The Prussian monarchy under Frederick the Great*. Aside from being a detailed economic survey the volumes are a manifesto for laissez-faire and against Frederick's efforts to develop Prussia. The count saw Frederick's state not only as an example of the phenomenon of 'too much governing' but also as an ideal study object for a 'science of despotism'. The work also contains a survey of the economic situation of all Prussian provinces, including Westphalia. About the inhabitants of this region, Mirabeau agreed with Voltaire in at least one respect. He saw the Westphalians as 'extraordinarily phlegmatic'. He also diagnosed much 'rudeness' and 'ignorance' in the whole region. Hardly encouraging was also the count's conclusion about the land of Arminius: 'The customs there are really bizarre.'[44] It may be mentioned in this context, that Mirabeau diagnosed slightly more apathy and ignorance among Catholic Westphalians than among their Protestant cousins. Max Weber would have been delighted.[45]

However, Mirabeau discerned traces of industry in 1786, which Voltaire did not see in 1750. While Mirabeau certainly did not foresee the steel and mining future of western Westphalia or the appearance of such industrious Westphalians as Carl Bertelsmann (1791–1850), he reported a considerable industry in two parts of Westphalia: the *Principauté* Minden and the *Comté* Ravensberg. Westphalia was, indeed, on the way to become one of the principal 'new' industrial regions of Europe in this period.[46] The two provinces Minden and Ravensberg, Mirabeau wrote, shared the same 'kind of industry'. That industry included a few French glove- and hat-makers but mainly an important linen production. Mirabeau calculated a yearly linen output of 921,000 *livres* for Minden and a considerable yearly production of 3,990,000 *livres* for Ravensberg. A propos of the latter he also noted a tax reduction that Frederick had given to the province: 'Frederick must have been struck by the industry of the small people of Ravensberg.'[47] The chronology evident in this observation is telling. Mirabeau sees the tax reduction as a bonus which follows the development of industry. In contrast to this view Frederick's policies in Westphalia and elsewhere were based on the notion that tax reductions would stimulate industry. The measures were intended to be financial incentives for the creation of manufactures. However, in Mirabeau's perspective, industry developed spontaneously and independently of tax incentives. The measure employed by the

Prussian administration did not help to create a sustainable industry. In his view, a tax reduction could at best be a superfluous bonus for a manufacture that operated successfully. However, historians of Westphalia have emphasised the significant difference in the economic development of the Prussian territories in Westphalia and the neighbouring territories where the administration was less concerned with the progress of manufacturing.[48]

Beyond the different views of political economy that underlie the remarks of Voltaire, Frederick, and Mirabeau, there is also a marked difference in the terminology. Voltaire uses the word 'industry' but not nearly as often as later during his stay in Prussia or, indeed, afterwards. In contrast to that, Mirabeau, who wrote his remarks about Westphalia almost forty years later, used the term frequently. Frederick, in turn, represents an interesting case. In his German language administrative writings of the period, the term does not appear. Accordingly, it is also absent from the writings of the lower administration where words like 'manufacture', 'factory', 'tradesman', or 'artisan' are used.[49] Their sum was simply referred to by the respective plural but no special term was used for the sector of manufacturing as a whole. Frederick's political and historical writings from the period, however, contain the word 'industry' frequently and prominently. These texts were written in French. It is significant that the term appeared in German later than in French and that the German language borrowed it from French. The details of this transition will not be explored here; however, it can hardly surprise that a country that imported French tradesmen and production techniques, and that followed Colbert's example of economic policies in order to develop industry, also adopted the French term for the sector that it sought to build up after the model of the principal industrial nation of the time. The fact that the French language was used to designate the abstract concept of industry might also be seen as reflecting contemporary perceptions according to which the German language was unsuited to express more complex concepts. Frederick's command of the German language remained poor throughout his life and he regarded the mother tongue of most of his subjects as greatly inferior to French. Thus, because of the perceived linguistic superiority of the French language and the economic superiority of France, a French term might have seemed more appropriate to contemporaries in Germany to designate a complex and sophisticated concept such as industry.

Voltaire continued his journey across Westphalia and onwards to Berlin without considering such linguistic differences between French and German. Equally, he did not take note of the considerable efforts that were made to establish more industry in Westphalia. He left Westphalia with the solid conviction of having crossed an industry- and culture-less desert that contrasted sharply with the prosperity of Paris. It is noteworthy that Voltaire's explanations for both the relative backwardness of Westphalia and the advanced development of Paris invoked the concept of industry in a prominent function.

The arrival in Berlin: 'The fairy-land'

The Westphalian experience left a deep impression on Voltaire. 'I have passed through purgatory', he wrote to his friend d'Argental after his arrival in Berlin. After this journey, Berlin was nothing less than 'heaven' to Voltaire.[50] His enthusiasm for his new home, however, was due not only to the 'Westphalian trauma' but also to the many splendid events that filled the first weeks of his stay in Berlin. A look at a diary of his host, Frederick the Great, compiled in the nineteenth century, makes it possible to reconstruct some of Voltaire's first experiences.[51] The diary notes not only the appointments and travels of Frederick himself but also frequently indicates the movements of Voltaire. After the entry 'today arrival of Voltaire in Potsd. from Paris', the entries that mention Voltaire in one way or another are legion.[52] In the weeks after Voltaire's arrival, Frederick presented to Voltaire everything that the arts in Berlin had to offer.[53] On 15, 19 and 21 July, for example, several Italian intermezzi were presented in the recently built Orangerie in Potsdam.[54] Like the château of Sanssouci – where Voltaire was lodged in the first days – the Orangerie had only been finished in 1747.[55] Both châteaux were new and had been built in record time – in just two years. Responsible for this speed was Frederick's architect Georg von Knobelsdorff who directed the works. The performances that Voltaire and Frederick saw in the Orangerie were called 'The imaginary count' and 'Don Tabarano' and were probably performed by '*la signora Astrua et i signori castrati*' whose voices Voltaire praised in one of his letters.[56] On the 22nd of the same month Frederick treated his host to the opera 'Phaeton'. The work was staged in Berlin's first opera house which was almost as new as the Orangerie. It had been finished by Knobelsdorff in 1743 and was, at the time, the biggest and only free standing opera house in Germany.[57] Voltaire apparently liked the building ('a Greek temple') but not the opera ('a Tartarian piece').[58]

This is despite the fact that Frederick had spared no effort to lure the best singers and dancers to his opera house. The cabinet files of the

1740s document the correspondence of Frederick with his ambassador Le Chaussier in Paris who recruited the famous Lany sisters as dancers. The promised salary for the next three years was a considerable 2000 *crowns* for the two sisters and a further 2000 for the brother who acted as their impresario.[59] As a point of reference it may be helpful to remember that Voltaire's novel *The man of forty crowns* has its name from the average yearly per capita income in French agriculture calculated by Voltaire.[60] For the singer Barberina von Palmanuova from Vienna, travel expenses alone were 750 *Imperial Thaler*. There were, however, not only financial hurdles to be overcome in the recruitment of artists for the opera. In the case of this singer Frederick had to compete with an 'enamoured English lord' who showered her with 'considerable gifts' and even followed her when she was already en route to Prussia. The romantic Englishman insisted on coming to Berlin and waiting for Frederick's death, which would free the object of his affections from her appointment.[61] The king, however, not only made great efforts to establish well-known artists in Berlin but was also involved in the most minute details of the daily business of cultural life in his capital. He thus commented, and decided personally, on the lighting in the theatre ('this candle ... illuminates badly') or the request for new costumes for the ballet dancers ('I will not do anything').[62]

The opera was by no means the only new building in the centre of Berlin. On his way to the opera Voltaire may have noticed two construction sites on the architectonic ensemble of the Forum Fridericianum adjacent to the opera building. Next to the opera the structure of the Catholic cathedral of Sankt Hedwig was taking shape in the heart of Protestant Berlin. Across the boulevard of Unter den Linden the construction of the *Prinz Heinrich Palais* – today home to the Humboldt University – was proceeding. Like the opera and so many other buildings of the period these two projects were designed and supervised by the ubiquitous von Knobelsdorff.[63] The important place that these building projects occupied in the government of Frederick II can be seen from a draft for the government budget for the year 1743 written in the monarch's own hand. In this year of peace between the two first Silesian Wars, Frederick attributed out of his private budget 20,000 crowns to Knobelsdorff 'for the buildings'. The sum represents a significant 1.25 per cent of that year's government budget. The duality of Frederick's reign, however, is well illustrated by the 200,000 crowns that were spent in the same year on gunpowder.[64]

When Voltaire arrived in Prussia the arts were thriving in Berlin. They were, however, clearly only thriving there since recently. Most of the new buildings mentioned here, in particular the château of Sanssouci, did not exist when Voltaire had visited Berlin for the first time in 1740. The rapid development of Berlin was palpable for Voltaire when he described it as a 'formerly savage place' that was had been 'embellished by the arts' and 'ennobled by glory'.[65] For Voltaire, Berlin was rising from the level of backward Westphalia to that of civilised Paris. Following the advice of Madame du Châtelet, Voltaire began soon to be interested in the role that the 'industry ... of a whole people' played in the progress of arts and sciences that he was witnessing in Prussia. However, before discussing Voltaire's observations about Prussian industry it is necessary to examine an event that took place in the first weeks of this stay in Berlin and that impressed him greatly. Voltaire's perception of this event – a *carrouzel* – is a concrete illustration of the close interrelation which he saw between art and industry.

The highlight of Voltaire's first weeks in Berlin: a *carrouzel*

The *carrouzel* was the highlight of Voltaire's first weeks in Berlin. Frederick's diary notes *carrouzel* for 25 and 27 August and adds 'in Lustg.', indicating the Lustgarten as the location. This garden was located in front of the Stadtschloss, the Hohenzollerns's residence in the city. What was a *carrouzel* in those days? If the reporters of the *Berliner Nachrichten* can be trusted, preparations for it had already begun well over a month before and if Voltaire's judgement can be trusted the long preparation was well worth it. In an enthusiastic letter, Voltaire gives a description of the scenery: the event involved not less than forty-six thousand glass lanterns and three thousand soldiers. The latter were divided into four small armies dressed up as Romans, Carthaginians, Persians and Greeks. Accompanied by 'martial music' the antique warriors paraded around the Lustgarten and 'fought' for victory in the shape of a golden apple from the hand of princess Amalia. The event ended with a gala dinner and a ball.[66]

Voltaire was so impressed with the presentation that he wrote to a friend in Paris: 'It is the fairy-land.' He did not, however, only communicate his enthusiasm to his friends in Paris but also to the readers of the *Berliner Nachrichten*: with a short delay of three weeks the paper printed a poem which Voltaire had been inspired to write by what the newspaper called a *Karussel*. The poem praised the greatness of the *carrouzel* and affirms that even Athens and Rome never saw a spectacle of that scale. Frederick was certainly pleased to see Berlin mentioned in one breath with the classic cities. However, the next poem of Voltaire, published in the same paper, resulted in a miniature literary scandal. On 15 August the paper carried a story about verses that Voltaire had addressed to the princess Amalia. Again, he praised his new home ('the supreme abode') and the princess ('your beautiful eyes'). The verses to the sister of the king did not go unnoticed. Only a week later the paper carried a swift denial: the poem was not addressed to the said princess, the chamberlain M. de Voltaire did not write it, nor would he ever write such a thing because he was both 'intelligent' and 'cautious'.[67]

Light verses were, however, not the only comments that Voltaire made on the *carrouzel*. Before the event itself he wrote to his friend d'Argental in Paris that the *carrouzel* was expected to be worthy in all aspects of the celebrations of Louis XIV. After having seen the *carrouzel*, he was even more emphatic: 'Frederic the Great is even greater than Louis 14.'[68] Certainly the question of whether Voltaire thought of Fredrick as greater, just as great or, slightly less great than Louis XIV is of lesser importance. The comparison itself is noteworthy, for he is comparing Prussia in 1750 with an era that he considered to be the era in which France acquired her greatness. As Voltaire was about to finish his *Age of Louis XIV* he saw in the king of Prussia a monarch in the same mould as the king whose reign brought culture and prosperity to France. (It will emerge in later chapters that this opinion was far from uncontroversial, but it certainly was Voltaire's.) If Frederick's Berlin looked to Voltaire like Louis's Paris, the possibility of a reflection of Frederick's reign on Voltaire's perspective on the age of Louis XIV must be considered.

It may be argued that Voltaire's enthusiasm for Frederick was not long-lasting. This is quite true and the compliments for Fredrick were less numerous after the first troubles occurred towards the end of 1751. By that time, however, the *Age of Louis XIV* was already written and printed. The period in which Voltaire wrote the work was one of enthusiasm for Frederick's reign that he shared with many contemporaries. The view of an 'age of Frederick' was a widespread concept at the time. Immanuel Kant, for example, called the eighteenth century the 'age of Frederick' in his *What is enlightenment?* However, no author linked Frederick's reign as directly to that of Louis XIV as did Voltaire. Considering the parallels that Voltaire saw between the two monarchs, the *Age of Louis XIV* may well be approached as an educational work, intended to encourage and guide the Prussian monarch. It is this spirit that reverberates from Voltaire's remark that his work about the age of Louis XIV should be of interest to Frederick who was about to form another great age. It may also be useful to remind the modern reader that only 25 years separated the end of the reign of Louis XIV and the beginning of Frederick's reign. Voltaire's work is thus to be understood as a piece of historiography that was related in more than one way to the place and time in which it was written. Such a perspective is, in fact, very close to the author's own understanding and to that of Frederick. In several instances Frederick suggested a certain continuity from Louis XIV to his own reign.[69]

Voltaire's considerations about the greatness of the two monarchs raise the question of why a spectacle like a *carrouzel* inspired this kind of reflection. In what way did a *carrouzel* represent the greatness of a monarch for Voltaire? First of all, it should be noted that the view according to which a great *carrouzel* was the sign of a great monarch was not an ephemeral idea for Voltaire. At least ten years after he had seen the spectacle in Berlin, Voltaire repeated this view in his great history of humanity, the *Essay on universal history*. The only difference was that there Voltaire added a third *carrouzel* to those of Louis XIV and Frederick II. It was an event staged by another great monarch of the period admired by Voltaire: Catherine II.[70]

The question remains: why did Voltaire see in these spectacles a sign of greatness? In order to understand the symbolism of these events, it is worth taking a look at Voltaire's representation on the *carrouzels* of Louis XIV. One description gives a particularly good insight into Voltaire's perspective on these matters: in 1685 Louis XIV gave a *carrouzel* on the occasion of the wedding of one of his sons. There were, in fact, all the elements present that for Voltaire formed the essence of the greatness of the reign of Louis XIV. The flourishing of the arts was represented by the performance of a new play by Jean Racine, an author revered by Voltaire. The achievements of architecture were represented by the venues of the performances, the gardens of Sceaux and Versailles. Both were designed by André Lenôtre who, according to Voltaire, perfected the 'art of gardens'. Finally, the event was completed by a display of the fruits of industry: 'Four pavilions were built, filled with most refined and rarefied products that the industry of the workers of Paris could produce.'[71] The *carrouzel* thus turned into something more than idle entertainment. It functioned as a display of the development of the country, namely its industry and arts. The event is remotely reminiscent of the world expositions of later centuries. These events combined fine arts, entertainment and the products of industry. A great age incorporated all these elements and a great *carrouzel* symbolised this greatness. If the *carrouzel* of 1685 symbolised the flourishing of arts and industry during the reign of Louis XIV, the 'carrouzel' of 1750 did the same for the reign of Frederick II.

Frederick's thought on art and industry

The association between the progress of arts and sciences and industry became an important notion in Voltaire's thought. During his stay in Prussia he was not only interested in the outward signs that announced the greatness of Frederick's reign. He took also an interest in the industry of the people that was the driving force behind the progress that he observed. Voltaire observed Frederick's active role in the development of Prussian arts and industry. He was at the same time exposed to Frederick's thought on the subject. Frederick's programmatic writings placed a special emphasis on the development of industry as the sole source of wealth of the Prussian state. In Frederick's perspective on the history of his nation, the protracted cultural progress that Prussia had made was closely associated to the keen interest that some of his predecessors took in the development of Prussian industry.

Frederick was not only closely involved in the promotion of the arts in Berlin. He and his administration also played an active role in the promotion of industry throughout the country. The list of Prussian companies that received governmental support in the form of subsidies, privileges, tax reductions and monopolies included many branches of industry. In fact, Mirabeau discerned 'a kind of passion' for privileged companies on the part of Frederick. The count clearly disapproved of companies and monopolies as the 'summit of error' among Frederick's attempts to encourage the industry of his realm.[72] The king, on the other hand, harboured a similar contempt for private individuals who were pursuing their economic advantage too eagerly for his taste. In the *Epistle against the gentlemen of finance* – the original draft in the king's hand is conserved in the Prussian archives – he calls them 'common carrot sellers' and worse. 'Insupportable mob', 'excrement' and 'brigands' are some of the other names that the king found for the speculators and financiers who exceeded what Frederick considered the limits of acceptable private economic initiative.[73] Frederick's poem suggests the difference between his and Mirabeau's approach to the matters of industry. Despite this clear disagreement, Frederick would hardly have objected to Mirabeau's 1788 statement: 'Frederick has tried everything to encourage industry; it was one of the principles of his administration'. Frederick himself had declared it a principle not only of his government but an eternal doctrine of the Prussian state. In 1752, in the middle of Voltaire's stay in Berlin, Frederick wrote in his *Political testament*: 'Prussia's power is not founded on any intrinsic power but solely on industry.'[74] This statement sums up the essence of Frederick's perspective on the historical development of Prussia, while at the same time it is a programmatic statement about the policies of his own reign and a recommendation for his successors. Prussia did not posses strong natural resources, nor was it favoured by its geographical position. It did not even have a compact territory. Prussian provinces were spread between the Baltic Sea and the Rhine. In this particular situation, Frederick saw the crucial importance of manufacturing as a source of wealth that could be developed on the basis of the population's labour despite these disadvantages.

In Frederick's view industry had brought progress to an otherwise sterile land. In his *Memoirs of the house of Brandenburg* of 1750 – Voltaire proof-read the work and re-read it while he was writing the *Age of Louis XIV* – Frederick traced the Prussian concern with industry back to the reign of his grandfather. In the programmatic introduction to the second volume of the work the king re-emphasised his concern with industry. This part of the work bears the indicative title: 'Of mores, customs, industry, and of progress in the arts and sciences.' In the introduction to the second half of the history of Prussia, Frederick promises special attention to 'the birth of industry' and to the 'causes that developed it'. He insists that it is the duty of any historian to enquire into matters of industry to obtain 'complete knowledge of a state'. While other aspects of history tended to be in the focus of historiography, he continues, the historian must turn his attention to the useful objects of enquiry. Frederick underlined that these aspects are of the greatest interest for 'politicians & philosophers'. Once again, as in Madame du Châtelet's writings, industry is declared to be a subject worthy of philosophical attention. It must be remembered that Voltaire observed Frederick's efforts to develop industry and read the monarch's writings about the issue while he was writing the *Age of Louis XIV*. Voltaire read Frederick's history soon after his arrival in 1750. In October of that year he made corrections to the second edition. He also wrote to his niece about his admiration for Frederick's work. Above all, he envied the monarch for his freedom to express his opinions about the history of his country openly. Voltaire's writings on Louis XIV were not welcome in France and he saw himself forced to write his praise of the French monarch in Prussia. Voltaire mentions only one criticism of Frederick's work. The monarch's perspective on his grandfather, Frederick I, seemed too critical to Voltaire. 'I quite like this grandfather', wrote Voltaire, 'because he was magnificent and he left beautiful monuments.' Voltaire's admiration for a monarch who founded the Prussian academy of sciences and created the Prussian silk manufacture comes as no surprise. One of the main reasons for Voltaire's admiration of Louis XIV was the splendour that he created. This splendour, Voltaire argued, led to the progress of art and industry in seventeenth-century France. In this context, Voltaire repeatedly pointed to the encouragement of the Académie Française and the progress of the French silk industry as two of the great achievements of Louis's reign. In 1751, Voltaire read the new edition of Frederick's work. He was enthusiastic: 'this is clear cut, elegant, precise, and above all philosophical!' Most of his praise was directed at part of the work which deals with the history of 'mores', 'government', and 'religion'. This part of the work also contained Frederick's arguments in support of the importance of industry. It emerges that Voltaire did not only reside in a country which impressed him every day with its economic and cultural progress. He also lived at the court of a monarch who declared industry repeatedly to be the sole source of this progress.[75]

Modern perspectives on Prussian industry under Frederick II

The promotion of industry was not only a prominent subject of Frederick's writings and his philosophical debates. The concern with industry also emerges clearly from his economic policies. In a period which saw an extraordinarily close connection between philosophers and monarchs, new ideas and new policies were equally intertwined. Frederick was perhaps the European monarch whose policies were influenced strongest by the thought of the enlightenment. Among his reforms as a monarch were the abolition of torture, cruelty in the army and press censorship. As Voltaire would find out later the abolition of censorship did not mean that it could not be re-established when the king deemed it necessary. However, the close association of Frederick's policies and enlightenment thought emerges clearly. This association also underpins the monarch's approach to the promotion of industry, one of the priorities of his administration. In June 1740 – only three months after he was crowned – Frederick created a new department within the Prussian central government administration, the Generaldirektorium. The new administration was the Departement für Kommerz-, Fabrik-, and Manufakturwesen, known as the fifth department. The sole task of this new organ of government was the promotion of manufacturing in Prussia. To what extent the promotion of industry was a personal concern for Frederick is illustrated by the subsequent developments. The new department was initially led by the minister von Marschall. When his term ended in 1749, however, the king did not appoint a new minister. Frederick took it upon himself to lead the fifth department. As with the promotion of the arts in his capital Frederick was personally involved in the specific details of the promotion of industry in Prussia.[76]

Frederick thus created the administrative tools which he needed to promote manufacturing. However, Frederick's policies for the encouragement of industry have to be seen in the context of the largely agrarian structure of the Prussian economy in the eighteenth century. Even towards the end of the eighteenth century the ratio between the population of the Prussian country side and the cities was 7:2. In 1800, 80 per cent of Prussians were still employed in agriculture and small rural trades.[77] With 100,000 inhabitants in the year 1755, Berlin was an extraordinarily large population centre.[78] Throughout the eighteenth century it alone accounted for one-third of the manufacturing output in Prussia. The economic situation of Berlin can therefore hardly be considered representative for the whole of Prussia. The city grew rapidly. In 1688 it had 20,000 inhabitants. By the end of the eighteenth century the city was populated by 172,000 inhabitants. Even compared to the significant population growth of the whole country, Berlin grew extraordinarily fast. The population of Prussia increased rapidly from 1.4 million inhabitants in 1688 to 3.4 million in 1784 – this increase was partly due to the annexation of Silesia with its 1.1 million inhabitants – and 6.2 million in 1800. Population growth in Prussia was significantly higher than in other European countries in this period.[79]

Prussia in the eighteenth century was, thus, still a largely agrarian state. But despite the continued importance of agriculture, extraordinary efforts were made for the development of manufacturing. During the reign of Frederick a total of 2.8 million *Thaler* was spent in direct subsidies for manufacturing. The Prussian government was involved in one way or another in the creation of 1302 manufacturing businesses in the period after the Seven Years War alone.[80] Productions of silk, velour, leather, porcelain, gloves, sugar, woollen and linen textiles, and many other goods were created. These efforts to promote manufacturing were important because of the sheer volume of resources employed. They were also noteworthy because they were intended to fundamentally change the economic structure of Prussia rather than improving an already dominant sector. The early stages of the growth of industry in Prussia are, not least, of particular interest because the country eventually rose to become one of the principal industrialised countries in Europe.

There has been considerable debate about the question whether the active role of the Prussian state helped or harmed economic development in Prussia.[81] A more differentiated analysis of the complex relationship between state and private enterprise in Prussia is necessary. A complementary relationship between private entrepreneurs and the Prussian state existed in the eighteenth century. The lack of skilled workers and financial resources for investment prevented many potential entrepreneurs from engaging in any form of enterprise. Frequently, private entrepreneurs could only pursue business activities with the help of the Prussian state. The Prussian state adapted its policies to the different local situations in the Prussian provinces. The development of the silk industry is a good example of this flexibility. The silk industry of Berlin was heavily subsidized and was run under close control of the government. At the same time, the prosperous private silk manufacturing in the western province of Mark was largely left unregulated and unprotected. The attempt to open East Friesia to trans-oceanic commerce is another example of the extraordinarily flexible approach to economic development. An enterprising spirit reigned in Prussia in the period. Many different roads to economic progress were explored in a pragmatic way and without much regard for economic dogmas of any kind.[82]

In what follows the complex interaction of private initiative and governmental activism in the creation of Prussia's industry will be further explored. In particular, Voltaire's perception of the rise of industry in Prussia in the light of the French experience will be discussed. In his account of the great age of Louis XIV, the French silk industry and the Compagnie des Indes played a crucial role in the creation of wealth and prosperity. From a similar perspective, Voltaire commented on the Prussian silk industry and the Prussian Asiatic trade company.

Merchant industry in Prussia: the new Asiatic trade company

One of the branches of industry which Voltaire saw at the origin of Prussia's progress was the newly founded Prussian Asiatic trade company. It was founded in the year of Voltaire's arrival in Berlin. He mentioned the Preußische Asiatische Handlungscompagnie in the same letter in which he compared Frederick II to Louis XIV. In the letter, he described the company as one of the signs of the great progress that Prussia was making thanks to Frederick's policies. After an enumeration of Prussian achievements such as the *carrouzel* and the recent military victories, Voltaire wrote to his correspondent in Paris: 'Add to this that we are going to have a company of the Indies.' The connection that Voltaire took for granted between the greatness of the monarch, the progress of the nation, the flourishing of the arts and the new trade company is not immediately obvious for the modern reader. Trade companies were of particular interest to Voltaire. The French Compagnie des Indes would feature prominently in the *Age of Louis XIV* as one of the institutions that made the greatness of that era, and that freed France from being 'tributary to Dutch industry'. In this context, industry was understood in a sectoral connotation but one that went beyond manufacturing. The 'merchant industry', as Voltaire called it, included not only manufacturing but also the activities that were related to the exchange and transport of goods. Trading companies were thus seen as a form of industry by Voltaire. On one hand these companies were associated to the encouragement of domestic manufacturing for exportation. On the other hand they were – like manufacturing – associated with the provision of the amenities of life or as Voltaire put it in the *Age of Louis XIV*, 'these goods from India that have become necessary'.[83]

The *Defence of the worldling* contains verses about some delicious coffee that is served at a bourgeois table thanks to the 'human industry' that fetched it from Arabia. This industry also provides the protagonists of the poem with wine from the Canary Islands, Chinese china, and silver saucers from Peru. Now, if one substitutes coffee with tea, one is already quite close to the cargo list of the first ship of the Preußische Asiatische Handlungscompagnie. In a memorandum that was submitted to Frederick II in 1750 in order to obtain the charter for the trading company, a view similar to that of Voltaire was put forward. The purpose of the trading company was not only to generate profits for the government but also to provide the subjects with exotic goods otherwise not available or at least to lower the prices for those goods. The company, the document states, was to procure the goods 'necessary for the consumption of the people of the north' such as wine, coffee, sugar, oil, cotton, wool, indigo and a long list of others. At the same time, the profits that trading companies generated for state and individuals remained the principal motivation for their creation.[84]

It may have been Voltaire's personal experience that convinced him of the benefits that were associated with the creation of a trade company. Not only was he a long-time shareholder of the French Compagnie des Indes but his secretary Sébastien Longchamp also maintained that the poet had acquired stock in the Prussian Asiatic trade company. In the list of the shareholders in the Prussian archives, however, he is not mentioned. It is possible, though, that he invested through an intermediary. However, his investments in the French East India trade are well documented and will be discussed later. Voltaire can thus be seen as an observer and commentator with some expertise in the matters of trading companies.[85]

Voltaire saw the creation of the company in the wider context of Frederick's efforts to promote domestic and international trade. Besides the wealth generating effect of trade itself, increased exchange was seen as a means to open up new markets for the products of Prussian industry. In the *Age of Louis XIV*, Voltaire described what he saw as the positive effect of the French trade companies during the reign of Louis XIV. In his opinion, this form of trade had made France rich by stimulating French exports. He vigorously opposed the critics who saw the East India trade as a drain of wealth and as a waste of money for luxury products that were quickly consumed. It was Voltaire's positive interpretation of France's historical experience with trading companies, together with his own successful investments in overseas trade that informed his enthusiasm for the new Prussian trade company. He saw this company as a part of the great progress that Prussia was making and that put the country on a par with the other great nations of the period who all had trading companies. For Voltaire, it was a crucial step in the development of Prussia that the nation would now participate in the flourishing overseas trade that had made other European countries wealthy and prosperous. A strikingly similar perspective appears in the remarks of the Prussian economist Gustav Schmoller over a hundred years later. Schmoller wrote about the economic policies of Frederick II: 'The task set before the men of that time was to secure for the ... Prussian state a share in the industries, and in the forms of industry, that constituted the essential features of the higher civilisation of western Europe.' While Schmoller had not only trading companies in mind, these comments aptly sum up Voltaire's views and those of his host Frederick. Voltaire was clearly convinced that an East India company was a branch of industry that was an essential feature of the higher civilisation of western Europe. This view is well illustrated by his description of the creation of the French Compagnie des Indes. 'Louis XIV who sought the glory and advantage of his nation in every possible way', writes Voltaire in his *Fragments on some revolutions in India*, 'founded in 1664, thanks to the efforts of the immortal Colbert, a powerful company of the Indies'. In contrast to this, the critics of trading companies were for Voltaire nothing less than backward looking opponents of progress. In the *Age of Louis XIV* he described the critics of trading companies as 'the advocates of the old timid, ignorant, and narrow-minded economy'.[86]

Seen from today's perspective the oceanic ambitions of the Prussian landlubbers may seem odd. However, Voltaire was not the only contemporary to take the latest project of Frederick very seriously. After the company had been chartered on 4 August 1750 in the East Friesian port of Emden the news spread quickly to the countries and cities bordering the north sea. The development was cause for serious concern among the established naval powers. Secret Dutch government reports warned that the company was the herald of 'the most far-reaching projects' for the expansion of Prussian commerce. British diplomats sent the alarming news to London and were instructed to gather further information 'in a secret manner'. Hamburg merchants read about the new competitor in the city's newspapers and the French minister of war learnt about the company from Voltaire. In 1750, diplomats, administrators, merchants and publicists across northern Europe watched with a mixture of fascination and concern as the young king of Prussia who had triumphed in the recent war of Austrian succession seemed to turn his mind and determination to the matters of overseas trade and commerce.[87]

There was genuine and widespread concern in 1750 that the creation of the company was the first step in a Prussian bid to become a major power in commerce and industry and to participate in the world of oceanic trade. This concern was not unfounded. In the period, Frederick II wanted his country to participate in overseas commerce on a larger scale and made this plan one of the priorities of his government. Largely situated in the heart of the European continent and traditionally oriented towards agriculture and expansion on the European continent, Prussia made a substantial effort to develop manufacturing and commerce also through the participation in the world of the Atlantic in the 1750s. Klaus Weber has argued that much of the Atlantic commerce in Hamburg, Bremen and other German ports had economic and social links that reached deep into the hinterland.[88] The Prussian example suggests that there were not merely strong links between Atlantic commerce of the coastal regions and the inland. In the 1750s the Prussian drive to participate in overseas commerce originated from the inland of a country which was traditionally oriented towards the continent. That government officials of Berlin rather than the merchants of Hamburg were the driving force behind a project to engage in commerce with distant shores is significant also in another respect. Much of the debates about the 'single functional unit' of the Atlantic has focused on the 'co-ordination provided by individual merchants'.[89] Weber, too, emphasises that the overseas commerce of Bremen and Hamburg was established by merchants who overcame the hurdles established by the mercantilist state. However, in the Prussian experience the initiative to develop industry and participate in overseas commerce must be largely attributed to the government bureaucracy in Berlin. The present study may therefore be a case in point to William O'Reilly's recent reminder to Atlantic historians that 'homogeneity was starkly absent in the past'.[90]

The Prussian decision to start a trade company in Emden was the result of an internal debate about the route that Prussia should take in the matters of industry and commerce. The actors in this debate were foreign merchants and merchants from Emden and Berlin local administrators of East Friesia, ministers in Berlin and, above all, Frederick II. The object of the debate was principles of political economy and their application. Should the largely agrarian Prussia develop this traditional source of income through domestic colonisation and improvement of agricultural techniques or should Prussia try to engage in manufacturing and overseas trade with the products of its growing industry? Could a nation without a powerful navy successfully develop overseas trade? Questions like these were controversial at the time in Prussia and elsewhere. The Prussian debate was intimately linked with the concerns and debates amongst its neighbours. While Prussian administrators were concerned with the further development of commerce the Dutch government was preoccupied with the question of how Dutch commerce could prevail over its foreign competitors, among them the new Prussian company. A substantial report was drawn up by the admiralty of Zeeland – one of five Dutch admiralties – which discussed the fundamental principles of commerce and the concrete steps to be taken. This report, however, was not only read by Dutch administrators. A copy was secretly obtained by the Prussian government and Frederick had the document translated into French in the greatest hurry. In a similar way, a copy of the charter of the Prussian company found its way into the British files. Together with reports about French commercial expansion in many parts of the world, the documents from Prussia fuelled the British preoccupation with the increasing commercial competition. And even the local East Friesian administration cited Dutch and English documents and policies in its writings to Berlin. A debate about the fundamental principles of commerce was associated with the creation of the Prussian Asiatic trade company. This debate was not limited to the national context of Prussia. It was a debate in which commentators in England, Holland, France, Prussia and Hamburg were concerned with the same events and often even read the same documents. Moreover, the debate took place largely in the offices of governments, embassies and trading companies. The actors were concerned with taking concrete policy decisions. For the nations bordering the North Sea, the early 1750s were thus not only an epoch of extreme insecurity about the political and commercial decisions of neighbouring nations but also one of insecurity about economic principles. In fact, as one Dutch report pointed out, Prussia was in this period not only trying to establish a trading company. Rather it was trying to uncover 'the most hidden secrets of commerce'.[91]

The decade preceding the establishment of the new trading company was one of extraordinary tension in international relations. The war of Austrian succession (1740–48) and Prussia's territorial expansion on shores of the North Sea contributed crucially to the dynamic that eventually led to the creation of the trading company in Emden. The foundations for new developments were laid by the Prussian acquisition of East Friesland – including the port of Emden – in 1744. The local ruling house had died out and with some manoeuvring the expanding Prussian monarchy was able to secure the territory for itself. The last prince of East Friesia – Carl Edzard – died in 1744. In the absence of male heirs, the Cirksena dynasty ended with him. Already in 1694, Prussia had obtained an *Exspektanz* from Emperor Leopold I, which assigned East Friesia to Prussia in the event that the local dynasty should remain without heir. In 1744, however, Prussia was not the only power interested in the acquisition of this territory. Hanover as well as the United Provinces tried to obtain control. Prussian troops finally took possession of East Friesia in 1744. In a sequence of events that was not altogether atypical for a trade company but that was usually reserved for coastal regions outside Europe, the arrival of the Prussian trade company in Emden was thus associated with the occupation of the surrounding stretch of coast by detachments of the marine infantry of a foreign power.[92]

Before these events, Prussia's 1740 invasion of Silesia had triggered the war of Austrian Succession with its volatile alliances. The two belligerent camps were composed of France, Spain and Prussia on one side and Austria, Britain, Sardinia and the Netherlands on the other. However, Britain joined the war only in 1743 and the Netherlands in 1744. Also Prussia did not continuously take part in the fighting. Between 1742 and 1744, and again after 1745, Prussia was not a belligerent party. In addition to the changing diplomatic constellations, the theatres of war moved through different regions of Europe, eventually leading to a French invasion of the Netherlands.

The French military threat to the Netherlands, together with the temporary Prussian neutrality, made Emden an attractive port for Dutch merchants. The now Prussian port was safe from French attacks and ships from Emden travelled under a neutral flag. As Frederick's ambassador

Ammon reported from The Hague in 1748, the security of ships under the Prussian flag from seizure by the British was the single most important issue for the merchants interested in trading from Emden. One of the interested merchants, a certain Jerome Jogues of Amsterdam, even insisted that Prussia obtain explicit guarantees from Britain that Prussian ships trading with France or carrying French goods would not be seized. Frederick's refusal to pursue the matter did not reduce the attraction that Emden exercised for Dutch merchants. One Dutch merchant offered to move there within two weeks and have his family follow in another six weeks. The Prussian government was, indeed, bombarded with proposals from merchants who wanted to settle in Emden. For the period 1744 to 1756 the Prussian archives conserve not less than nine proposals of foreign and local merchants for the establishment of trade companies.[93]

Among those who sent their projects to Frederick were the merchant Pedro Slayer from Antwerp, Borgers from Emden and Berlin, a certain Abbé Mercenati, Jerome Jogues, the Dutch Heinrich Thomas Stuart, the Frenchman Chevalier de la Touche, Capitaine de Ruvyuer, a certain Harris and finally a merchant by the name of Buzaglo. The scope of the proposals ranged from a privilege to send two ships from Emden to Canton to the idea of conquering the whole of Bengal. While the former plan eventually came to fruition, the latter was shelved by the Prussian government, abandoning therefore the intriguing prospect of a Prussian East India. The conquest of Bengal was proposed by an Englishman who called himself Clerck but whose real name, according to the Prussian representative in Paris, was Mill. Clerck's, or Mill's, argument for the conquest of Bengal was clear: on the one hand the European merchants had been carrying bullion to Bengal for decades. In fact, the author maintained that all the gold and silver that circulated in European commerce was 'in the end swallowed up by the Indies'. On the other hand not even an ounce of gold ever left Bengal. Therefore, he claimed, the land was clearly filled with treasures. Whoever was to conquer it would be in control of more gold and silver than the Spaniards took from their mines in South America. Fortunately for the King of Prussia, Bengal was not only 'hardly capable of defending itself' but Clerck knew also 'exactly' where the treasures of Bengal were hidden. For this information, he asked for 50 million *pounds* sterling and for a monopoly for the trade with the future Prussian East India. This was but a small premium considering that the conquest would procure the King of Prussia 'one hundred million crowns'. Frederick's ambassador was not convinced by Clerck's plan to conquer the riches of Bengal. 'I have to admit', he wrote to Berlin, 'that I was flabbergasted when he explained to me the means of obtaining them.' Frederick's reaction was probably not much more favourable and the plan was abandoned. Similarly unsuccessful was a proposal to conquer a port in Morocco to rival Gibraltar. As the proponent, a Portuguese merchant from London, pointed out, the conquest would cost 'a mere nothing' and yield enormous benefits by opening the trade with everything from wheat to opium. He also tried to tempt the Prussian government with the low local prices for black slaves of the highest quality. Unimpressed, Frederick instructed his ambassador not to pursue the negotiations any further. Frederick's comment was 'it is nothing more than a pipe dream'. Aside from these adventurous projects, most of the Dutch, English and French merchants who were offering their services to the Prussian crown were not asking for much more than the right to settle in Emden and use Prussian flags and passports for their ships.[94]

Of the many projects that were sent to Berlin the Prussian government chose that of Chevalier de la Touche for the creation of a Compagnie des Indes. The Frenchman – 'a very sensible man but whose head is constantly fill'd with schemes', as Albermarle, the British ambassador in Paris reported to London – did not promise to conquer Bengal or procure enormous treasures for Prussia.[95] However, with de la Touche's proposal Frederick opted for one of the most comprehensive concepts. The Compagnie was to build its own ships with Prussian timber. French experts were to teach the necessary skill to local artisans. The constructed ships would then carry Prussian linen, tar, hemp and timber to Spain. Having exchanged these goods for Spanish silver they were to continue to Canton and return with loads of silk, tea, china and exotic spices.[96] The Dutch diplomats were indeed right when they wrote about vast projects being 'on the table' in Emden.[97] La Touche's scheme not only foresaw a large-scale participation in Atlantic and Asian trade; the project paid particular attention to the sale of Prussian products and the development of manufacturing in Prussia. The trading company was to be linked with the other sectors of the Prussian economy and constituted a far-reaching development effort. Mainly it was a way to promote domestic industry through trade and to create a centre of manufacturing in a province of Prussia which had hardly any noteworthy industry. The encouragement of exchange of foreign and exotic goods against the fruits of domestic industry was one of the development measures that Voltaire and Frederick admired in Colbert's administration. When the Prussian company was chartered on 1 September 1750 neither the Dutch nor the British government had a clear picture of what was happening in Emden but there was considerable nervousness about the development. 'The Dutch', the secretary of state Holles Newcastle wrote, 'are a great deal alarm'd at this intelligence'. Newcastle himself expressed concern to Albermarle in Paris 'that something of a commercial nature was negotiating between the courts of Berlin and Versailles'.[98]

It may seem puzzling that the strongest naval powers of the period feared the competition of a trading company which, at this point, did not even own a ship and which was based in a second rate port in an enclave far way from the centres of Prussian industry which could supply it with goods to trade. However, Britain was far from feeling secure in its commercial and military position. Newcastle's correspondence of the period illustrates the omnipresence of commercial conflict with France. Alone in the month when the Prussian company was founded, the secretary of state was simultaneously concerned with a confrontation between the British and French East India Companies over stores in Madras, a whale that French whalers had stolen from a certain Elias Bland in the Davis Strait, the territorial boundaries in Nova Scotia, the conflicting claims of the French and English crown to the island of St. Lucia and 'disputes in America' in general. Small conflicts were thus taking place from the shores of the gulf of Bengal to the North Atlantic and the Caribbean.[99]

If France and the Netherlands were the main commercial rivals, the British concern with Prussia's military might was equally strong. In 1745, during the second Silesian War, Newcastle had warned of the desperate position of Britain in the conflict. But even after the peace treaty of 1748 Prussia was perceived as a threat. In the most vivid words Bedford warned of Prussia's plans to raise 'a Flame in the north'. Besides disturbing 'publick tranquility in the north' Prussia was also seen as 'instigating' France to re-start the war.[100] In a situation of military insecurity and tight commercial competition the creation of a trading company in the nation that had just proved itself as a superior military power in Europe aroused the greatest preoccupation in the British government. The spirit that reverberates from the diplomatic correspondence of the time reflects the growing concern that any project – military or commercial – that the Prussian King laid his hands on was bound to be a success threatening British positions. These concerns were reinforced by intelligence suggesting that the new commercial enterprise was a joint effort of France and Prussia. However, while La Touche's company stirred up worries with Prussia's neighbours the project came to nothing. The Frenchman failed to raise the necessary capital and Frederick issued a charter to another company with a more limited scope.[101] The official name of the company was Prussian Asiatic Company in Emden to Canton in China. It was a brainchild of the merchant Heinrich Thomas Stuart who – as Dutch intelligence reported – was from the Dutch city of Groningen.[102] Stuart was not the only foreign investor. As well as a number of Prussian shareholders, the main participants in the enterprise were foreigners from Rotterdam, Antwerp, Gent and Hamburg.[103] The significant presence of foreigners in the company's operations can also be seen from the list of officers on the companies ships. Out of 16 officers on the first ship, the König von Preußen, five were Dutch, two Swedish and one Spanish. On the second ship, the Burg von Emden, five out of eleven officers were Dutch.[104] In addition to being a commercial competitor for the Netherlands, the Prussian company was also a competitor for capital and skilled labour. The already mentioned report of the Dutch admiralty emphasised in its conclusion that it was vital for the Netherlands to make sure that no Dutch merchant participated in any form in 'any foreign company'. Among the competing companies also the company of Emden was mentioned.[105] In the same spirit the report praised a law passed in December 1750 – immediately after the creation of the Prussian company – which made it illegal for anybody who 'earned their living through any form of manufacturing, commerce, or trade' to offer their services to foreign companies. Specifically, the report speaks of wood cutters, rope-makers and weavers. Offenders were to be punished by death. This Dutch threat corresponded to an offer made on the eastern shore of the Ems. The charter of the Prussian company specified that any craftsman – rope-makers and carpenters are mentioned explicitly – who settled in Emden would be allowed to exercise his trade without having to join the city's corporations. It may surprise that the Dutch resorted to such heavy threats in this situation. However, the report of the admiralty specified that nothing less than the 'happiness of our Republic' depended on the success of Dutch trade. In addition, there was no question as to who the new Prussian company was competing with. 'It is mainly against us that they have a grievance', noted a Dutch diplomat in Hanover concerning Stuart's company.[106]

The British government, too, took material steps against the new competitor. As a director of the Prussian company reported from London to one of his colleagues, the British parliament was contemplating a bill making it illegal to insure assets of any trading company founded after 1747. As the director pointed out, the legislative project was clearly directed against the Prussian company. The significance of the threat may be seen from a promise made in the brochure that advertised the creation of the Prussian company and invited investors to buy shares.

All ships of the company, the brochure stated in order to boost confidence of potential investors, would be insured with respected foreign insurers. Another hostile British measure was reported by the *Berliner Nachrichten* in 1752. One of the company's first vessels to leave Emden was searched by the British navy. The British sailors who were found aboard were forced to leave the vessel as it was illegal for them to sell their skills to foreign trading companies.[107]

The specific details of the Dutch and British reactions to the new competitor are a good illustration of the interrelation that contemporaries saw between individual industry and the development of industry as an economic sector. The administrators in Holland and England were mainly concerned that skilled woodcutters, weavers, rope-makers and sailors would migrate to Prussia and contribute to the growth of manufacturing there. The same reasoning underlies the Prussian policies. Foreigners were offered to exercise their trades outside of the straight-jacket of the regulations of the guilds of Emden in order to attract as many foreign workers as possible. Administrators on both sides of the Ems and the British Channel shared the view that the growth of industry mainly depended on the supply of skilled labour or, in other words, on individual industry.

The strong reactions of Prussia's neighbours indicate that the naval powers were taking the new projects very seriously. 'Our neighbours are interested', stated the Dutch report, 'in watching carefully any new developments that might be undertaken'.[108] Given the uncertainty about the nature and scope of the Prussian projects both England and Holland decided to hit the new competitor as hard as possible. Their nervous reaction was partly due to the extremely tight commercial competition of the period. Any new competitor would probably have met with stiff opposition. However, the reaction to the Prussian case goes beyond that. The economic progress of Prussia and above all its recent military triumph had raised the sensitivity to any move or project that could be undertaken by that nation. In particular, the Dutch and English government took very seriously the possibility of Prussia using its bridgehead on the North sea to participate on a larger scale in overseas trade. The possibility that this was a fundamental change in the Prussian economic and strategic orientation was at the origin of the strong reactions.

The change associated with the creation of the trading company in Emden led not only to insecurity among Prussia's neighbours. In Prussia itself, more precisely in the province of East Friesia, new concerns emerged with the creation of the company. Associated with the new role of Emden as the port of an overseas trade company was increasing fear of epidemics and disease. In this period the Prussian administration in East Friesia began to be preoccupied with alleged outbreaks of plague in the Levant in 1752, on the coasts of Africa in 1753 and in Rouen in 1754. The administrative files reflect a new sense of exposure to the threat of epidemics carried to Emden from distant regions of the world by the ships of the new company.

In 1754 news of an outbreak of plague in Rouen arrived in Prussia. On 17 January, the central government in Berlin ordered severe measures to prevent the epidemic coming to Prussia. The measures were published in printed advertisements. French ships and other unknown or suspicious ships were not to be allowed to enter the harbour or unload their cargo. The pilots of the small island of Borkum were threatened with the death penalty should they help any ship to approach Prussian territory. In the event that foreign ships should come near Emden the instructions were detailed. The officials were to approach the ship against or over the wind. Then passports were to be handed over from the suspicious ship with long poles. The documents were then – 'before they are opened', as the instructions from Berlin specified – to be soaked in vinegar.[109] The measures were to be implemented strictly but without noise. Exceptions were possible for returning Prussian ships, which were apparently considered to be a lesser health hazard. Soon the local administration began to petition Berlin for such an exception. Two Prussian ships, one from Emden and one from Leer, had departed from Rouen with destinations in the Netherlands and England. It was feared that the Prussian ships would be barred from entering foreign ports if the same rules that were in place for the treatment of foreign ships in Emden were applied there. Permission for the ships to return to East Friesia was solicited. The files do not indicate whether the permission was granted. The local administration used the case to ask for a general loosening of the disruptive measures. Letters from Holland were cited where the threat of disease from Rouen was considered less serious. In addition a letter from London was produced which stated that quarantine measures had been abolished in England. In the correspondence with Berlin the local administration referred in several instances to the more relaxed behaviour of the authorities in the experienced naval nations – Holland and England.[110]

With scares of foreign epidemics in 1752, 1753 and 1754 coming from the European and African coasts of the Atlantic and from the Mediterranean, a Prussian concern emerged with the new situation in which Prussian territory was for the first time directly linked to these distant coastal provinces on a larger scale. Prussia's only direct naval commerce of any significance had been on the Baltic sea.[111] Most of the

Prussian commerce with the nations bordering the Atlantic Ocean or with Asia had previously been carried out by foreign merchants. The question of how to deal with ships arriving from Rouen or other even more distant ports had not been a concern of Prussian authorities but of the authorities in the ports of Amsterdam, Antwerp or Hamburg. Despite the fact that the volume of trade in Emden remained small compared to its foreign competitors, the new Prussian overseas commerce was associated to a range of concerns with infectious disease and epidemics. If the creation of the trade company in Emden was considered to be a serious change by Prussia's neighbours, the new challenges associated to the company's creation were not taken less seriously by the Prussian administration itself.

The development of manufacturing in Emden outside the system of guilds and the exposition of East Friesland to epidemics from distant shores are but two aspects of the changes that were associated to the new trade company. On a small scale Emden was experiencing the 'revolution' in industry, commerce, customs and government that Raynal described roughly twenty years later. He was most likely not thinking of Emden but of the great coastal cities of Bordeaux, Cadiz, Liverpool, Havana and New York when he wrote about the change that was associated to the development of overseas commerce. However, the creation of the trade company brought a small revolution to East Friesland.

In the period of the early 1750s great expectations for change were associated with the new company inside and outside Prussia. In 1752, Frederick II noted about the enterprise in his *Political testament*: 'This project could become very important if it were realised.' The king's caveat proved to be farsighted. After having sent 16 ships to Canton the company's operations were brought to an end by the Seven Years War. In 1756, tensions between Britain and France, and the opposition between Prussia and Austria led to the outbreak of the war. Fighting took place in Asia, America and Europe, and also East Friesia became one of the battlefields of this war. When French troops occupied Emden in 1757 one of the company's directors was able to leave the port in the last minute on one of the company's ships. Together with the ship he saved all liquid assets of the company from the French invaders. At the same time, another vessel of the company, the Prinz Ferdinand, was on its way back from Canton. It was diverted to Plymouth and sold together with its cargo. These fortunate circumstances meant that the company could pay its shareholders their capital back and even distribute a per annum dividend of two percent. While the shareholders did not make a loss, the company did not survive the war. The Prussian Asiatic trade company which was born in the context of a large European war eventually also failed because of a European or even global conflict.[112]

Other forms of overseas commerce and trading companies continued to exist in Emden. However, the perspective of the Prussian government on Prussian commerce had changed significantly after the experience of the Asiatic trade company. This big commerce, Frederick noted pessimistically in his second *Political testament* of 1768, is not 'within our reach'. This fundamental policy change was the result of the first-hand experience with commerce in Emden and of the exchange of ideas, which had been associated to the creation of the company. The period was one of increased Prussian interest for the matters of commerce. For establishing a trading company was not only a logistical problem. It was also about knowledge of the principles of commerce. In 1750, Dutch concerns were not only with the improvements of the basin of the port of Emden and the storage facilities there that the Prussian king was undertaking. Preoccupation was not only focused on the loss of Dutch capital and skilled labour to Prussia. Dutch diplomats were also worried that Prussia might discover 'the most hidden secrets of commerce'. The enquiries into the principles of commerce were compared to Newton's efforts to understand the laws of physics. More specifically, there were concerns that an agent of the Prussian king who played a role in the establishment of the Prussian company could have procured 'all the memoirs and explanations necessary to this end' in Amsterdam.[113] As has been mentioned, the Dutch concerns about what may today be called 'industrial espionage' were well founded. The memoir of the Dutch admiralty, which ended up on Frederick's desk in 1751, was a detailed analysis of all matters regarding Dutch trade in that period. One of the principal concerns that were discussed in the report was the issue of military protection for overseas commerce. Arguing for an increase of the admiralty's budget, the report concluded that commerce was fragile and would decline or even collapse 'at the slightest blow'. The means to prevent this was to ensure that 'the flag of our Province appears frequently in the Mediterranean', or, for that matter, in Africa, Curacao, Surinam, The Barbary Coast, and Esquebo. This view strikingly resembles the assessment of an anonymous French navy officer whose correspondence was intercepted by the British in 1750. The officer was part of a French navy squadron in the Mediterranean. The French war ships were on their way from Cadiz to Malaga, Algiers, Tunis, Malta and Toulon. The purpose of this peculiar tour of the Mediterranean was made clear in the intercepted correspondence. The letters were bound to cause concern in London. 'The king', wrote to the French officer about the motives of his master, 'wanted to show that he was able to support commerce as well as the English who claim that France no longer has sufficient vessels'. And in another letter from Alicante: 'The main objective of our mission [is] to maintain a presence on foreign shores'. To show the might of the nation's navy on distant shores was considered necessary – a condition 'sine qua non', in the words of the Dutch admirals – for the development of commerce. In 1750, such considerations did not prevent Frederick seeking a place for Prussia in the network of overseas commerce. However, in 1768 the Prussian inability to militarily protect its merchant vessels had become Frederick's principal argument against a large-scale engagement in commerce. 'Prussia is a power on dry land', he noted in his discussion of commerce, 'it needs a good army but no navy.' Frederick's 'landlubber attitude' reflected first-hand experience. The vulnerability of Prussian vessels had become painfully clear when the first ship of the Emden company was stopped and searched by the British navy. Prussia had no means to prevent such hostile interventions in the North Sea and much less in the Gulf of Bengal or in other places where Prussian merchants were lured by lucrative commercial opportunities. In the Seven Years War, Prussia almost collapsed and could not even prevent the occupation of the Friesian port of its trading company. Much less would it have been able to protect any commercial establishments or possessions overseas. Frederick's line of reasoning necessarily led to the conclusion that the lack of a powerful navy prevented Prussian trading companies from becoming a major player in overseas commerce. The king was well aware that by 1768 significant currents of economic thought suggested other approaches. Trading companies and their monopolies had fallen in discredit with many authors of the time and in France a controversial debate raged over the future of the French East India company. The king shared some of the concerns with commercial companies but maintained that all companies of this type had at least in their beginning had monopolies and that there was no other way to compete with the established competitors. Based on this view, which seemed powerfully confirmed by the Prussian experience, there was no prospect of Prussia making a new bid to engage in overseas commerce on a large scale.[114]

However, even after the experience of the 1750s Frederick did not advocate a complete neglect of international commerce. Rather, the perspective on the function of Prussia's commerce changed. Frederick had justified the establishment of the Asiatic trade company with five motives: (1) to provide an investment opportunity, (2) to increase the volume of money circulating in the kingdom by adding the shares of the company as a form of paper money to the existing currency, (3) to take away a branch of commerce from the Dutch, (4) to obtain 'the drugs from India' at a cheaper price, (5) to increase Prussian commerce at the expense of that of Hamburg, Poland, Bohemia and Moravia. The goals were far reaching and were associated to fundamental change. In a largely rural economy like that of Prussia the project of introducing a paper currency must be considered a bold plan.[115] It is equally noteworthy that the king saw the company as a tool to provide the Prussian population with exotica at a cheaper price. This argument echoes Voltaire's views expressed in the poem *The Worldling* where he contemplated how the goods from India and other distant destinations had become necessary to the people of Europe. However, Frederick's principal motive for the establishment of a trading company, which appears twice in the king's programme is the increase of Prussian commerce at the expense of foreign merchants. The company was meant to compete with other enterprises of the same type and bring wealth to Prussia by developing its commerce. In 1768, the benefit that Prussia could derive from a trading company in Emden was not seen mainly in the increase of commerce itself anymore but in an ancillary function of that commerce. 'This company', the king wrote, 'will be useful in order to facilitate and increase our exports in linen, woollen fabrics, amber, cloth, and china.' Providing an outlet for Prussian products had become the only acceptable purpose of trading companies and one of the main objects of commerce. As discussed earlier, the focus of Prussian economic development policies was on industry. Manufacturing was not only prioritised over trade but much of the manufacturing was oriented to substitute imports and thus limit import trade. These policies have become one of the trademarks of Frederick's reign. However, even in one of the most advanced commercial nations of the period similar policies were advocated. Frederick and other readers of the report of the Dutch admiralty of 1751 were told that the only way to save that nation's commerce was for the inhabitants to dedicate themselves more intensely again to 'manufacturing and fabrics'. For without any products of domestic making to trade with Dutch commerce would be destroyed by the 'cancer' which had already afflicted it. England was cited in the report as a shining example of joint progress of manufacturing and trade.[116] While there is a strong concentration on manufacturing in the second political testament of Frederick there is no mention anymore of using commercial companies to compete with foreign merchants or to introduce a paper currency. On the issue of investment in commercial companies Frederick equally reversed his judgement. While the companies of 1750 were to provide investment opportunities, the king argued in 1768 that Prussian investments in overseas trading companies should be forbidden. In particular in times of war, investments in overseas commerce were simply too risky. This argument leads back to the king's initial assessment that overseas trade could not succeed without the protection of a potent navy. The impact of the failure of the Asiatic trade company went beyond the liquidation of a single commercial enterprise. In the end, the first-hand experience with overseas commerce and the views and arguments received through the commerce of ideas associated to the creation of the company in Emden led the Prussian government to the conclusion that there was no place for Prussia in the world of oceanic commerce. The concentration was now fully on the development of domestic industry. A road which Prussia pursued with great success.

'A new industry' in Prussia: the silk manufactures

Another more domestic form of industry that was at the heart of Frederick's development efforts and that attracted Voltaire's interest was the silk industry. This branch of manufacturing was not geared towards exportation but it fitted equally in the logic that underpinned the creation of trade companies. Whereas the company in Emden was intended to promote Prussian industry by increasing exports of manufactured goods, the Prussian silk industry contributed to the same goal by substituting imported manufactured goods. In particular, the Prussian government wanted to reduce the costly imports of French, Italian and other foreign luxury textiles. In 1753, Voltaire described the royal efforts to revive the Prussian silk industry with a bon-mot of great insight: 'Here in Berlin we have transplanted silk worms and wits.'[117] Much like Voltaire's observations on the trade company, this comment combines the progress of fine arts, culture and industry in a way that needs further explanation. What was the link between wits and the silkworms of the Prussian capital?

In order to answer this question it is necessary explore the situation of both species in Prussia in 1753. The second part of the bon-mot does not need much explanation: Voltaire's transfer to Berlin alone was probably the single greatest example of a transplanted 'wit' in that period. Alongside Voltaire, Frederick had attracted such prominent academics as the Frenchman Pierre Maupertuis, who had proven certain theories of Newton about the shape of the earth, the Italian Francesco Algarotti who had had a considerable success with his work *Newtonianism for the ladies*, and the eminent Swiss mathematician Leonhard Euler who – among other achievements – discovered the number which bears his name and which has since become a staple of secondary education.[118]

The first part of Voltaire's bon-mot points to a branch of industry that was not only of the highest priority in Prussia in the 1750s but that also played an important role in Voltaire's admiration of the reign of Louis XIV. In the seventeenth century, Voltaire pointed out in the *Age of Louis XIV*, that silk manufacturing had created 'a new industry' in Lyon and Tours. The silk industry that Voltaire saw in Prussia, and the French silk industry that he wrote about in Prussia, however, were not only abstractly linked: on 18 November 1747, Frederick was offered the services of a French expert in the matter of silk production by the name of de Barry. This de Barry claimed to posses the secret of how to make mulberry trees and silkworms survive in the cold climates where they had been transplanted. As a recommendation and reference for the applicant, the official who submitted the proposal to Frederick emphasised that de Barry was the son of 'Pierre de Barry, royal inspector of Mulberry tree seedlings & plantations for King Louis XIV in Languedoc.' The files are silent about the outcome of de Barry's proposal but one would suspect that Frederick was delighted. The industry of skilled workers was attracted to Prussia from other European countries at a considerable price. Usually the Prussian government bought the necessary equipment and paid the travel expenses of the immigrants who were also compensated with high wages once they had arrived. In the Berlin silk industry, immigrants played a particularly important role. In the year 1769 the large majority of the 583 workers who were employed in the silk manufactures of Berlin were French. In the production of silk stockings the French workers were even stronger represented. Of a total of 85 workers, 55 were French and 30 Prussian. The picture is slightly different for the entrepreneurs in this branch. Of 33 entrepreneurs, eight were French, four Jewish, and 21 Prussian.[119]

At the beginning of his reign, in the middle of the first Silesian war, Frederick had started to promote the silk industry with his customary combination of carrot and stick. In order to substitute raw silk imports with domestic production, for example, he had decided that the local administration of the Kriegs- und Domänen Kammern – that of Minden and Ravensberg has already been mentioned – were to make land available to anyone who wished to establish a mulberry plantation. Those who maintained a plantation of one thousand or more trees out of private means were entitled to wage-subsidies for an employed gardener for as long as the enterprise ran at a loss. When the trees were old enough, Frederick's edict promised Italian silkworm eggs free of charge to anybody interested. Finally, the government guaranteed to buy all the silk that the silkworms would produce once they had hatched from their government-subsidized eggs. These measures to promote the silk industry were complemented by the threat to have anybody run the gauntlet who damaged a mulberry tree.[120]

In the *Age of Louis XIV*, Voltaire emphasised the importance of the similar development that had been encouraged in the French silk industry. Under Louis XIV the importation of raw silk had been increasingly substituted through the development of a domestic raw silk production. Overall he saw the silk industry as one of the principal branches of industry during the reign of Louis XIV. He estimated their annual output in the seventeenth century at a considerable 50 million *livres* and praised the support that had been provided in France to the establishment of this industry. But while Voltaire was praising the promotion of silk manufacturing as a sound economic policy, other authors disagreed strongly. Mirabeau, for example, condemned Frederick's efforts to establish a silk industry in the provinces surrounding Berlin. The opinions of economic historians on governmental efforts to develop industry in Prussia remain controversial to this day. In the case of the Prussian silk manufactures at least one prominent economist shared Voltaire's views about the benign effect of the promotion of industry on the development of the Prussian capital. Schmoller saw the Prussian silk industry as an important contribution to the economic and cultural development of the nation and its capital: 'Berlin in 1780–1806 stood almost on a level with all other places where the silk industry was carried on. It was mainly through the silk industry that Berlin became an important factory town, and the town whose inhabitants were distinguished by the best taste in Germany.' In analogy to Voltaire's argument, Schmoller not only praised the promotion of the silk industry but also associated it with simultaneous development of a cultivated and elegant way of life in Berlin.[121]

The relation that Voltaire saw between the Prussian silk industry and the progress of culture in the Prussian capital is to be seen in the context of the common origins of the silk industry and the academy of Berlin. Both establishments go back to an initiative of Gottfried Wilhelm Leibniz. For some time the thinker had been trying to convince the elector Frederick III and his wife Sophie Charlotte to establish a Prussian academy of arts and science. In 1700, his efforts were crowned with success and an academy was established in Berlin. This academy, however, was not only to be a benign institution for fine arts and sciences. Its founder and first president, Leibniz, had given it a very distinct mission. In a handwritten memorandum for the establishment of the academy Leibniz introduces his argument with the following observation: 'All enlightened and well-informed persons agree that countries flourish when, in addition to the produce of nature, there is labour and industry.'[122] Leibniz's understanding of the term 'industry' in this context is not entirely clear. On the one hand, the opposition of 'industry' with the products of nature suggests some form of sectoral connotation. It is, however, not clearly defined as manufacturing. On the other hand, 'industry' stands alongside 'work' which associates it with a personal quality, perhaps that of inventiveness.

While Leibniz's 'industry' seems still closer to the connotation of an individual quality than to that of a sector, he considered the connection between prosperity and industry to be obvious. He went on to describe that this important connection was ignored in Germany for far too long. Only after witnessing how the Dutch and the French 'became virtuous' in the matters of 'industry' did the Germans start to understand the importance of industry. Leibniz, however, was not inclined to wait until his compatriots would develop the virtue of industry by themselves. Instead, 'making young people hardworking and industrious' was to be a principal goal of the new academy. The order in which the academy's goals appear is telling: Leibniz's first priority was 'that which regards factories and commerce'. Then follow agriculture and the education of the young, and only after that Leibniz mentions: 'Finally, it will also have as an objective the arts, sciences, experiments, and study.' These, however, were only to be admitted to the extent that they procured 'the comfort and ornaments of everyday life'.[123] Leibniz's academics – Voltaire was going to be one of them – were to push his project of cultivation on all levels: economic, artistic and scientific. One of their main goals was to improve 'everyday life' rather than to engage in lofty artistic activity or in enquiry that satisfied only scientific curiosity. The role that Leibniz ascribed to his academy bears a striking resemblance to the effect that Voltaire associated with the development of industry. As has been pointed out, he saw industry as the source of everyday 'comfort'.

Leibniz's concern with matters of industry was, in fact, so prominent that he has been referred to as the first writer to use the word *Industrie* in the German language. There can be no doubt about his concern with the issue and about his use of the term in French. The passage, however, in which Leibniz allegedly uses the term for the first time in German appears to be the result of a nineteenth-century translation mistake.

The curious history of the passage in question is an intriguing journey through the complexities of academic footnoting but it also illuminates the complexity of the changing meaning of the term industry. The starting point for the modern reader is the 1982 article for the entry *Industrie* in a standard encyclopaedia of German historiography. The article presents a German quotation in which Leibniz describes the goals of the academy and allegedly uses the term *Industrie* for the first time in German. Leibniz is quoted as attributing the following tasks to the new academy: 'to unite practice and theory and to improve through arts and sciences everything that is of interest for the land and the people, agriculture, industry, commerce, foodstuffs'. The reference for this quotation is to a work from 1967 which presents the passage as the first use of *Industrie* in the German language.[124] In this work, Leibniz's alleged passage is given in German and two references can be found in the relevant footnote. One is to Christian Bartholmèss's French work *Philosophical history of the Prussian Academy* of 1850, the other one to the anonymous German volume *Memoir of the royal Academy for useful sciences in Erfurt* of 1854. In the 1967 work the quotation is taken from the *Memoir* where it appears in German as a direct quotation from Leibniz.[125] The reference in the *Memoir*, in turn, is to Bartholmèss's *Philosophical history*. There, the passage appears in French and is given as a translation from a German quotation from Leibniz. The footnote of Bartholmèss's French translation refers to G. Guhrauer's 1838 edition of Leibniz's German works.[126] Here, one finally approaches the 'epicentre' of the story. The German original of the Leibniz text does not contain the word *Industrie*. Instead Bartholmèss translated – not inaccurately and certainly innocently – the word *Manufacturen* in Leibniz's text with the French word *industrie*. When the French text was re-translated into German by the author of the *Memoir* in 1854, he translated the French *industrie* with the Geman *Industrie*. Again this was certainly done innocently. By that time the term *Industrie* had become common also in German and was without any doubt an appropriate translation for the French *industrie*.

Besides being a curious episode, this story of translation and re-translation is a good illustration of evolution and continuity in European debates about industry in the eighteenth and nineteenth century. Continuity is documented by the fact that Leibniz' early eighteenth-century text was cited in nineteenth-century debates. However, Leibniz was not only quoted incorrectly but above all his ideas were taken out of context. He had written about the necessity to develop 'manufactures' in the early eighteenth century. In 1854 he was cited as writing about 'industry'. This was nine years after Engels's *Condition of the working class in England* had brought the term *Industrie* to the centre of a heated public debate in Germany. Industry was by this time closely associated with the social consequences of nineteenth-century industrialisation. Leibniz' 'manufactures' were without any doubt the establishments that formed the early foundations of what came to be called industry in Engels's day. However, both writers were concerned with very different concepts. The transplantation of Leibniz's views from the early eighteenth to the middle of the nineteenth century render them virtually nonsensical. In a very similar way it is impossible to understand eighteenth-century comments about industry with the economic reality of the nineteenth or twentieth century in mind.

The distinct practical spirit of the Prussian academy and its first president is best illustrated by the involvement in the establishment of silk production in Prussia. After the academy had been formed, its president did not primarily put his talents to further the knowledge in mathematics, physics or philosophy but he turned to the establishment of a Prussian silk industry.[127] Leibniz thus became the father of the Prussian silk industry and the Prussian academy. However, it must be said that Leibniz's projects did not succeed after their hopeful beginnings. He died in 1716 and the successor of Frederick I, Frederick William II, cared more for soldiers and guns than for academics and their silkworms. During Frederick William's reign from 1713 to 1740 Leibniz's projects fell into decay. It was left to the next Prussian monarch, Frederick II, to revive the academy and the silk industry. Voltaire's bon-mot reflected these renewed efforts that Frederick started after his accession to the throne.

Looking back on Voltaire's observations about the silk industry and the trade company, the close association between industry on the one hand and enlightened culture, arts and science on the other hand is striking. For him, where there was no industry, as in Westphalia, there was no culture and no progress. Analogously, where there was culture and an enlightened ruler, as in Berlin, there was also industry in the shape of a trade company or silk manufacturing. For Voltaire, progress such as the one he witnessed in Berlin was closely related to the concept of industry. This perspective is well illustrated by a historical comparison between London and Paris that he undertook in the *Essay on universal history*. Sixteenth-century London, he wrote, was still badly built and life there was hard. At the same time in Paris, industry had already transformed 'huts made of wood and plaster' into 'sumptuous palaces'.[128]

The examples of the Prussian silk industry and the trade company illustrate how the progress of industry and the progress of arts and science were closely associated. The products that industry brought to the population of

Prussia were beautiful and refined. They were silk fabrics, exquisite china and exotic spices. The industry that Voltaire saw and commented on was a source of art and culture and had little to do with smoking chimneys, pauperism and cheap textiles that came to be associated with industry in the nineteenth century. Voltaire's industry was not the industry of the nineteenth century that Engels associated to a 'mortal pressure' on workers and that Wilde singled out as the 'source of all ugliness'.[129]

While industry was seen by Voltaire as associable with art, culture and the general progress of reason, it was at the same time dependent on the spread of certain forms of culture. Industry required, after all, men with the right skill and mentality. Leibniz outlined how his academy should contribute to the development of industry by teaching the Prussian population the necessary skill and discipline. The academy was thus geared at promoting a culture that was seen as necessary for economic development. Significantly, economic historians have ascribed a similar educational function to the Prussian silk industry. While the industry had been prosperous in the eighteenth century, it started to disappear in the 1860s and 1870s. However, those who had been associated with the silk industry turned to other industrial activities. The development of many other industries thus benefited from those whose skill had been schooled in Frederick's silk industry.[130]

Voltaire had left Paris with a notion that industry was the source of many beautiful and useful products that made life more comfortable. In Prussia, however, he began to realise that industry had a greater importance. The Prussian stay made it palpable for him that the development of industry could bring progress and prosperity to a whole nation. From Voltaire's perspective, Frederick's efforts to develop various branches of Prussian industry brought prosperity, arts, sciences and culture to a nation that had been backward and poor. Even if certain parts of Prussia – namely those situated in Westphalia – had not yet been affected by these changes, Voltaire still remained impressed with what he saw. Based on the progress that he observed, he predicted a great age for Prussia.

If one adds to Voltaire's first-hand observations that his host Frederick did not miss any occasion to point out just how important industry was for the development of Prussia, it can hardly be surprising that the phenomenon of industry found its way into Voltaire's writings of the period. In particular the *Age of Louis XIV* needs to be read in the light of the Prussian experience. If industry played a fundamental role in Prussia's ubiquitous progress, how could any serious historical analysis of France's great age neglect that phenomenon? Voltaire did not ignore

Frederick's call on historians, politicians and philosophers to enquire into the origins of industry and 'the causes that developed it'. In fact, contemporary readers of the *Age of Louis XIV* noticed the work's unusual concentration on matters of industry. Condorcet praised Voltaire's concern with the progress of 'commerce' and 'industry' in the book and excused Voltaire even for defending Colbert's economic policies which Condorcet normally abhorred.[131]

Voltaire's admiration for Colbert and the philosopher's thought about industry had become inseparable. Voltaire's stay in Prussia had not done anything to dilute his opinion that it was the systematic efforts of great administrators that brought industry to a nation. If the trade company and the silk manufactures of Frederick helped to bring about a great age in Prussia, Colbert's Compagnie des Indes and his silk manufactures in Lyon and Tours could not have been without relevance to the splendour of that age. Similarly, if France's greatest cultural development in the seventeenth century took place simultaneously with the growth of the French silk industry and trading companies these branches of industry would certainly help Prussia's progress a century later.

Voltaire saw the success of Colbert and his policies confirmed by the example of Frederick's Prussia. At the same time he held up the development of France under Louis XIV as an example for Prussia and other nations of his day. Colbert thus became the hero of Voltaire's Prussian work, the *Age of Louis XIV*. A minister of finance was certainly an unlikely hero of a work that set out to explain how the 'most enlightened age that has ever existed' was brought about in France. The reader encounters the famous minister throughout the book relentlessly working for the promotion of industry, arts and sciences. So important was the role that Voltaire assigned to the minister that he had to clarify in a letter why the period ought to be called the *Age of Louis XIV* rather than the *Age of Colbert*. While the minister was responsible for many of the achievements of the time, Voltaire argued, it was only because the king had approved his policies that he could implement them. Therefore, Louis XIV was deserving of the praise.[132] With this perspective Voltaire reconciled the strong role of the minister in his account with the principle of undivided monarchical authority that he supported. However, this perspective leaves the role of the administrator who was actively involved in the concrete policies for the promotion of arts, commerce and industry to Colbert. It is helpful to see this emphasis on the active administrator in Voltaire's perspective on the reign of Louis XIV in the light of the Prussian experience.

3
A European Debate about Colbert

Chapter 2 focussed mainly on the relation of Voltaire's larger perspective on industry with the specific and often minute experiences in Paris and during his stay in Prussia. This chapter will adopt a different perspective. It will place Voltaire's views on industry in the context of a European debate about the legacy of Jean Baptiste Colbert. Many contemporaries did not share Voltaire's admiration for the minister and his policies were the subject of controversial debate throughout the eighteenth century. This debate about Colbert involved many French authors but it also extended across Europe. Adam Smith – after having read Voltaire's praise of Colbert in the *Age of Louis XIV* – did not only criticise the minister's policies for the promotion of industry himself, but he also pointed out that 'the most intelligent men in France' were severely criticising 'Mr. Colbert'.[1] Voltaire's support for the minister thus raises the question of why the most celebrated European poet of the eighteenth century defended the legacy of the most prominent administrator of the seventeenth century.

It is remarkable in itself that a finance minister who had died in 1683 was still at the centre of heated debate seventy years later. Even today opinions about Colbert diverge sharply. Some economic historians call him the godfather of France's industry while others see his policies as the single most important reason that hampered France's economic development and led to Britain's alleged superiority in industrial development. No other figure in French history – with the possible exception of Robespierre – has remained as controversial. Colbert may, indeed, lay claim to being called the most controversial finance minister ever. After all, most of his colleagues are not even remembered after a decade and hardly any minister is still controversially discussed over three centuries after his term of office ended. Colbert's prominence may also be seen from the fact that a whole current in political economy developed from the rejection of his policies: the origins of the concept of laisser-faire seem to go back to a conversation in which a group of merchants told the minister not to meddle with their interests. Since that time Colbert has remained the favourite bête noire of liberal political economists and their ancestors.[2]

Nothing in the life of the young Jean Baptiste Colbert indicated that he would rise to such prominence: his career as an administrator had begun as an aide to cardinal Mazarin, the powerful minister of Louis XIV. However, Colbert was not himself from the circle of courtiers. He was born in 1619 to a family of textile merchants. Initially he was trained in business and was thus well acquainted with contemporary practices. After Mazarin's death and on recommendation of the latter, Louis XIV appointed Colbert to the position of comptroller general in 1665. Four years later he was also made minister of the navy. His reforms addressed a broad range of issues. Some of his most characteristic policies were the introduction of an efficient system of accounting for the government finances (or any system, for that matter); the promotion of many branches of manufacturing in order to substitute imports and increase exports of manufactured goods; and the encouragement of arts and sciences. He also aimed at increasing internal trade by abolishing trade barriers within France. Overseas trade was encouraged through the creation of trading companies and the construction of new ports. In fiscal matters the minister concentrated on reduction of tax fraud and tax exemptions. Not all of Colbert's reforms were successful. Most importantly, he did not achieve a fundamental revision of the fiscal system. However, his overall successes cannot be denied. In 1661 total receipts of taxation were 80 million *livres* of which less than half actually reached the treasury. The budget deficit was of 22 million *livres*. At the end of Colbert's administration France had a budget surplus of more than 29 million *livres*. The streamlined administration of Colbert had increased receipts and had dramatically reduced spending. Colbert's authority rested on the firm support of Louis XIV but his policies also antagonised many. As Lionel Rothkrug points out, the growing opposition to Louis XIV towards the end of his reign was closely associated with the rejection of Colbert's policies. In particular, the aristocracy and many merchants strongly opposed the minister's reforms which interfered with their interests. However, the critique of Colbert was not limited to these groups. Voltaire reports that the 'senseless people' wanted to dismember the minister's body after his death in 1683. The widespread critique against monarch and minister was echoed by a number of writers on political economy who Joseph Spengler has called 'reformers'.[3] The authors who criticised the economic policies of Colbert before the end of the reign of Louis XIV include Boisguilbert, Vauban, Boulainvilliers, the Abbé de Saint-Pierre and the Archbishop of Cambrai, Fénelon. Of these authors, Voltaire commented on the views of Boisguilbert, Fenélon and Saint-Pierre. Their relationship with Voltaire will be discussed in this study. After the end of Louis's reign the critique continued. The *Persian Letters* of Montesquieu were not concentrating on Colbert but they were the most prominent critique of the reign of Louis XIV as a whole. The defence of Louis XIV and Colbert which Voltaire completed in Prussia in 1751 was written as a contribution to this long-standing public debate. In Voltaire's admiration of Colbert and for the debate as a whole, the concept of industry played a crucial role. It is therefore helpful to consider the controversial perspectives on the minister in the light of fundamentally diverging views on industry that were held by the debaters.

The concept of industry in the debate about Colbert

One of the most striking features of the debate about Colbert is that its nominal subject was virtually absent from it. This is certainly true of eighteenth-century debates and would probably also emerge from a careful reading of today's controversies about the minister. Not that Colbert's name is not ubiquitous, or that his policies are not heatedly discussed, but the historical personality 'Colbert' is absent from the arguments to such an extent that his name seems to have been reduced to a mere cipher. It is as if the minister's name ceased to be that of a person but instead became the designation of an abstract principle that was either defended or contested.

This is particularly true of Voltaire's writings: despite the ubiquitous praise for Colbert, the hero's personality remains largely in the dark. The reader of the monumental *Age of Louis XIV* is given not even the most basic biographical information about Colbert. The date and place of Colbert's birth are not mentioned, nor his family background, nor the details of his life before becoming an administrator. It almost seems as if Colbert had entered this world as a perfect minister. Consequently, Voltaire does not mention any development of Colbert's personality or principles in the course of his career: the great administrator is not enthusiastic and motivated at the beginning of his career, nor is he tired or disillusioned towards the end. The apparent lack of interest for the personality of Colbert was later confirmed explicitly by Voltaire: 'I paid attention to the memorable things that he did ... not to the manner in which he tied his cravat'.[4] The near complete silence about Colbert's person is all the more significant in a work that talks about the life of artists and aristocrats in great detail and that devotes entire chapters either to the most minute details of court life, or to speculations about the identity of the 'Man in the Iron Mask'. From the picture that Voltaire paints, or rather does not paint, of Colbert it becomes apparent that Voltaire admired him not as a historical figure but rather as the embodiment of a certain spirit or a set of principles.

If the person Colbert was virtually absent from the debate, Voltaire's defence of the minister centres around one particular achievement of the minister: 'Colbert ... brought about the birth of industry in France'.[5] For Voltaire, the minister was simply 'the man who brought about the birth of so much abundance by reviving so many industries'.[6] Note that the use of the plural of 'industry' makes it clear that Voltaire is praising Colbert not only for the animation of an individual virtue but of entire branches of production.

The concept of industry was at the heart of Voltaire's defence of Colbert. However, the minister's promotion of manufacturing, arts and sciences was also the target of harsh criticism at the time. Much of the contemporary controversy about the administrator is best understood through the diverging contemporary perspectives on the concept of industry. Voltaire saw a twofold relation between progress and industry: not only does the peaceful progress of humanity depend on industry but this progress also constitutes the normative orientation and ultimate goal of 'human industry'. This view was far from controversial. Many commentators saw in industry a source of moral and economic decay and in Colbert's economic policies the reason for the almost uninterrupted series of wars under Louis XIV.

However, it was not a keen interest in the past that inspired heated debates about Colbert and his master. The previous reign and its actors served mainly as a projection screen for a debate in which political and economic decisions of the eighteenth century were at issue. That writings about the reign of Louis XIV were understood as statements about current political questions in the 1750s is well illustrated by the hostile official reaction to Voltaire's *Age of Louis XIV* in France. Publication of the work in France was unthinkable. When the introduction had been published there in 1739, it was immediately banned. This first publication of a part of the work came seven years after Voltaire had first mentioned his plan to write the work. In a letter in English of 1732 he wrote: 'I never go out of doors. I see nobody but at home. I hope to employ such a studious leisure with Eriphyle, the English letters and the Age of Lewis the Fourteenth'.[7] After the publication of the introduction in 1739 the project did not make much progress until the 1750s. When Voltaire took up the work again in Prussia in 1750 he had at least produced a significant body of excerpts and notes on the topic which he could use to complete the work. He mentions these papers in a letter from Prussia in October 1750. In December of the same year he wrote to his niece that he was writing about the battle of Hochstedt. This indicates that he had arrived to chapter 19 of 49 and that he was about to conclude the first part of the work which was formed by a chronological account of the events of the reign of Louis XIV. This part is followed by a section with anecdotes about court life. The chapters about development of finance, administration, arts and science are in the last part of the book. These chapters contain most of the comments about the development of industry and related matters. In the original two-volume edition they were part of the second volume. Voltaire proposed the publication of the *Age of Louis XIV* in Prussia to Frederick in May 1751. The first edition was then printed in Berlin towards the end of 1751. On 24 December 1751 Voltaire sent six corrected copies of the work to Paris. However, it was impossible to obtain permission for the publication of the work in France. The praise for Louis XIV was inevitably understood as a critique of the reign of Louis XV. This understanding was not entirely unintended. Voltaire himself regarded the work as an 'encouragement' for the French nation and the reign of Louis XIV as an 'example' for the future. The work was both a piece of historiography and a contribution to debate about contemporary policies concerning matters of industry.[8]

The arguments about industry that were put forward in the debate about Colbert addressed a wide range of economic, moral, religious and political issues. It is, however, possible to structure the controversy around three fundamentally contentious questions. Does an active role of the government administration help or harm the progress of industry? How big should the sector of industry be in relation to agriculture in order to benefit the prosperity of the nation? Does the progress of industry help the cultural progress of a nation or does it make a people weak and morally corrupt? The last two questions reflect a central concern of enlightenment debate with the moral and economic implications of the rapid growth of industry. However, the battle-lines of these debates often followed unfamiliar patterns: Voltaire was a champion of industry but believed in the importance of an active government while the Physiocrats, for example, called for laisser-faire but insisted that the growth of industry should be limited for economic and moral reasons. Others, like Saint-Pierre, called for a strong role of government to guide the development of industry towards 'useful' applications precisely because they feared the harmful moral effects of certain branches of industry.

Voltaire's defence of Colbert during the stay in Prussia

During his stay in Berlin, from 1750 to 1753, Voltaire was involved in controversies with two rather different critics of Colbert. The first was Pierre de Boisguilbert (1646–1714), a pious Jansenist administrator and pamphleteer from Rouen. The second was Angliviel de La Beaumelle (1726–73), a Protestant French publicist who travelled to Potsdam on a diplomatic mission for the Danish court. Boisguilbert had already died over three decades before Voltaire responded to his criticism in the *Age of Louis XIV*. Nevertheless, his writings had remained the most powerful attacks on Colbert that circulated in France. Voltaire took up Boisguilbert's criticism in the first edition of his *Age of Louis XIV* and in a number of related writings. Their disagreement was rooted in the question of how the industry of the individual should be directed to the branch of industry where it was best used. Mainly they disagreed over the question on what role ministers and their administrations should play in this context. Boisguilbert's answer to these questions differed strikingly from the practices that Voltaire admired in Frederick's Prussia and Colbert's France.

While Boisguilbert was arguably one of the most radical critics, he was certainly not the only writer who took part in what Voltaire called a 'plot to diminish all that made those memorable times glorious'.[9] Soon after the *Age of Louis XIV* was published a rather colourful contemporary author prepared a vicious response to Voltaire's work. After a literary scandal in Potsdam which involved Frederick, Voltaire and La Beaumelle, the latter decided to take revenge on Voltaire. He published an edition of the *Age of Louis XIV* along with a commentary. This edition – printed in Germany like Voltaire's original – was filled with the most acerbic footnotes. Voltaire responded with additions to a subsequent edition of the work, a *Supplement to the Age of Louis XIV* of 44 pages, and many other comments in other writings, stretching from the 1750s until the death of La Beaumelle in 1773. Voltaire and La Beaumelle were clearly separated by more than their views on Colbert and industry. However, this aspect played a significant role in their quarrel. La Beaumelle's Montesquieuean views on government and the development of industry were diametrically opposed to Voltaire's. For La Beaumelle, the monarchs and ministers whom Voltaire admired as the creators of industry were mere despots and the policies that Voltaire praised were at best indifferent to the development of industry. Despite their mutual dislike, La Beaumelle and Voltaire shared a similar fate in Potsdam. Not long after La Beaumelle's disgrace, Voltaire's friendship with Frederick II went sour. In 1753, the philosopher gave up his post as chamberlain and left Prussia.

Before going on to explore the exchanges between Voltaire and his opponents a remark must be made about the terminology employed in this debate. As regards the term 'industry' it was an uneven controversy. In Voltaire's defence of Colbert, the term appears prominently. In contrast to that, it appears only rarely in the language of the minister's critics Boisguilbert and La Beaumelle. This is despite the fact that they were concerned with the same policies of Colbert that Voltaire was writing about. Thus, while they were talking about the same manufactures, products and administrative measures they only rarely employed the term industry to denote their sum.

Voltaire used the term for the changes that Colbert created in France. For the critics the minister did not create anything new but was only responsible for countless vexations. They did not see in him the promoter of a new spirit of industriousness, new ways of manufacturing and new products. In short, they did not see him as the creator of a new phenomenon. Voltaire, however, saw the minister at the origin of a profound transformation. This transformation was composed of countless changes small and large. Voltaire described many of them individually in his works. However, he also summed up the many transformations that the minister brought about in one phrase: 'Colbert ... brought about the birth of industry in France'. At this stage of the debate about Colbert, the term industry was thus clearly associated with a positive view of the minister's policies. It was not until the Physiocrats entered the debate that the critics of Colbert appropriated the term industry. Finally, it may be remarked that the tone between Voltaire and the critics of Colbert was not always polite. The 'French Virgil' accused Boisguilbert of losing house, home and wife through gambling and La Beaumelle of being a 'deeply disgusting object'.[10] While this certainly illustrates that the controversy was more than an academic debate for Voltaire, it does not make it easier to bring out its substance. The question, however, remains: why was Colbert a genius to Voltaire but much hated by so many contemporaries and what was the role that industry played in this debate?

Voltaire's response to Boisguilbert

After Voltaire had finished the *Age of Louis XIV* in Berlin the first copies were delivered to the Prussian public in the last months of 1751. The success of the work was impressive. The first edition was quickly sold: within one year the book had gone through seven further editions that were printed in Berlin, Rouen, The Hague, Leipzig, Dresden, Edinburgh and Paris. In Prussia Frederick II was enthusiastic about the *Age of Louis XIV* and in Scotland Adam Smith apparently read the book from cover to cover: in his 1756 *Letter to the Edinburgh Review* he quoted from its very last paragraph. The impact of the *Age of Louis XIV* is underlined further by a statistical study. In 1910 Daniel Mornet found that the work was among the ten best represented works in French private libraries in the period between 1750 and 1780. Voltaire's work was more frequently found than the *Encyclopaedia* or the *Social contract*.[11]

Immediately after the publication, Frederick II wrote to Voltaire that he was impatiently reading the two volumes of the work simultaneously. And while he praised both volumes, he declared that he preferred the second one because of the subjects that it treated.[12] Apparently, the king was less interested in the countless anecdotes about the court of Louis XIV in the first volume. The second volume treated topics that were of much greater concern to Frederick. This part of the work – written by Voltaire only a few months earlier in Prussia – began with chapters about the 'Interior government' and 'Finance'.

In these first chapters of the second volume Frederick and other readers of the *Age of Louis XIV* found Voltaire's defence of Colbert's policies against the attacks of 'a certain Bois-Guillebert'.[13] Boisguilbert was, indeed, one of the harshest and most prominent critics of the great minister. From his post as a provincial administrator in Rouen he had observed the financial crisis of the last years of the reign of Louis XIV of France unfold. During these years Boisguilbert wrote tracts about the economic situation of France under such telling titles as *France ruined during the reign of Louis XIV*.[14] The author left no doubt as to when the decline of France began or who was responsible. On the eighty-four pages of one of his other pamphlets, he repeated it well over two dozen times: it was since Colbert had begun to interfere with the matters of commerce that the population of France had been 'slowly but surely burned'.[15] However, Boisguilbert was not merely a critic. He also proposed policy alternatives with great confidence. Once – in a letter to a successor of Colbert – he declared: 'I have the key to all sorts of industry'.[16] However, Boisguilbert's key to industry had not much in common with the policies that Voltaire saw in Prussia or that were described in the *Age of Louis XIV*. Boisguilbert had the greatest confidence in the importance of his discovery. In the opening paragraphs of one of his books he likened himself not only to Copernicus and Columbus but also to Virgil. The comparison with Virgil is particularly surprising. Despite a distant family relationship to Corneille, Boisguilbert's writing style can hardly be called elegant. Ironically, Boisguilbert's opponent in this controversy, Voltaire, has also been called 'French Virgil'. In this case, however, the comparison was not made by himself but by a later biographer.[17]

'Nothing could be more wrong'

As has been pointed out, Boisguilbert's criticism of Colbert was already over thirty years old when Voltaire wrote his response in the chapter 'Finance and regulations' of the *Age of Louis XIV*. Even if several decades separated the critique from the response, Voltaire could not have rejected Boisguilbert's attacks any more emphatically. 'Nothing could ... be more wrong', wrote Voltaire about Boisguilbert's assertion that a severe financial crisis had developed in France after the appointment of Colbert. Similarly categorical is his choice of words in the rejection of Boisguilbert's pretension that France had become decadent under Colbert. 'It was exactly the opposite' is the opening of Voltaire's reply.[18] This rejection of Boisguilbert's statements suggests at first glance a simple disagreement about the actual economic situation of France under Louis XIV. However, the disagreement about the facts constitutes only a minor part of what separated the author of the *Age of Louis XIV* from the author of *France ruined during the reign of Louis XIV*.

Surprisingly there was little disagreement about the facts between the two authors. In the chapter 'Finances', Voltaire concedes a deterioration of the financial situation of France in the last decades of the seventeenth century. After a period of prosperity during Colbert's ministry, Voltaire admits to economic problems after the war of 1689. But he is quick to add that it was only possible to sustain the war effort because of the 'vigour' that Colbert had previously created in all members of the 'body of the state'. Voltaire certainly used a much milder vocabulary than Boisguilbert to describe the situation in France. But he still could not avoid admitting a certain 'slowing down' towards the end of the reign of Louis XIV. That the different assessments of the factual situation of France was not at the heart of their disagreement is also underlined by what seems to be the only positive comment that Voltaire ever wrote about Boisguilbert. 'That Bois-Guillebert', he admitted, 'had a great knowledge of the finances of the kingdom'.[19] However, if Voltaire had to concede that Boisguilbert's criticism was based on a sound knowledge of France's financial situation, what separated the two authors?

Voltaire gives the answer after the compliment just quoted: 'the passion for criticising every act of the great Colbert carried him too far'.[20] The half-hearted compliment for Boisguilbert reflects the arguments put forward in the *Age of Louis XIV*. While admitting that economic problems had started to affect the 'body of the state' during the war of 1689, Voltaire argued that they started only after the end of Colbert's ministry, that they were due to the war rather than to Colbert's policies, and, finally, that if the state could sustain the war effort at all, this was only thanks to Colbert's wise policies. While the first two points are of a rather defensive character, the third is a positive argument in favour of Colbert that hints at what Voltaire admired in the minister. In an earlier passage, Voltaire is more explicit about what he means by the 'vigour' that Colbert created in the body of the nation: 'The French certainly owe him their industry and their commerce.' Here, the essence of the argument is the same except that Voltaire does not use the body analogy to illustrate his point. Thus, 'the body of the state' turns into 'the French' and 'vigour' becomes 'industry' and 'commerce'.[21]

The concrete details of the animation of 'industry' and 'commerce' by Colbert are described in great detail in the *Age of Louis XIV*. Much of the chapters 'Of interior government' and 'Finance' is devoted to Colbert's creations such as the Compagnie des Indes, the ports of Marseilles and Dunkirk, the export subsidies and – above all – the manufactures of fine fabrics, mirrors, silk, tapestry, lace, tin-plate, steel, earthenware and morocco leather. 'From the year 1663 until 1672', Voltaire marvelled, 'each year of this ministry was marked by the creation of some factory.' It is through these creations that Colbert made France prosperous. While there is no doubt for Voltaire that Colbert 'revived industry', he laments the ingratitude towards the minister: 'he worked for ungrateful people'.[22]

As the reasons for Voltaire's admiration for Colbert begin to emerge, it is useful to return to Boisguilbert's arguments. While Voltaire complains about the lack of gratitude for the minister's work, Boisguilbert sees a lack of gratitude towards quite a different authority: nature. After having criticised the regulations and interventions of Colbert's administration in his *Treatise on nature*, Boisguilbert goes on to denounce the outrageous 'ingratitude' in France towards nature. Because the people of France trusted the interventions of Colbert more than the fundamental rule of 'leaving nature to its own devices', he argued, the nation saw itself as punished by nature. In fact, Boisguilbert compared the experience of France with the fate of the Israelites in the desert. As the reader may recall the latter were deprived of the manna because they had failed to obey God's commandments.[23]

The difference between Voltaire and Boisguilbert emerges clearly: Voltaire believed that France should be grateful for the industry that Colbert created and the prosperity that resulted from it. Boisguilbert, however, saw Colbert's efforts to control and create prosperity as a blasphemous distrust of nature. According to him, this blasphemy was subsequently punished by nature and resulted in a profound financial crisis. The blasphemy insulted nature and prevented it from giving its manna to the people. Boisguilbert's passage about the vengeance of nature deserves to be quoted in full: 'Nature herself, jealously protecting her work takes immediate revenge in a general upheaval as soon as she sees her insight and the sagacity of her acts being challenged by external interference.'[24]

French and Prussian anecdotes about administrators and merchants

The different perspectives on Colbert and his interventions into the matters of commerce and industry are well illustrated by two anecdotes reported by Voltaire and Boisguilbert. It should be pointed out that the factual accuracy of the anecdotes is questionable. Their accuracy is, however, less relevant in the present context. The anecdotes are revealing because they were told by the authors with a specific intention. Voltaire's and Boisguilbert's stories about the interaction between administrator and merchant are indicative of their perspectives on the kind of authority that the administrator should exercise over matters of industry.

In one of his books, Boisguilbert reports the famous encounter in which the merchant Thomas Le Gendre is said to have coined the phrase 'laissez-faire'. Colbert had asked Le Gendre how to make the country prosperous. The merchant's answer, as reported by Boisguilbert, was that it would be enough if the minister 'and people of his kind' kept out of these matters. Le Gendre went on to explain to the minister that the individual's 'eagerness to earn' was the only ingredient needed to create prosperity. Guided by their respective 'personal interest' individuals would naturally act in such a way that 'everything will go perfectly well'. Ministerial interventions guided by 'indirect interests' rather than by the 'personal interests' were bound to be harmful for commerce.[25]

The essence of the anecdote is that Colbert's work is not only futile but even harmful because it collides with the working of nature. Note that the episode is not only directed against Colbert but against the intervention of administrators in general. The merchant is quoted as specifying that not only Colbert but also 'people of his kind' should keep out of matters of commerce. The efforts that Voltaire praises as being at the origin of France's industry are in the eyes of Boisguilbert nothing more than disrupting interventions. Rather than a minister who animates it, commerce needs no more than the 'personal interest' as a driving force.[26] However, Boisguilbert's positive assessment of the 'personal interest' and 'eagerness to earn' contrasts sharply with Voltaire's views about what he calls the 'individual interest'. In the *Age of Louis XIV* Voltaire reports a similar anecdote about an encounter between Colbert and a merchant. The story is prefaced by a short reflection about selfish behaviour. 'Individual interest', Voltaire warned, 'fascinates the eye and narrows the mind'. The story itself unfolds in a similar way to Boisguilbert's. Again, Colbert meets with a merchant – this time by the name Hazon – and asks for advice on how to promote commerce. The merchant replies that the minister was overstepping the mark with his activism: 'You found the coach fallen over onto one side and you have turned it onto the other.' Voltaire qualifies this answer as scandalous and 'rude'. To him such a comment shows how little the merchant, guided by his 'individual interest', is able to appreciate Colbert's work for the 'general good'. According to Voltaire, it was only with the introduction of the 'philosophical spirit' in his own times that this ingratitude ended and the people started to appreciate the memory of Colbert.[27] Considering the debates of the decades after the publication of the *Age of Louis XIV* it seems safe to say that this was a misjudgement on the part of Voltaire. Many of his fellow philosophers were highly critical of Colbert and his master. The anecdote about the encounter with Hazon seems to have been at least as well known in the eighteenth century as the story about Le Gendre. The French diplomat Amelot de la Hossaie, for example, reports it in a more detailed and colourful version in his *Historical memoirs*. Voltaire also indicates that the story was reported in one of the most popular dictionaries of the time, Louis Moréri's *Great historical dictionary*. In Amelot's version it can be seen that the original tendency of the story was strongly against the minister.[28] It was without any doubt this tendency and the prominence of the anecdote that prompted Voltaire to comment on it in his work.

It is important to put in relief the fundamental difference between Boisguilbert and Voltaire that is expressed through these anecdotes. The difference lies not in the way the two merchants think: both are guided by their self-interest. Rather, the difference lies in the judgement of the respective authors about the merchant's attitude. Boisguilbert agrees with the merchant that any intervention that is not clearly guided by 'personal interest' will ruin commerce. Voltaire, to the contrary, condemns the pursuit of the 'individual interest' as insufficient. He emphasises the need for a minister with the 'general good' in mind in order to create industry and commerce.

It is revealing to read the anecdotes about the interaction between Colbert and the merchants in the context of similar stories that were told about Frederick II in the eighteenth century. Voltaire's host travelled frequently through the Prussian provinces in order to inspect the progress of manufactures, ports and new settlements. Anecdotes about Frederick's travels and his encounters with his subjects circulated even during his reign. After his death, printed collections of these episodes became available. In many of these stories a similar constellation as in Boisguilbert's and Voltaire's anecdotes can be found: they are about the travelling administrator who encounters local merchants.

Some of the most telling anecdotes of Frederick's interaction with the Prussian Hazons and Le Gendres stem from his travels through Silesia. The region was one of the most developed regions of Prussia where Frederick made significant efforts to further the development of the local industries. On one of Frederick's annual travels he passed through the town of 'A'. There he asked about a large building. He was told that it was a woollen mill which had been built with government subsidies. The king then enquired about the produce of the mill and was told that it made light woollen fabric. Frederick demanded to know why it did not produce heavy woollen cloth, too. The answer was that there was no water in the region to power the mill. In response, the king pointed to a large body of water near the town and remarked that it was 'big enough to drown the whole ... bench of aldermen'. On another travel the king told the manufacturers of cloth near the Polish border to dye fabrics in yellow and light red. According to the monarch the two colours were particularly popular in Poland and would help to increase sales across the border. Another anecdote tells how Frederick tried to convince the merchants of Landshut to open up a new lace manufacture with royal subsidies. According to his observations the demand was strong. The women of Breslau and Berlin consumed lace worth 60,000 *Thaler* annually. However, the merchants stubbornly resisted his encouragement. With an ironic comment he eventually gave up on the project. Frederick's travels to Silesia were also a topic in his correspondence with Voltaire. In 1773, after Frederick's return from Silesia and other parts of Prussia, he wrote to Ferney about his accomplishments. In that year he had opened a canal that joined a number of smaller rivers to the Elbe, supervised the reconstruction of several cities, dried a swamp and ordered the construction of new roads 'to facilitate commerce'.[29]

The stories from Silesia illustrate what Voltaire meant when he described administrators like Frederick or Colbert as creators of industry. The king is depicted as taking decisions about new manufactures, the extension of old ones and the fabrication of new products. Like Colbert in Voltaire's anecdote, Frederick emerges from these stories as the wise administrator working for the 'general good'. Without a direct interest in the manufactures, he tried to encourage and assist their development. The merchants and local administrators, however, are shown as ungrateful and stubborn. In his 1963 study of the Prussian economy under Frederick II William Henderson paints a similar picture of the local entrepreneurs: 'New industrial processes and methods of business organisation and finance were held up by the inertia of manufacturers, merchants and artisans who were as hidebound in their ways as landowners and peasants.'[30]

The merchants in the Prussian anecdotes were also less self-conscious than their French counterparts in the stories of Boisguilbert and Voltaire. Hazon and Le Gendre were not afraid to antagonise the minister and tell him to keep out of their business affairs. No similar behaviour is reported in the Prussian anecdotes. They convey a picture in which Frederick's authority is too strong to be contradicted. But they do not only reflect the king's strength. At the same time they illustrate Prussia's relative backwardness. Even compared to France under Louis XIV, Prussia under Frederick II was far less developed. The merchant class was less established, less influential and less able to stand up against the royal administration.

The relative backwardness is also illustrated by the lack of imagination and entrepreneurial spirit among the merchants encountered by Frederick. They were depicted as being unable to take even the most basic decisions about new production facilities, new techniques or a new product. Certainly the most striking example for their lack of entrepreneurial spirit is the episode about the cloth for exportation to Poland. Significantly, it is the king who had to suggest to the merchants that a change of colour could help to increase sales. The Prussian anecdotes document a contemporary understanding according to which Frederick's interventions were not disturbing but rather helpful and even necessary for the creation of new manufactures. This view also corresponded to Voltaire's observations about the new Prussian industries which he saw closely associated to the activism of Frederick. Like Voltaire's story about Colbert and the merchant Hazon, the anecdotes about Frederick express a contemporary experience in which the 'individual interest' of the merchants alone was seen as insufficient to create industry. In sharp contrast to this, Boisguilbert maintained that the free pursuit of 'personal interest' was all that was needed to create industry and commerce. However, Voltaire's and Boisguilbert's anecdotes about the interaction between merchants and administrators illustrate that they agreed on one point. The pursuit of 'personal interest' – as Boisguilbert called it – or 'individual interest' – as Voltaire referred to it – was for both authors a constant of human behaviour. However, they fundamentally disagreed on the mechanism that was needed to create a flourishing industry out of the selfish behaviour of the individuals.

Two different keys to industry

When Boisguilbert bragged that he possessed the 'key to all sorts of industry' he had a new and surprisingly simple concept in mind. He was convinced that 'eagerness to earn' was a sufficient motive to create flourishing industry and commerce. However, in his view, the generalised pursuit of self-interest also gave rise to a conflict of interests: everybody tries to buy cheap and sell dear. In this critical moment, nature intervenes. Out of conflicting self-interests, she creates prosperous order: 'It is only at point of the sword that justice is maintained in these encounters; nevertheless this is the charge that nature and providence have taken upon themselves.' Nature-Providence thus balances the interests and establishes an order that brings about 'opulence'. However, Nature-Providence can only fulfil its benign role, 'as long as nature is left to its own devices' ('laisser faire la nature'). All human interventions to balance the conflicting interests will disturb nature's work.[31]

The bold notion of a mechanism that spontaneously creates harmonious order and prosperity out of antagonistic interests has become a familiar idea since, but it was certainly a revolutionary idea in Boisguilbert's day. However revolutionary, his idea did not fail to convince a growing number of readers in the course of the eighteenth century. But at the same time there was a strong current in eighteenth-century thought that remained sceptical about this notion. Notions of laisser-faire in seventeenth- and eighteenth-century thought have received much scholarly attention partly because of the success of liberal economic thought in later periods. This emphasis may at times lead to an unbalanced picture of the importance of these notions in eighteenth-century thought. Voltaire and many other prominent contemporary authors agreed that every human was bound to (and should) pursue his or her self-interest, but they did not agree to the simple solution that Boisguilbert offered to the problem of how to make the many selfish individuals engage in an orderly, prosperous and peaceful industry.

Since Boisguilbert's concept of Nature-Providence has a significant religious dimension it is helpful to explore Voltaire's religious views in order to understand his perspective on this aspect of political economy. In particular, his deistic cosmology underlies his mistrust of a nature that actively intervenes in economic affairs. In fact, Voltaire not only mistrusts nature he flatly denies its existence: 'There is no such thing as nature, ... all is art'. The meaning of this radical statement is explained in Voltaire's *Second dialogue about divinity*. Voltaire's answer to the initial question 'Is there a Theos?' is a variation of an argument that is familiar from Cicero's *On the nature of the gods* or Hume's *Dialogues concerning natural religion* of 1779. The key notion is that the orderly composition of a building reveals an architect. Accordingly, the order that exists in the universe can only be attributed to an eternal, supremely intelligent and powerful 'maker'. This also means that the whole universe created by this supreme 'artisan' is art rather than nature. One of the characters of Voltaire's *Dialogue* raises the objection that 'artisan' was nothing but another name for the secret power that in reality is nature. But for Voltaire nature was only 'an assembly of things that exist' or 'a word that designates the universality of things'. Nature, he was sure, could not be the secret force that created the order of the universe.[32]

The impossibility of spontaneous order is a favourite topic of Voltaire. In the *Letters from Memmius to Cicero* he vigorously opposed the idea that the universality of things could have developed movement, order and life by itself. The notion of spontaneous order was nothing less than 'absurd' to him.[33] If spontaneous order seemed absurd and if the order of the universe just like the orderly structure of artefacts could only be the work of an intelligent creator, how could there be prosperous order in industry without the intervention of an enlightened minister like Colbert? This line of reasoning was particularly prominent in Voltaire's thought but it was not unique to the philosopher.

The banker and later minister of finance Jacques Necker was originally from Geneva. In 1750 he moved to Paris where he started a successful career in banking. He founded his own bank and became one of the directors of the East India Company. In 1776 he became director of the treasury and exercised the function of comptroller general, a position which he could not take on officially because he was a foreigner and a Protestant. He lost his position, was recalled in 1788, and played a crucial role in summoning the generalstates. His downfall in 1789 contributed to the escalation of the revolutionary situation in Paris. He was recalled once more but resigned finally in 1790 and retired to Switzerland.

In 1773, Necker wrote one of the most famous praises of Colbert. In the *Eulogy of Colbert,* Necker compared the minister to the creator of the universe. If man was God's image on earth, he wrote in 1773, the individual who could lay the best founded claim to this title was the 'administrator of finances'. Only the monarch, he added, might be more worthy of the title. It remains questionable how serious Necker was about putting the monarch first. He might have found himself in the same situation as Voltaire when he struggled to justify the proposition that despite the important role of the minister the period was the age of Louis XIV and not the age of Colbert. Necker and Voltaire attributed a very important role to Colbert. Necker specifically pointed out that it was the task of the minister to direct the passions in order to create 'public happiness'. Voltaire wholeheartedly agreed to the analogy between the order creating function of the minister and the creator of the universe. In a letter to Suzanne Necker about the book of her husband, Voltaire repeated the comparison between 'God's governance' and the 'administration of J.-B. Colbert'. Both had flaws, he admitted, but both deserved praise, the former in the form of adoration and the latter in the form of esteem.[34]

The notion that a guiding hand was needed to create industrious prosperity out of the many individual interests in a society was also a topic of discussion between Voltaire and Frederick. In 1770 they discussed the issue in several letters. Frederick had composed a ten page dissertation under the title *Essay on self love as a moral principle.* The text was written for the Prussian academy. In it, Frederick examined the relation between 'self love' and – he used the same words as Necker – 'public happiness'. As one may guess from his policies, his was not an attitude of laissez-faire. The common good could only be achieved if the selfishness of the individuals was administered ('maniée') by the hands of an able philosopher. The task of the philosopher was to 'regulate' and 'direct' the selfishness of individuals in order to ensure an orderly balance. Quite clearly an ordinary philosopher would hardly be up to the task. Most likely, Frederick had in mind a philosopher on the throne. Voltaire was delighted when he received Frederick's essay. Their friendship had recovered by this time from the events that had led to Voltaire's departure from Prussia in 1753. Voltaire used a nautical analogy to illustrate that he shared his friend's views. Self-love, he replied to the king of Prussia, was the wind that filled the sails of a ship. Nevertheless, a helmsman was still needed for the vessel to reach port. Voltaire apparently found Frederick's essay particularly inspiring since he added a second metaphor. For Voltaire, 'well-directed self love' was similar to a marriage between self-love and reason. The offspring of the happy union would be 'virtue' and 'happiness'. Voltaire has made clear repeatedly that the role of the administrator was to regulate self-love but not to repress it. Albert Hirschmann has characterised approaches that were similar to those of Frederick and Voltaire as the 'harnessing' of individual interests. In fact, Voltaire considered self-love to be a useful and even necessary instinct for the preservation of society. Merchants, Voltaire argued, would not go to India out of charity and masons would not cut stone to please their neighbours. The argument is reminiscent of Adam Smith's famous observation that it is not 'from the benevolence of butcher, or the baker, that we expect our dinner, but from their regard to their own interest'. However, as far as industry was concerned the agreement between Voltaire and his famous admirer ended there. As we will see later, Smith's views about the development of industry was much closer to Boisguilbert's views. Voltaire considered self-love a necessary condition for the merchant to go to India and the mason to cut stones. But he did not consider it a sufficient condition for the merchant's and the mason's trades to develop in the first place and to flourish. In other words, he considered self-love a motive for the encouragement of industriousness or of the industry of the individual. However, for a sector of industry to be established, the guiding hand of an able administrator such as Frederick or Colbert was necessary.[35]

Self-love and the branches of industry

The importance of the administrator for the creation of industry in Voltaire's thought is best illustrated by contrasting it to Boisguilbert's views. The latter believed that an actively intervening Nature-Providence establishes a balance between the various personal interests. According to Boisguilbert providence creates the balance that is best for commerce and industry. As Marx pointed out in his observations on the history of economic thought, Boisguilbert's providential balance determines the optimal proportions in which the working hours of the individuals are assigned to the different 'branches of industry'. This insight is emphasised by Marx as the foremost contribution of Boisguilbert to economics.[36]

When Adam Smith contemplated the problem of the distribution of labour to the different branches of industry in the *Wealth of Nations*, he put forward a similar view to that of Boisguilbert. In 1776 he argued that the balance between buyers and sellers distributes 'the whole quantity of industry annually employed in order to bring any commodity to the market' to the different 'species of industry'. The distribution of labour or individual industry would be such, Smith predicted, that every branch of industry meets the demand for its product. One of the well-known examples that Smith uses for the working of this mechanism is the rising demand for black cloth in the case of a 'publick mourning'. The demand for 'coloured silks and cloths' falls in such a case and the change influences the behaviour of labourers and merchants.[37]

At least in Silesia the behaviour of contemporary merchants seems to have followed different principles. In the anecdote about Frederick's travel to Silesia and his encounter with the local textile merchants, the demand for coloured cloth existed in Poland but the Silesian textile manufacturers did not respond to it in the way that Smith would have expected. Frederick II had to step in to direct the Silesian industry to the demand that existed in Poland. The different contemporary perceptions reflect the significant differences between Prussia and Britain. Smith's example may have been a good illustration of how merchants and labourers reacted in one of the most advanced commercial societies of the eighteenth century. The anecdote from Prussia reflects a perception in which the local merchants of a less advanced European country depended on the helping hand of the administrator.

Not surprisingly, Smith was just as critical of Colbert's policies as Boisguilbert. The Scottish author had read the *Age of Louis XIV* but disagreed with Voltaire on the merits of the minister. In particular, Voltaire's work failed to convince Smith about the effectiveness of Colbert's policies for the creation of industry. In the *Wealth of Nations* the minister is criticised for regulating the 'industry and commerce ... upon the same model as the departments of a public office'. Instead of allowing 'every man to pursue his own interest', the minister privileged some 'branches of industry' and submitted others to 'extraordinary restraints'.[38]

For Voltaire, this was precisely the achievement of Colbert. The crucial task of distributing individual industriousness among the branches of industry could not be entrusted to a spontaneous order brought about by Providence or an invisible hand. Voltaire assigned this task to a worldly 'mind behind the work'. In the pamphlet *Dialogue between a philosopher and a comptroller of finance* – published in the same year as the *Age of Louis XIV* – Voltaire argued his view of how the nation's industry developed. Already the opening question of the 'philosopher' is programmatic: 'Do you know that a minister of finance can do much good'? While Boisguilbert's answer would probably have been in the negative, Voltaire goes on to explain how the minister can contribute to making the nation prosperous. Not surprisingly the model that Voltaire holds up for all future finance ministers is 'the great Colbert' who made France rich by developing her industry.[39]

The point of departure is Voltaire's postulate 'to be rich is to enjoy'. Consequently, the increase of 'enjoyment' is the 'general good' that the minister ought to be striving for. As Voltaire emphasises, it is not the increase of money in the nation that procures a better life for the population, but the perfection of its industry. While the amount of money in the country has not increased in the last eight hundred years, France is 'in real terms' a hundred times richer than in the times of Hugh Capet. The reason for this hundredfold increase in the nation's wealth is the increase in 'industry'. As has been pointed out, Voltaire uses his own coach as an illustration for the progress that industry brought to France. The basis of this industry is the great number of industrious men, but their individual industriousness is merely the raw material in the able hands of the minister. Without the minister, 'oaks were rotting in the forests' and 'sand remained useless in the earth'. What makes 'hard working men' turn oak trees into parquet and sand into mirrors is the guidance of the minister, the 'mind behind the work'. It is only because Colbert directed the industriousness of the French to the mirror industry that the nation is enriched by the 'enjoyment' of being able to look at herself and the prosperity that this new branch of industry created. The production of mirrors is, indeed, one of the most prominent examples of the industry that Colbert created in France.[40]

Voltaire's equation of the wealth of a nation with well-being, enjoyment and the development of industry rather than with the amount of specie in the country is noteworthy. Classical economists, most of all maybe Smith, have been quick to condemn their predecessors for the bullionism which allegedly pervaded their thought. However, as the example of Voltaire shows bullionism was far from being a universally accepted concept among pre-Adamite thinkers. Homogeneity was strikingly absent in the thought of the different thinkers who are often lumped together under the label of 'mercantilism'. Not much is gained from using this summary label but much of the complexity of pre-classical thought is obscured. Eighteenth-century views on industry are a good illustration of the multi-layered complexity and variety of arguments of economic and political thought in this period. Voltaire's view on industry was strikingly different from Boisguilbert's 'key to all sorts of industry'. The latter believed that individual greed was sufficient to make workers turn trees into parquet and sand into mirrors. Quite clearly, this perspective conflicted with what Voltaire observed in Prussia. If the silk industry was developing in Prussia it was because the king had used resources and authority to direct parts of the workforce to this undertaking. In Berlin Voltaire saw a development of the silk industry that was hardly left to private initiative. As has been documented in the previous chapter many measures were taken to encourage the production of silk: silkworm eggs were distributed free of charge, experts were recruited from France, the government guaranteed the purchase of the produced silk and anybody who damaged a mulberry tree was severely punished.

At the same time, Prussian merchants were going to Bengal with the support of Frederick II. This is not to say that Prussian merchants were lacking the necessary self-love as a motivation for their risky journeys. But without the – however limited – backing of Frederick's administration it is unlikely that a Prussian ship would ever have reached India. Voltaire admired the Prussian Asiatic trade company just as he admired the French Compagnie des Indes. He regarded both as new prosperous branches of industry that Frederick and Colbert had helped to create in their countries.

The anecdotes about Frederick tell a similar story about the development of more domestic forms of industry. The wool mill of 'A' existed because of Frederick's subsidies and, if it ever started to produce heavy woollen cloth, it was because the king directed the workforce to that task. Both Colbert and Frederick were thus seen by Voltaire as introducing whole new branches of industry as well as helping to further the existing ones. It becomes clear that the Voltairean 'mind behind the work' has an important function in his perspective on progress and prosperity. He – that is assuming that the 'mind' would in the eighteenth century most likely be imagined as a male minister or monarch – guides the industry of the individual to the branch of industry where it creates new enjoyment and prosperity. Moreover, the minister also created whole new branches of industry. This view was diametrically opposed to Boisguilbert's. For him it was the active intervention of a supernatural entity, Nature-Providence, that assigned individual industriousness to the right branch of industry. The disagreement between Voltaire and Boisguilbert went far beyond admiration or dislike for the 'historical' minister Colbert. More profoundly, both were at odds over the relation between individual industry and the development of the sector of industry. Boisguilbert relied on a solution that evoked religious categories. Voltaire lacked the necessary faith and preferred a worldly solution. At a time when many religious explanations for natural phenomena and historical developments were challenged it is hardly surprising that Voltaire rejected Boisguilbert's views. The rule of Nature-Providence was not only a religious concept, it also removed an important sphere within the nation from royal authority. While Smith criticised Colbert for treating the branches of industry like 'departments of a public office', Voltaire regarded it as necessary that the royal authority fully extend over the matters of industry. This was necessary for the development of industry but it was also unacceptable from Voltaire's point of view that the prerogative of royal authority should be curtailed in any way.

Moreover, Voltaire's focus on the *progress* of industry set him fundamentally apart from Boisguilbert. The latter presents the reader with an essentially static perspective that does not cater for great leaps of progress. However, the increase of 'enjoyment' carried by the development of 'industry' is constitutive of Voltaire's views. For the creation of new branches of industry with new products, techniques, facilities, sources of raw materials or markets, the guidance of a minister was required. Voltaire did not trust that 'self-love' would teach the inhabitants of rustic regions such as Westphalia how to make better carriages, cloth, porcelain and mirrors. Only the efforts of Frederick could bring industry to this remote region and improve the living condition of its frugal inhabitants.

Enter La Beaumelle

In the same year in which Voltaire praised monarchical authority in the *Age of Louis XIV* for its benign role in the creation of industry, arrived an author in Potsdam who had a distinctly different perspective on these matters. For La Beaumelle, Louis XIV was nothing but a despot and his minister Colbert did not create anything but vain pomp. But La Beaumelle did not only disagree in silence. A series of events prompted him to publish in 1753 an edition with commentary of the *Age of Louis XIV* in Frankfurt on Main. This edition contained some of the harshest criticism that has ever been directed at Voltaire's works. In fact, the controversy – or rather feud – that developed between Voltaire and La Beaumelle in Potsdam is even by Voltairean standards a particularly nasty quarrel. La Beaumelle summed up the character of the dispute quite aptly when he wrote to Voltaire in 1753: 'between us there can be no question of politeness'.[41]

The personal tone of the pamphlets and footnotes that were exchanged makes it difficult to uncover the substantial aspect of the dispute. Of the complex relationship between La Beaumelle and Voltaire only a part will be discussed here. What is relevant for the present enquiry is Voltaire's defence of the strong and uncontested 'sovereign authority' of Louis XIV – or Frederick, for that matter – which, in his view, was a necessary condition for the development of industry.[42] For La Beaumelle the authority of the government of Louis XIV was excessive and not much more than simple Montesquieuean despotism.[43] This form of government inspired complete horror in La Beaumelle and was for him certainly not the source of any sort of industry. In fact, he maintained that the form of government was altogether unrelated to the progress of industry.

It should be added that both authors did not only discuss the impact of monarchical authority controversially. Both of them – first La Beaumelle and later Voltaire – did also experience great difficulties with the Prussian authorities. Their perspectives on despotism also have to be seen in the context of these events that eventually forced them to leave Prussia. However, before exploring further the controversy that unfolded in Potsdam between Voltaire and La Beaumelle, it is necessary to pause for a moment in order to shed light on the chain of events that caused Voltaire to regard La Beaumelle as the 'the last of writers' and that prompted La Beaumelle to attack the *Age of Louis XIV* so ferociously.[44]

La Beaumelle between Voltaire and Montesquieu

Laurent Angliviel de La Beaumelle – sometimes referred to as 'Angle-Vieux' by Voltaire – was a truly European thinker and pamphleteer.[45] Born in 1726 to a Protestant family in the Cevennes, he moved to Geneva at twenty-one years of age and became, as Condorcet puts it, an 'apprentice pastor' in the city of Calvin.[46] Two years later, he accepted a position as a private tutor in Copenhagen where he was subsequently appointed royal professor of French. Before taking up this academic position, he made a brief but fateful trip to Paris. In the capital of his native France, he met two men who were to profoundly influence the rest of his life: Voltaire and Montesquieu. The Paris encounter with Voltaire was polite and harmless. On 17 June 1750 – Voltaire's departure to Prussia was imminent – La Beaumelle presented himself with a letter of introduction from one of Voltaire's correspondents in Copenhagen. In the following week, the two went for a walk in the Tuileries and La Beaumelle was invited to a performance of Voltaire's latest play, *Rome Saved* (which he did not like). Any further contact was then interrupted by Voltaire's departure to Potsdam, the place of their next – and much less courteous – encounter.

La Beaumelle remained in Paris where he met the man whose thought was to form the foundation of his criticism of Voltaire's *Age of Louis XIV*. Not only did Montesquieu become La Beaumelle's intellectual mentor in this period, but a close friendship and durable collaboration also grew out of La Beaumelle's admiration for the great thinker and Montesquieu's esteem for the young author.[47] Most noteworthy in this context is the *Second part of the defence of the Spirit of the laws* of 1751 in which La Beaumelle responded to attacks against Montesquieu. The pamphlet was written in co-operation with Montesquieu and at the time frequently attributed to the latter. Montesquieu, in turn, supported La Beaumelle in his later quarrel with Voltaire and, in 1753, helped him to get out of the Bastille where certain careless remarks about the royal family had landed him.

The close relationship with Montesquieu is of particular interest because it places La Beaumelle's confrontation with Voltaire in the larger context of two diametrically opposed judgements about the reign of Louis XIV that dominated the eighteenth century: the fundamental critique of Montesquieu and the eulogies of Voltaire. Montesquieu's Louis XIV is far from the great monarch that is Voltaire's Louis XIV. In the *Persian letters*, Montesquieu ridiculed the vanity and decadence that characterised society during the reign of Louis XIV. He accused the king of being a deceiving 'magician' who exploited the vanity of his subjects and blinded them with his splendour.[48] Under this cover of superficial glamour, however, the monarchy degenerated into a despotism that astonished even the oriental observers of the *Persian letters*. Montesquieu's judgement is reflected in the writings of La Beaumelle, for whom the reign of Louis was simply 'Persian'.[49] Voltaire opposed the judgement of Montesquieu in several instances. In his article 'Contradictions', for example, he asked why Montesquieu was accepted to the Académie Française after having criticised Louis XIV in the *Persian letters*. Voltaire pointed out that another author – the Abbé de Saint-Pierre who will be of interest for the present enquiry in Chapter 4 – was expelled from the academy for his much milder criticism of Louis XIV.[50]

Voltaire's perspective on the reign of Louis XIV was fundamentally different from that of Montesquieu. The flourishing arts and the splendour of the monarch, which, for Montesquieu, merely create the deceiving façade of a decadent monarchy, are for Voltaire the very characteristics of the progress of humanity. While the splendour of Montesquieu's Louis XIV is only a fatal illusion, Voltaire depicts the reign of Louis XIV in a different light. He considers Louis XIV a great monarch whose splendour stimulated the industry of his subjects and thus guided them to a new pinnacle of human progress. Voltaire's insistence that real progress of humanity was made under Louis XIV must be understood in the light of Montesquieu's critique. Voltaire argues against Montesquieu that the French nation not only achieved unparalleled progress (rather than a mere illusion of vain splendour), but that this progress was achieved by the guidance of the government that Montesquieu attacks as oriental despotism.

Voltaire presents his argument against Montesquieu in two forms. He published a series of direct comments on the *Spirit of the laws* such as the *Republican ideas*, the article 'Laws (Spirit of the)' in the *Philosophical dictionary*, and the *Commentary about the Spirit of the laws*. Parallel to the direct comments, Voltaire argued his own perspective on history in several works. Most prominent is the *Age of Louis XIV*, which Antoine Adam calls a 'defence' against Montesquieu's criticism. After the publication of the *Age of Louis XIV*, Voltaire added to this 'faithful picture of the progress of the human mind among the French' the *Essay on universal history* which covers the history of the world since the times of Charlemagne. Laurent Versini sees in this work 'Voltaire's *Spirit of the laws*'. In the light of Voltaire's defence of Louis XIV it is ironic to remember that Montesquieu had ridiculed his eulogies before they had even been written. In letter CXXX of the *Persian letters* – published exactly 30 years before the *Age of Louis XIV* – Montesquieu mocked an imaginary writer who maintained that 'Louis the Great was the greatest of all princes'.[51]

La Beaumelle clearly preferred Montesquieu's perspective on Louis XIV to that of Voltaire. This sympathy and the close relationship that connected La Beaumelle and Montesquieu will have to be kept in mind when analysing the quarrel between La Beaumelle and Voltaire. La Beaumelle was more than a mouthpiece for Montesquieu but his positions are clearly informed by Montesquieu's thought.[52]

Frederick, Voltaire and La Beaumelle's edition of the *Age of Louis XIV*

When La Beaumelle arrived in Potsdam in 1751 he was on an official diplomatic mission for the Danish court. In his luggage he carried several copies of his latest work, *My Thoughts*. Despite an introductory remark in the book, according to which the author was 'incapable of offending anybody', the book contained a number of thoughts that were bound to get him into trouble in Potsdam.[53]

First of all, there is more than one derogatory comment on Voltaire's idol Colbert in the book. According to La Beaumelle's 'Thought CLXXII' the minister had not only 'little knowledge' and 'no taste' but his policies were also completely wrong. La Beaumelle's *Thoughts* paint a picture of Colbert's ministry that could not have been more different from the one that Voltaire painted in the *Age of Louis XIV*. 'His first steps', writes La Beaumelle about the minister, 'were wrong, his first choices were ridiculous, his first enterprises were mistakes, & his last one[s] were vexatious.' Now, this perspective on Colbert was certainly not welcomed by Frederick II and his chamberlain. While these thoughts on Colbert might have been enough to ruin La Beaumelle's credit with Voltaire, the young author's work contained other remarks about the poet and his relation to the king that proved to be fateful. In 'Thought CCCCXXV', La Beaumelle declared that 'there have been greater poets than Voltaire but none as well paid'. To that he added less than flattering comparisons between Voltaire and a 'buffoon', and between Frederick and a minor German prince. The literary scandal that resulted from this 'thought' is beyond the scope of this project. For the present purpose, it is sufficient to note that practically all of Potsdam's small literary world were involved and that neither Voltaire nor the king was convinced by La Beaumelle's attempts to explain the harmlessness of the remarks.[54]

In addition to this, a pamphlet attributed to La Beaumelle circulated in Potsdam at the time. The hand-written brochure was entitled *Short account about the person and lifestyle of the King in Prussia* and contained a great number of ironic remarks about Frederick. Voltaire, too, was ridiculed on the 32 pages of the pamphlet. Besides the German version, the Prussian archives conserve a French version. It was seized from Voltaire when he was arrested in Frankfurt after his escape from Berlin in 1753. The pamphlet circulated not only in Prussia but also in France, England, the Netherlands and Sweden. Whether the pamphlet was actually written by La Beaumelle can not be said with certainty. However, many contemporaries believed that he was the author and the mere fact that it was circulating under his name certainly made his situation more difficult.[55] The result of La Beaumelle's literary activities was that he was forced to leave Prussia after a brief incarceration in Spandau. As he was convinced that Voltaire was responsible for his disgrace he prepared his revenge. It is at this point that the quarrel becomes germane to the present enquiry.

La Beaumelle decided to take revenge on Voltaire by attacking his latest literary success, the *Age of Louis XIV*. The form of attack that La Beaumelle chose was to publish in Frankfurt on Main an edition of the work under the title *The age of Louis XIV with a great number of additions and comments by M. de la B****. The subject of Colbert was not new to

La Beaumelle and Louis XIV, too, had been the target of his writings previously.[56]

Most of the footnotes that La Beaumelle added to the *Age of Louis XIV* are of little interest for the present enquiry as they attack either Voltaire's character or his writing style. What remains, if personal insults and literary criticism are disregarded are only a handful of notes. These, however, target some of the most important passages of the work concerning the role of the 'sovereign authority' in the development of industry. One of Voltaire's arguments in particular attracted La Beaumelle's criticism: on the first pages of the *Age of Louis XIV*, Voltaire considers the question of why no 'age of happiness' had occurred in France before the century of Louis XIV. He leaves no doubts as to the sorry state of France before Louis XIV. In this period, he writes, the Italians used to refer to those 'on the other side of the Alps' as 'barbarians'. As he adds, they were deserving of this name.[57]

Voltaire starts his discussion by postulating that a powerful and prosperous state can either be based on 'freedom founded on laws' or on an uncontested 'sovereign authority'. This maxim immediately provoked a footnote from La Beaumelle. While he agreed with the first part, he strongly rejected the uncontested 'sovereign authority' as despotism. This form of government, he added, never made a state powerful. Not surprisingly, Voltaire saw things rather differently. While he mentioned 'freedom founded on laws' as one option in his maxim, he does not seem to seriously consider it a viable way for France. He did not elaborate at all on it. Almost certainly the reference was a nod to the commercial success of Britain. However, the first part of the maxim seems to be forgotten when Voltaire constructs his answer to the question of why France had not flourished before Louis XIV. The reason, according to Voltaire, was quite simply the weakness of 'royal power'. The kings of France before Louis XIV were continuously busy imposing their authority on their vassals. Consequently, they did not have the leisure and the power make their subjects happy. What exactly were the consequences of this weakness of the royal authority? Voltaire's answer is clear. Because 'the genius of the French' suffered under a 'gothic government' for over nine hundred years, the people found themselves 'without industry' and in great misery.[58]

What has to be understood by 'industry' in this context is elaborated in Voltaire's next paragraph. The lack of industry manifested itself in the absence of great 'discoveries' and 'inventions', a large number of which were made outside France. He lists the art of printing, gunpowder, mirrors, telescopes, the compass and the pneumatic pump. Because of its unstable government France did not make any inventions that contributed to its progress and prosperity. Again, La Beaumelle commented in a footnote. First of all he objected to the notion that the 'inventive nations' were any happier than other nations. Even more importantly, he maintained that there was no relation between the 'constitution of these people' and the discoveries that they made. Inventions, he added, were exclusively determined by chance.[59]

Aside from the question of whether more industry made a nation happier, the crucial disagreement lay in the link between the form of government and the development of industry. As is clear from the examples given by Voltaire, the term is used in this context principally in the sense of inventiveness. It is a form of progress of industry that includes innovations regarding the techniques of production, such as the printing press, and innovations that resulted in new products, for example, mirrors. The mirror industry is one of Voltaire's favourite examples to illustrate the connection between the powerful government of Louis XIV and the creation of a new industry. Due to the weakness of France, Venice had developed a monopoly on mirrors in the sixteenth century and produced mirrors for all of Europe. This changed only under Louis XIV and his able minister. Colbert established a French mirror production. Clearly, France could not invent the mirror for a second time. But from the beginning of Colbert's ministry on, French mirrors began to improve. Voltaire points out that French mirrors were, soon, superior in size and quality to the Venetian produce. Since that time, the French mirrors had not been surpassed.[60] French mirror production was tied to the power of the government of Louis XIV in more than one way. Besides being an industry that was created by the intervention of Colbert, mirrors also became one of the principal consumer goods associated with the brilliance of the reign of Louis XIV: while the minister was the father of mirror production in France, his master was without any doubt its best customer. The hall of mirrors of Versailles is a 73-meter-long illustration of Voltaire's thesis of the interdependence of royal power, splendour of the court, perfection of the arts and the development of industry in the age of Louis XIV.

It may be added that, in a curious way, one of the other inventions mentioned by Voltaire was equally related to the royal splendour of Versailles. It was with gunpowder that the royal physicist Christiaan Huygens wanted to create a particularly impressive fountain for the gardens of Versailles. The motor of the pump had already proved its power in a demonstration for Colbert where it easily lifted up 'four to five footmen'. The work on the gun powder pump was, however, not finished when Louis's fear of internal opposition interfered with his taste for glory. After the revocation of the edict of Nantes the Protestant Huygens was no longer welcome in France and the fountain was never built.[61] It should be noted, however, that the gunpowder consumption in Louis's many wars was without any doubt much higher than the amount that would have been used in even the most elaborate fountains of Versailles.

While Prussia had nothing to offer that could rival the gallery of mirrors in Versailles, it still had Sanssouci, the new opera house of Berlin, its newly revived silk industry and a military with an enormous consumption of textiles and many other products of Prussian industry. Some of the largest manufactures in the Berlin area worked exclusively to produce supplies for Frederick's army. In particular the rise of textile and metal manufactures was closely related to the continued demand of Prussia's extraordinarily large army.[62] On a smaller scale, but much in the same fashion as in France, Voltaire saw Frederick's autocratic government associated not only with the production but also with the consumption of the products of industry.

The question of whether the form of government and the development of industry were related was not only an issue of dissent between Voltaire and La Beaumelle. In Voltaire's comments on Montesquieu's works the question is equally present. Like La Beaumelle, Montesquieu did not think of the government of Louis XIV as a source of industry. If anything determined the occurrence of industry it was not the government but rather nature and geography. Montesquieu discerned a balance between the nations of the north and those of the south. The balance was established as follows: nature had given to the nations of the south 'all sorts of commodities' and 'few needs', while she gave to the nations of the north 'many needs' and 'few commodities'. The balance between the north and the south is then established by the 'laziness' that nature has given to the nations of the south and the 'industry and activity' that the people of the north were given.[63]

The form of government does not factor as a determinant in this theory. Industry – here clearly in the sense of industriousness – and laziness are instead given out by nature once and for all. In fact, the form of government is equally given out by nature so that it fits best with the mentality of the people. The inhabitants of the north who were endowed with more industry need also more freedom to exercise their industriousness. As the opposite applies to the south, the people of these regions tend to be in a state of oppression if they are not simply slaves.[64]

Clearly, this line of reasoning does not leave much leverage for the government to influence the development of industry. If one can discern any causal relationship between industry and the form of government at all in this thought, it is the inverse of what Voltaire postulated: a population is given certain needs by nature. Together with a certain resource endowment, again given by nature, this determines the level of industry. If this level of industry is high, the population requires freedom to pursue its industry, otherwise it will be submitted to a regime of slavery. From this perspective the form of government does not only not influence the development of industry but it is reduced to a function of what might be called a 'natural' level of industry.

Note that Montesquieu's conception of 'nature' was different from Boisguilbert's. In Boisguilbert's view 'nature' actively intervened in order to fulfill the specific function of establishing a balance between the individual interests. Montesquieu's 'nature' is not less powerful but he elaborates far less on the details of the mechanism through which she intervenes. However, his notion of nature is much closer to that of a principle or set of natural laws which provide a framework for human agency than to Boisguilbert's 'activist' nature. Moreover, Boisguilbert's 'nature' is associated with providence while Montesquieu's is lacking that religious connotation. However different the concepts of 'nature' of the two writers were, they had in common the fact that Voltaire had not agreed with them.

Voltaire did not only ridicule the fact that Montesquieu tried to prove his theories by experimenting with a frozen sheep's tongue but he also presented an already familiar historical counterexample in the *Commentary on the Spirit of the laws*. After a colourful description of the barbaric state in which France had remained for many centuries, he concluded that the French had become 'industrious and docile, educated and kindly' under Louis XIV. In an ironic remark, he added that the climate of France had not changed between the reign of Clovis and Louis XIV.[65]

Voltaire's Prussian observations about the contrast between the backwardness of Westphalia and the progress of Berlin mesh with this view. After all, the new opera house, the château of Sanssouci and the new Prussia Asiatic trade company were closely linked to the government of Frederick and not to a change of climate. There was no doubt for Voltaire that its form of government strongly influenced the level of industriousness of a people and many of its other characteristics: 'Climate makes men blond or brown; it is the way they are governed that makes their virtues and their vices.' Industry figures prominently among the virtues inspired by the right government. In his *Observations about Mssrs Jean Lass, Melon and Dutot* he stated 'the peoples are what their kings or ministers make them' and continued to list a number of talents that stayed buried unless they were animated by a king or a minister. These talents were 'courage', 'strength', and 'industry'.[66]

Aside from the substantial disagreements between La Beaumelle, Montesquieu and Voltaire, significant differences in the use of the term 'industry' can be noted. Most significantly, La Beaumelle does not use the term in his attacks against Voltaire's views on industry. The term features in the passages that La Beaumelle tries to refute but he does not use it himself. This is all the more significant since La Beaumelle wrote his footnotes only shortly after Voltaire had finished the *Age of Louis XIV*. Similarly, Montesquieu's arguments about industry in the *Spirit of the laws* were written not long before the publication of the *Age of Louis XIV*. In his writings the term is present but his use of the term differs from Voltaire's. Montesquieu's arguments about the relation of climate, geography and industry focus on industry as an individual quality. Without using the term itself the thrust of La Beaumelle's objections to Voltaire is the same. La Beaumelle's and Montesquieu's concern was with the determinants of industriousness and inventiveness. The development of branches of industry or industry as a sector of activities does not feature prominently among their arguments. This perspective differs significantly from Voltaire's writings of the same period. He, too, was concerned with the determinants of individual industry. However, the individual quality of inventiveness was seen by Voltaire in the larger context of the development of new branches of industry. For him, the individual industry that led to the invention of larger and better mirrors was only the first step of a development that eventually led to the creation of a mirror industry. In Voltaire's arguments this complex relationship between the industrious inventor of mirrors and the industrial production of mirrors is captured in the two semantic dimensions that the term industry takes on in his writing.

Against Boisguilbert, Voltaire had argued his view of the policies that were needed to successfully develop France's industry. In the confrontation with the arguments of La Beaumelle and Montesquieu, Voltaire defended not only the view that the form of government mattered for the development of industry. He also defended the only form of government that he believed to be capable to promote the progress of industry. Given the far-reaching tasks that Voltaire assigned to the administrator in the progress of industry, only a government with an uncontested 'sovereign authority' could fulfil this role. While Voltaire did not elaborate on the question of whether only a monarchy could be a sufficiently strong authority, it is clear from the context that a strong monarchy was the form of government that he was contemplating.

The opposition to a strong role for royal authority in the matters of industry was in this debate closely associated to dissenting religious tendencies. Boisguilbert did not only evoke a religious concept in his views on political economy. He and La Beaumelle also belonged to religious groups that were oppressed in France. Jansenists and Protestants had both been persecuted under Louis XIV. This certainly contributed to a general distrust of royal authority. Voltaire's relation with authority, in turn, was not a simple one. However, despite his own fights with worldly and ecclesiastical authorities he still believed in the benign effect of this authority on industry. This paradox is well illustrated by Voltaire's experience in Prussia. When he arrived in Prussia in 1750 he was – and remained for the rest of his life – enthusiastic about the benign effects of Frederick's authority on the progress of industry, arts and sciences. However, it was a conflict with the king's authority that eventually led to his departure from Prussia in 1753. The details of the rupture between the king and his chamberlain cannot be discussed here. However, a brief sketch of the situation will be useful: Voltaire supported the physicist König in a quarrel with the president of the Prussian academy, Maupertuis. Frederick was unhappy with the attack on the president of his academy and tried to silence Voltaire. The conflict escalated and a pamphlet of Voltaire was publicly burned on the Gendarmenmarkt in Berlin – an extremely rare procedure in Prussia. Voltaire then decided to leave Prussia. Initially, he was at a loss where to turn. He was still not welcome in France. After some hesitation, he decided to go to Geneva where he subsequently settled for several years. On his way there, however, he made one last acquaintance with Prussian authority. On Frederick's orders, Voltaire was arrested for several days in Frankfurt on Main by the Prussian resident in the city. During the arrest, Frederick's representative, Franz von Freytag, was assisted by a certain Johann Friderich Schmid. Ironically, the latter was a representative of a Prussian institution which Voltaire greatly admired. Documents from the Prussian archives indicate that Schmid was, since 1751, one of the directors of the Prussian Asiatic trade company. The episode illustrates the contradicting tendencies in Voltaire's thought. On the one hand the development of industry and with it the progress of civilisation were closely associated with the concept of an activist authority. On the other hand, Voltaire's life was characterised by the defence of the freedom of speech and other individual freedoms against oppressive authorities. Pomeau has pointed out this conflict between authoritarian activism and liberal humanism in Voltaire's thought.[67] The heterogeneity of Voltaire's thought illustrates that he was not an uncritical admirer of royal authority. He personally experienced the oppressive character of the French monarchy in many instances: he was imprisoned in the Bastille, spent most of his life in various exiles inside and outside France, and had a large number of his writings banned in France by the royal censor. Despite his own negative experiences with authority, his observations convinced him that 'sovereign authority' also brought about positive results, namely the progress of industry.

4
How Much Industry Does a Nation Need?

After Voltaire left Berlin in 1753, the controversy about Colbert and the continued growth of industry reached a new stage. A highly critical account of the age of Louis XIV by the Abbé de Saint-Pierre (1658–1743) was published in 1756. In the same period, the Physiocratic school with its strong views about industry and marked dislike of Colbert rose to dominate the debates on political economy. However, in the period was also published an eloquent defence of Colbert. In Jacques Necker (1732–1804) – the author of the 1773 *Eulogy of Jean-Baptiste Colbert* – Voltaire finally found an ally in the defence of the minister. At the centre of the debates was the question of how much industry a nation needed in order to be prosperous and virtuous. The relative sizes that the sectors of industry and agriculture should have were controversially discussed and moral arguments were fielded alongside with political economy arguments. It was in this period that Diderot accused his opponents of wanting to 'build industry on the ruins of agriculture'.[1]

In this stage of the debate about Colbert, new criticism was put forward. Boisguilbert and La Beaumelle had mainly attacked what they saw as wrong policies to develop industry. The minister's critics of the late 1750s and 1760s concentrated more on the question of whether the development of industry itself was desirable. Economic and moral arguments were put forward for a limitation of the size of the sector of industry. Saint-Pierre emphasised the negative moral effect of some branches of industry. He also described them as a waste rather than a source of wealth. The Physiocrats, in turn, concentrated on the alleged sterile character of industry. To the fresh criticism of this period Voltaire responded with a new round of writings in defence of Colbert.

The debates of the 1760s also emphasise further that the debate about Colbert was far more than a controversy about the past. In this period, one of the minister's most prominent projects, the Compagnie des Indes, found itself in great difficulties. Its crisis was among the principal topics of the political controversies of the day and gave rise to new criticism against the minister. Almost exactly one hundred years after the beginning of Colbert's ministry one of his creations was thus still among the principal topics of public debate. Voltaire had already shown a keen interest in the Prussian trading company and he was actively involved in the debate about the future of the French company.

The period also saw a further step in the development of the use of the term 'industry'. Boisguilbert and La Beaumelle had used the term rarely. Similarly, it is largely absent from Saint-Pierre's writings. A significant increase in the use of the term among the opponents of Voltaire occurred only in the late 1750s in the writings of the Physiocrats. Their use of the term sometimes differed from Voltaire's and they profoundly disagreed with him on the economic benefits of industry but they surprisingly agreed with him in one important respect: like Voltaire they increasingly saw industry as an economic sector and they associated the concept of industry with the name of Colbert. However, what was a praise for the minister in Voltaire's writings amounted to a devastating critique in their treatises. In contrast to this perspective, the term 'industry' can be found as a concept associated with the success of Colbert's ministry in Necker's *Eulogy of Colbert* of 1773. There, the creation of industry featured as prominently as an achievement of the minister as in Voltaire's writings.

In this period falls also the publication of the *Encyclopaedia*. Some of the period's most prominent authors – including Voltaire – contributed to this work edited by Diderot and d'Alembert. The first volume was published in 1751. In 1759 the official permit for the publication was withdrawn because of the allegedly anti-religious tendency of the work. The work was then continued clandestinely. The last volume was completed in 1772. Articles about the trades and techniques of manufacturing were an important part of the work. D'Alembert explicitly emphasised the importance of the 'mechanical arts' in the *Preliminary discourse of the Encyclopaedia*. However, he did not use the term 'industry' for the sum of activities in manufacturing. The sectoral connotation of 'industry' did not play an important role in the *Encyclopaedia*. The article 'industry' discussed industry primarily as a 'faculty of the soul'. However, this individual quality is seen as one that extends mainly to the 'mechanical productions & operations'.[2] This perspective illustrates the semantic transition of the period. The term was no longer understood solely as an individual quality but at the same time there was not yet a clear concept of it as an economic sector. However, at this time – the *Encyclopaedia* was completed in 1765 – the perception of industry as an economic sector distinct from commerce and agriculture had already emerged more clearly in the writings of Voltaire, Turgot, many of the Physiocrats and many other contemporaries.

Saint-Pierre's critique of the reign of Louis XIV

After Voltaire had left Berlin, a small odyssey brought him to Leipzig, Gotha, Kassel, Frankfurt, Mainz, Schwetzingen, Strasbourg, Colmar, Plombières and Lyons, before he arrived in Geneva in December 1754. Although it was not initially his intention, he soon decided to stay and bought the house Les Délices. Most likely it was in this house that Voltaire read Saint-Pierre's *Political annals (1658–1740).* The Abbé had died in 1743 and his last work was published posthumously. Like Boisguilbert, Saint-Pierre had seen the controversial age of Louis XIV with his own eyes. But while Boisguilbert observed it in provincial Rouen, Saint-Pierre was much closer to the centre of the power and splendour of this era. The position of chaplain of the Duchess of Orléans that the Abbé had bought in 1702 gave him a singular opportunity to observe the reign of Louis XIV from an insider's perspective. As the function of chaplain did not absorb his attention – both the duchess and he were largely non-religious – Saint-Pierre used his time to write about the shortcomings of the reign that he could observe so closely. The result of his observations was a flood of pamphlets treating subjects as diverse as the quality of roads, taxation, the threat of pirates in the Mediterranean and the creation of perpetual peace. The choice of his subjects may seem rather random but they are more coherent than they initially appear to be. What unites his numerous writings is that they all sprang from problems that Saint-Pierre observed in the reign of Louis XIV. Unfortunately for the Abbé, his reformatory zeal did not coincide with a great literary talent. It was rumoured that Saint-Pierre never found a publisher and had to print all his works at his own expense. This possibility is confirmed by Voltaire's assessment that the Abbé 'wrote in a way that made nobody jealous'.[3]

Despite this verdict, Voltaire praised the Abbé for the substance of some of his projects. Above all, the project for a taxation proportional to income and wealth, the Abbé's *taille tarifée*, had Voltaire's full support. Because of Saint-Pierre's call for the abolition of the tyranny of arbitrary taxation, Voltaire classed him, together with Locke, as one of the great champions of mankind. This support of Voltaire's is noteworthy because the project of the *taille tarifée* was tied to a radical critique of the taxation system under Louis XIV. This critique of the existing fiscal regime had almost cost the Abbé his seat at the Académie Française in 1717. On this occasion, he was able to save his position, but his next pamphlet brought him into trouble again. The publication that finally led to Saint-Pierre's removal from the academy was the *Discourse on Polysynodie*, which criticised the structure of government under Louis XIV. On that occasion, no less than three members of the academy were dispatched to the regent in order to apologise for their unruly colleague. Voltaire sharply criticised the expulsion of Saint-Pierre. As has been pointed out earlier, Voltaire believed that Saint-Pierre's criticism was far better founded than that of the *Persian letters*.[4]

'Half fool and half philosopher': ambiguous perceptions of Saint-Pierre

While Voltaire approved many of the Abbé's projects he never took him entirely seriously. The ambiguous perspective on Saint-Pierre is best summed up by Voltaire himself. Once, in a letter to his friend d'Argental, he called the Abbé as 'half fool and half philosopher'. Saint-Pierre was frequently the target of Voltairean mockery: in one of Voltaire's epigrams, for example, a sculptor creates a bust of the Abbé. The work of the artist is so true to reality that Voltaire cannot tell whether he has in front of him the Abbé or a sculpture. After some hesitation, Voltaire is sure that it is a bust. The reason that Voltaire was able to tell the difference, he added, was that the real Abbé would have uttered something foolish while the bust remained silent.[5]

Voltaire was not alone in mocking the Abbé. Bruyère nicknamed him 'Mopse' in his *Characters*. Even outside France, Saint-Pierre had a reputation as a curious figure. Herder talked about the 'stunning naivety' of the Abbé and Wieland mentioned him in a hardly flattering way in his 1766 novel *Story of Agathon*. In order to illustrate just how nonsensical the undertakings of the novel's hero were, he compared them to the projects of the Abbé de Saint-Pierre.[6]

One of the reasons for the contemporary perceptions of the Abbé might lie in the somewhat curious nature of some of his projects. There is, for instance, the Abbé's 'postal chair', a monument to the Ancien Régimes's 'fascination with the medical and physiological process of digestion', which may justify a brief digression. A certain Dr Chirac had discovered a salutary effect of the movements of stage coaches on the human body. Saint-Pierre realised the importance of these medical findings and swiftly designed a machine that – albeit stationary – produced the same effect. In other words: the Abbé's 'postal chair' or 'Trémoussoir' (literally 'shaker') was a machine that shook the user as if he or she was travelling in a stage coach. In the December 1734 edition of the *Mercure of France*, Saint-Pierre explained the benefits of his invention. According to him, the 'Trémoussoir' was an ideal remedy against many illnesses associated with 'melacholy', 'vapours' and 'glands of the lower stomach'. However, the 'Trémoussoir' benefited not only those who suffered from 'obstructions of the small canals of the glands', but was also useful to maintain good health. Short exercises on the machine twice or thrice a week would be enough. The Abbé described the target group of his invention as those who ate too much and had too little exercise. He named 'studious people', 'religious communities' and 'ministers'. Unfortunately, the opinion of the notorious hypochondriac Voltaire about this machine has not survived. It is therefore not known whether this invention further discredited Saint-Pierre's reputation in Voltaire's eyes. It is almost tragic that the 'Trémoussoir' may be the Abbé's project which is most widely remembered. While most of his other projects are long forgotten the 'Trémoussoir' even achieved literary fame. In 1881 when Flaubert thought of yet another ridiculous enterprise on which his fictional heroes Bouvard and Pécuchet could embark he let them build a make-shift version of the Abbé's 'Trémoussoir'.[7]

There are a number of other sources that make it possible to understand why Voltaire and others did not take Saint-Pierre seriously. In the first edition of the *Age of Louis XIV*, Saint-Pierre was described with only two sentences couched in Voltaire's typical mix of appreciation and mockery. After praising the project for fiscal reform, Voltaire continued to say, 'his political ideas were not always fantasies'. Unsatisfied with this brief description, Voltaire started to gather additional information. In September 1752, for example, he wrote to Argental in Paris to find out the year of Saint-Pierre's death. Voltaire himself was in Potsdam at the time, where he was revising the first edition of the *Age of Louis XIV*. He could also have asked his host Frederick about his impression of the projects of the Abbé. After the coronation of Frederick, Saint-Pierre had travelled to Potsdam to convince the young king of his views. The Prussian files preserve the abstracts of four projects that the Abbé submitted to Frederick. Most prominent among them was the 'European Arbitrage', the project of a league of European nations for the preservation of peace. Apparently the projects of the Abbé did not convince Frederick. To the contrary: the monarch even commissioned the composition of a book called *Anti St. Pierre*.[8] Frederick's policies made it equally clear that he did not believe in the Abbé's peace project. Shortly after his coronation, he invaded Silesia and remained one of the most belligerent monarchs of his day. Saint-Pierre's travel to Prussia may not have been successful but he fits into a series of more or less prominent foreign visitors in Prussia. The visits of Voltaire, Helvetius, Mirabeau served as part of a tight knit European communication on political and economic questions. As an emerging political, economic and military power Prussia was, in many respects, at the centre of interest of the thinkers who wanted to see their ideas and projects applied. Prussia was rapidly changing at a time when many other European countries, in particular France, were stuck in political inertia.

The result of Voltaire's research for the *Age of Louis XIV* was a considerably extended description of Saint-Pierre, in which Voltaire revealed the reasons for his ambiguous feelings towards the Abbé. As Voltaire saw it, the main problem with Saint-Pierre was that 'he almost always proposed impossible things'. While he emphasised that Saint-Pierre always had the public good in mind, Saint-Pierre's projects were not more than 'fantasies of a good citizen'. It emerges that Voltaire was not opposed to the reformatory substance of Saint-Pierre's views. The real barrier between the two men was Voltaire's pragmatism which prevented him from taking most of Saint-Pierre's laudable projects seriously. The Abbé had many 'philosophical views' but they were simply not 'practicable'. It is important to note that, at this stage, Voltaire did not reject the goals of the Abbé's projects and he certainly did not question the need for reform that they addressed. If Voltaire was more amused than impressed with Saint-Pierre, it was because of what Voltaire considered to be the naive and utopian character of Saint-Pierre's projects. 'He has rendered himself ridiculous in France', Voltaire concluded, 'through the excess of his good intentions'.[9]

Voltaire's response to the *Political Annals*

Saint-Pierre's critique of the reign of Louis XIV in the *Annals* made a strong impression on Voltaire. After having read the work in August 1756 Voltaire responded without losing any time. In the same month he added several footnotes to a new edition of the *Age of Louis XIV* in response to Saint-Pierre. That the *Annals* made such an impression on Voltaire is all the more significant since he was well acquainted with the Abbé and his works. However, none of the Abbé's views had provoked such a strong reaction from Voltaire before. Voltaire's attitude towards the Abbé's ideas changed radically in 1756. If he had previously called the Abbé 'half fool and half philosopher', he now started to call him a 'complete fool'.[10]

What in the *Political Annals* of the Abbé could have provoked an immediate and angry response from Voltaire rather than yet another satirical epigram? It was a passage about Colbert's policies in the *Annals* that triggered Voltaire's polemical reaction. In the passage in question, Saint-Pierre argued that Colbert's trading companies were an imitation of the English and Dutch example while the fine arts were encouraged by the minister to measure up to the Italian model. He praised the establishment of the trading companies but criticised Colbert for the promotion of the arts. For him, painting, sculpture, music, poetry, comedy and architecture were merely outward signs of a nation's prosperity. They did not contribute to the nation's happiness or wealth. Saint-Pierre argued that flourishing arts only meant that one 'kind of layabout' was maintained and fed by another. He suggested that the arts led to moral corruption. Saint-Pierre cited the example of the Italian people, 'these miserable successors of the highly estimable Romans'. Because the fine arts had flourished there, the country had declined and had become a nation of 'beggars' and 'layabouts', who were 'lazy', 'vain' and 'cowardly' and who were mainly occupied with 'silliness'. By concentrating on sciences and fine arts, Saint-Pierre concluded, Colbert had neglected the trading companies and thus mistaken 'the shadow for the body'.[11]

Two arguments of Saint-Pierre can be distinguished. They are interrelated, but in order to facilitate the discussion they will be treated separately. The first, could be called the 'political economy argument'. It maintains that fine arts and sciences do not contribute to the nation's wealth and prosperity. The second argument, which may be called the 'moral corruption argument', attempts to demonstrate the harmful effects of arts and sciences on the morality of a nation. For Voltaire, both arguments were equally flawed and he took on both in a whole set of notes which he added to the *Age of Louis XIV*.

Saint-Pierre's political economy argument

Voltaire did not agree with Saint-Pierre's notion that there existed a trade-off between trading companies and fine arts in the sense that one was a producer of wealth while the other was a consumer of resources. Voltaire started his counter-argument by rejecting the allegation that Colbert neglected the French trading companies. He inserted a footnote in the chapter of the *Age of Louis XIV* where he described how the minister freed France from being 'tributary to Dutch industry' by encouraging the trading companies. In the note he quoted Saint-Pierre's critique and called the whole of Europe as his witness that the minister did not in the least neglect the overseas trade.[12] Saint-Pierre's allegation seems, indeed, curious in the light of the subsequent debates. When the fate of the Compagnie des Indes was controversially discussed in the 1760s, Colbert was mainly attacked for devoting too many resources to the trading companies.

Voltaire went on to dispute Saint-Pierre's perspective on the fine arts. According to the Abbé fine arts were the 'shadow' because they were merely signs of prosperity, while trading companies were the 'body' because they contributed to the nation's prosperity. In this view, fine arts only consumed resources but did not create wealth. Voltaire did not agree with this distinction. He had agreed that trading companies were highly profitable, but he also saw fine arts as the product of often prosperous trades. In particular, he saw fine arts as closely associated with many branches of industry that brought prosperity to a nation. In a further footnote that Voltaire wrote in response to Saint-Pierre, he pointed to the historical example of Venice: despite the flourishing of the arts, Venice was 'the most opulent of all republics'.[13] More specifically he elaborated on the relation between arts, prosperity and industry in his description of the reign of Louis XIV. The king's 'lavishness' and liberal expenditure did not impoverish the nation. On the contrary, the king's expenditure on 'buildings, fine arts, and pleasure' enriched the country, for all 'expenses that encourage industry enrich a state'. It is one of Voltaire's key arguments that the growth of industry depends on the stimulus of liberal spending for 'lavishness'. Stimulating expenses could take various forms and went far beyond the immediate consumption of the king. In the context of the establishment of new textile, mirror, iron and leather manufactures by Colbert, Voltaire describes how Louis XIV bought each year 800,000 *livres* worth of their products in order to give them out as gifts. In this way, the king not only guaranteed a certain demand but also helped to popularise the products of the new manufactures.[14]

Among the useful 'lavishness' of Louis XIV that is praised by Voltaire one also finds an already familiar form of entertainment: the *carrouzel*. Voltaire reports an anecdote about Colbert's great skill as a financial administrator. In the story, the minister is said to have created revenue for the king even out of the expenses for a *carrouzel*. Despite his great admiration for Colbert, Voltaire has to concede that this story is an exaggeration. However, he adds, the story expresses 'a palpable truth', namely that the liberal spending of Louis XIV on arts and entertainment had enriched the country.[15]

Voltaire saw the expenditure for arts, buildings and products of industry as a model for his own times. In a letter to the comptroller general Machault d'Arnouville, Voltaire suggested an increase in government expenditure to improve the capital, finish the Louvre, build roads, subsidise manufactures and encourage the fine arts. He even encouraged the minister to raise taxes to pay for the new expenses. An increase in taxes, he argued, would eventually enrich the nation as long as the money was spent 'in order to encourage industry on all sides'. As much as Voltaire saw a positive effect of liberal spending on the establishment of new branches of industry, he condemned any restriction on luxury spending. Sumptuary laws, for example, meant for him nothing less than 'the suffocation of industry'. He argued that such restrictions with their negative effect on industry were in the end equally vexing for the rich and the poor.[16]

Voltaire has repeatedly described the different ways in which spending stimulated industry and created prosperity. Most prominently he called for an improvement of the urban infrastructure of Paris in several pamphlets. In particular, the one-page-tract *What is not done and what could be done* of 1742 was an emphatic call for action. The great number of 'lazy' people should be employed to repair streets and squares, to drain swamps, to built fountains, theatres, palaces and statues. This would not only allow them to earn a living, but it would also make the country 'flourishing'. He argued that the money used for these projects was not lost. The workers would spend their wages immediately, thus creating new prosperity throughout the country. In this way, the fine arts contributed at the same time to the glory and wealth of the nation. Moreover, this course of action would also turn the mass of unemployed workers into a prosperous and industrious population.[17] Expenditure for the fine arts thus had a double function: it allowed the fine arts to flourish and created an opportunity for the individual to sell his industriousness. It is important to note that for this effect to occur the motive for the expenditure was irrelevant. If the monarch spent for himself he showed his 'greatness', if he spent for the public he showed his 'generosity'. In both cases he encouraged the arts and created prosperity because he let money circulate.[18]

While Voltaire defended all types of expenditure that Colbert undertook as a stimulus for industry, Saint-Pierre distinguished between useful and harmful expenditure. In the expenses of Louis XIV he saw a 'bad use of the surplus' and thus a violation of one of the two principles of government that he postulated. In his view, the first goal was the 'increase of work' because work was the source of 'abundance' and 'surplus'. The second goal was the good use of the 'surplus' thus produced. While luxury expenditure was a bad use of the 'surplus' for the Abbé, it was for Voltaire the only way to attain Saint-Pierre's first goal of government, the 'increase of work'.[19]

In this context, it should be mentioned that Saint-Pierre recognised the importance of the arts for the flourishing of a nation in his own way. However, Saint-Pierre had 'useful arts' in mind, close to what today may be called 'technical know-how'. The examples he cited were mills, ships and the printing press. Voltaire was certainly not opposed to these 'useful arts'. In the debate with La Beaumelle he had strongly emphasised the importance of inventions such as the printing press or the compass. However, he saw them as insufficient to bring about opulence. He insisted that it was 'impossible to have a surplus at home only through the abundance of the arts of primary necessity'.[20]

It is quite clear from the above discussion that for Voltaire the expenditure of Louis XIV on 'buildings, fine arts, and pleasures' were an indispensable stimulus for French industry and thus a source of prosperity for the whole nation. However, for Voltaire, fine arts were not only a stimulus for industry. Instead, arts and industry were mutually dependent. It was 'human industry' that pushed the development of arts and sciences to ever new heights.[21] To the Abbé de Saint-Pierre this did not make matters any better. For him, fine arts were not only a waste of resources but they also had another negative effect. They degraded the nation's morals.

Saint-Pierre's moral argument

According to the Abbé de Saint-Pierre, the perfection of art, sculpture, music, poetry, comedy and architecture had reduced the proud Roman nation to a bunch of corrupted 'layabouts' with nothing but folly on their minds. Saint-Pierre's perspective is to a certain extent similar to that of Montesquieu. The latter had published his *Considerations on the causes of the greatness of the Romans and of their decadence* in 1734. Mainly as a reaction to providential explanations for the decline of the Roman empire both authors, Saint-Pierre and Montesquieu, put forward a cultural explanation for the historical development. In the centre of the considerations was the effect of increasing prosperity on the morals of the individual. Voltaire did not share this fear of moral degradation through industry. In the 1756 edition of the *Age of Louis XIV*, he contested the historical evidence of the Abbé and pointed out that Italy had produced great warriors – who he took to be examples of virtue – and great artists at the same time.[22]

However, Voltaire did not only dispute the alleged decadence of Italy. For him, the arts had generally a benign effect on humanity. Voltaire's perspective has been summed up aptly by one of his most avid readers. In the papers of Frederick II a draft for an introduction of Voltaire's epic poem to Henri IV can be found. On Voltaire's thought on the process of cultivation, Frederick noted: 'The sciences make the greatest contribution towards men becoming polished; they render them more docile, more just'. Rather than corrupting the people, arts and sciences made 'citizens' more 'reasonable'. Frederick explained how the process of cultivation took place: inspired by a small number of thinkers at the court 'this way of thinking' spread first to the cities and from there into the provinces. The progress of arts and sciences thus brought about – now in Voltaire's own words – a 'general revolution' of the 'mind', 'customs' and 'government'. The fundamental difference between the perspectives on art and industry in the *Age of Louis XIV* and the *Annals* was also pointed out by Voltaire himself. The Abbé, Voltaire remarked, only ever spoke of fine arts 'in order to vilify them'.[23]

In Voltaire's thought, the development of arts and sciences was carried forward by industry. However, industry did not only help the development of culture. The process of cultivation also helped the further development of industry. The progress of industry was associated to the application of the achievements of science and culture to the activities related to the production of goods. Industry and enlightenment progressed jointly. In the article 'Academies' in the *Philosophical dictionary*, Voltaire offers a glimpse of the effect of the academies on culture in provincial France. His perspective is, indeed, similar to that of Leibniz. Voltaire emphasised that the provincial academies forced people to work, introduced young people to reading, made people more polite and reduced prejudices and ignorance.[24] This description of the achievements of the provincial academies gives an insight into the nature of the project of cultivation that was on Voltaire's mind. That eradication of ignorance and prejudice feature among the goals of the academies is certainly not surprising. More noteworthy is the prominent place that Voltaire attributes to the concept of 'work' in the process of cultivation. Clearly, industriousness is not only a motor of culture but also one of the core values of Voltaire's idea of culture.

The prominent place of industry in the canon of values that cultivation was to spread among the population can also be seen in Voltaire's ironic *Of the horrible danger of reading* of 1765. High up on this list of the 'dangers' that reading may excite was the industry of 'farmers' and 'manufacturers'. Here, Voltaire defined the essence of the culture that he wanted to be spread by the power of the printed word. He cited 'industry', 'elevation of the soul' and 'love for the public good' as the ingredients of his cultural project. Pomeau's dictum that Voltaire's was a 'culture of work' thus proves to be true in more than one sense.[25] Not only did Voltaire envisage a culture that was carried to ever new highs by 'industry' but this culture also features 'industry' among its most cherished values.

In the 1773 *Eulogy of Colbert*, Necker reasoned in a similar fashion about the interrelation between fine arts and industry. Yet again, it was the omniscient Colbert who pulled the strings in this elaborate process. According to Necker, the minister realised that the masterpieces of Racine and Molière were connected by 'invisible strings' to the progress of the nation's industry. Their daily performance gave instruction to the people from which 'French industry' profited without realising it. Only because of the influence of fine arts on the 'nation's spirit' were the French triumphing in all 'works of industry'.[26]

This process of cultivation in which Colbert formed not only manufactures but also the ethics of the manufacturer was compared by Voltaire to the developments in the world of music: when Colbert came into office, he was in the same situation as the composer Lully. When the latter arrived from Italy in France, he could initially not find musicians who were able to play his music. However, this changed subsequently. With the general progress of culture, Colbert and Lully were also able to find skilled personnel to execute their respective projects. Voltaire even boasted that in the France of his day there were a great number of musicians who could play 'the most learned music'.[27] The process of the cultivation of the arts and sciences was thus seen not only as a process which was carried forward by industry. It was at the same time a process that imprinted industry as a way of life on the individual and even on the 'nation's spirit'.

Gareth Stedman Jones has pointed out a similar perspective in Jean Baptiste Say's writings. Say regarded 'industry' as 'the sole legitimate activity in modern society' and, indeed, the 'industrious' as the sole legitimate members of that society.[28] In quite a similar way, Voltaire was concerned with the progress of a 'society of industry'. While a reader of Saint-Pierre had to be concerned about the moral consequences of any industry that he was involved with, the reader of Voltaire did not have to worry. The moral doubts of Saint-Pierre about the desirability of some forms of industry were for Voltaire quite out of place. The philosopher king made it clear that industry was, indeed, the sole legitimate way of living. After all, the progress of industry and the progress of culture were inseparably intertwined. Voltaire's perspective thus contains a paradox.

On the one hand he insisted that the pursuit of industry derived its legitimacy from the fact that it served the progress of culture. Industry was a phenomenon that had to be judged also as an ethical issue. But on the other hand, Voltaire's view that all forms of industry served progress *de facto* freed industry from the limitations of ethical considerations. No matter how decadent a specific form of industry may have seemed, by adopting Voltaire's perspective one could rest assured that it ultimately served the progress of humanity. He thus contributed considerably to creating an attitude in which the development of industry was not hampered by moral objections.[29]

The controversy between Voltaire and Saint-Pierre is exemplary but not unique. It illustrates the struggle of the contemporaries to arrive at a moral judgement of the new and expanding sector of industry. Voltaire and Saint-Pierre are exponents of different tendencies of thought about industry that sought to influence the judgement of their contemporaries. That Voltaire was on the winning end of this struggle is well illustrated by the changing definitions of industry in the dictionaries of the time. As has been pointed out, industry was still described as an immoral activity in the dictionaries of the first decades of the eighteenth century. In the light of controversies like the one between Voltaire and Saint-Pierre this judgement began to change.

A revolt against Fenélon's frugality

Saint-Pierre's mistrust of industry and the complete rejection of industry by the Physiocrats, which will be discussed soon, fit into a long-standing intellectual tradition in France. One of the earliest and maybe the most radical advocate of an agrarianisation of France was another eye witness of the reign of Louis XIV: Archbishop Fenélon (1651–1715). For his quietist tendencies Fenélon had been banned from Paris to provincial Cambrai. Nevertheless he was made the tutor of the grandson of Louis XIV who was expected to become king: the young Duke of Burgundy. While an infection ended the Duke's life prematurely in 1712 Fenélon had enough time to compose a lengthy educational novel for the prince. The *Adventures of Télémaque*, son of Odysseus, are interspersed with a great number of episodes which were intended to teach the prince and turn him into a good king of France. How much the prince enjoyed the reading is not known: Fenélon has been called the 'Swan of Cambrai' but Madame de Deffand – one of Voltaire's sharp tongued correspondents – declared the *Adventures of Télémaque* to be 'deadly boredom'.[30]

Irrespective of its literary qualities the novel was arguably the greatest plea ever written for an agrarianisation of France. It was one of the most widely read texts of the eighteenth century. In many respects it was more radical than the writings of Saint-Pierre and more appealing to a broader public than the sectarian pamphlets of the Physiocrats. Many educational episodes that are woven into the story: the longest and most important experience of the prince is a visit to the fictional kingdom of Salente. Administered by a king who loves luxury and warfare, Salente is a not too subtle reference to France under Louis XIV. Télémaque arrives there accompanied by Minerva who, for the purpose of guiding the prince, had adopted the shape of an elderly man called Mentor. Not surprisingly, Mentor's views bear striking resemblance to those of Fenélon himself. When Mentor becomes the trusted advisor of Salente's king he carries out a complete agrarianisation of the realm: the splendid public works in the capital of Salente are given up. The artisan who used to produce works of luxury in marble, silver and gold are now employed in the fields outside the city. The trades that produce refined goods are banned from Salente. Instead of being corrupted by luxury the inhabitants are guided back to working the soil, this 'good mother' of humanity. They are not made unhappy and weak anymore by their desire for the superfluous but live in happy frugality. The idea of the poor being fed by the expenses on luxury by the rich – one of Voltaire's topoi – is nothing but a sham for Fenélon. Rich and poor alike, Mentor convinces the people of Salente that they can gain their living on the fields and avoid the contagious vice of luxury. According to Fenélon and in stark contrast to the views of Frederick II the strength of a nation lies in the great number of men and the abundance of fertile soil and not in industry. The work of artisans, tradesmen and manufacturers does not enrich a country and is the source of many moral perils. It is only the 'necessary arts' that will not harm the morals and the well-being of a nation. This distinction of luxuries and necessary arts is echoed in Saint-Pierre's writings and lives on in the thought of the Physiocrats which, as we will see, allowed for a limited sector of manufacturing.[31]

The principal difference between Fenélon and the later advocates of agriculture is the language that he uses to conceptualise the nature of the 'contagion' that is threatening the nation with corruption and impoverishment. Fenélon does not have a single term or concept for the 'contagion' but he gave a colourful description of the way it appeared in Salente: already from far away the visitor to the capital noticed 'glowing furnaces', 'eddies of smoke' and fires similar to the subterranean fires of the volcano Etna. The sound of the hammer beating on the anvil resounded from the surrounding mountains. To today's reader and to the readers of the second half of the eighteenth century this sounded a lot like a description of industry. Fenélon, however, does not use the term. He sometimes refers to the 'harmful arts' and the 'superfluous artisans' employed in these activities. However, the term 'industry' does not appear in Fenélon's book as a description of the damnable sector of activities. He only uses 'industry' in the older meaning of 'industriousness': when Télémaque falls in love with the princess of Salente he marvels at her 'industry' in the handicrafts. The novel also speaks about the industry of the scheming Pinochles whose intrigues bring about the downfall of his competitor Protésilas at the court of the king of Salente. However, this 'industry' is much closer to Voltaire's qualitative use of the term in the play *The Eavesdropper* of 1725 than it is to the sectoral meaning that became dominant in the second half of the eighteenth century.[32]

One reason for which Fenélon did not have a term for the sum of the pernicious activities in manufacturing was that he, like Saint-Pierre, did not see them as a single sector. For Fenélon and Saint-Pierre there was a fundamental difference between harmful arts which produced superfluous products and useful arts which were at the origin of necessary products. This distinction is at the heart of Saint-Pierre's argument and Fenélon, too, makes it clear that in his agrarian utopia there would only be space for the arts that provide the most basic products: workers would not be employed in the harmful arts anymore but only in the necessary arts – which are small in number, as he points out – and in commerce and agriculture. Here Fenélon uses the sectoral terms 'agriculture' and 'commerce' but splits the activities that would later be called 'industry' into two sectors using a distinction based on the assumed moral effects of the products of different arts.[33]

The making of a simple clay pot and the weaving of a luxurious silk scarf could only be seen as a part of the same sector of industry once moral distinction between the different acts of production and different products had been superseded by an analytical approach which emphasised the common economic function of the different branches of manufacturing. Voltaire's sectoral use of the term 'industry' was not conceivable without his universal moral approval of all forms of manufacturing or without his conviction that all manufacturing contributed to the creation of wealth. However, as the arguments of the Physiocratic thinkers will show that it was not necessary to see industry as a source of wealth in order to conceptualise all branches of manufacturing as a single economic sector. The strictly sterile character which the Physiocrats attributed to all forms of manufacturing and the resulting condemnation of all forms of industry had a similar effect. This uniformly negative view of industry contributed as much to the rise of the sectoral concept of industry from the 1750s as did Voltaire with his universal praise of industry.

Physiocratic industry and Voltairean industry

The question of whether industry promoted wealth and virtuousness or whether it did quite the opposite was at the centre of controversy throughout the 1750s and 1760s. Physiocracy was the latest economic theory that was debated in France and across Europe from the late 1750s onwards. It was based, in part, on the notion that industry did not create any wealth. Not surprisingly, the Physiocrats also chose Colbert as their bête noire. Thus, when Voltaire returned to France in 1760, he returned to a country where the criticism against Colbert reached new heights. As Voltaire was still not allowed to return to Paris, he settled in Ferney, situated close to Geneva but on French territory. From there, he closely followed the debates that were going on in Paris and intervened whenever he felt that the policies of Colbert needed to be defended.

In the present context, it is impossible to treat Physiocracy or even Voltaire's attitude to it in an exhaustive manner. The secondary literature on François Quesnay's sect is impressive; many articles, books and dissertations have been written on Voltaire's quarrels with the Physiocrats. While these publications contain a great number of relevant observations, some aspects of debate, namely the disagreements on the issue of industry, have been neglected. There is a tendency in the literature to minimise the disagreement and emphasise the issues on which Voltaire agreed with the Physiocrats, such as the need for tax reform or a liberalisation of the internal grain trade. The disagreement is often portrayed as being largely based on a misunderstanding. Voltaire's not entirely disinterested pupil and editor Condorcet seems to be at the origin of this view. In editorial remarks to the 1784 Kehl edition, Condorcet wrote that the controversy between Voltaire and the Physiocrats could have been avoided if the former had studied Physiocratic theory more closely and if the latter had explained it better.[34] Through the study of the role of industry in this debate, it is possible to arrive at another perspective. After all it seems rather unlikely that in the course of a debate that lasted well over a decade Voltaire or the supporters of the Physiocratic school would not have noticed that it was all merely a misunderstanding.

Voltaire contributed to this debate in various forms: in 1768 he made extensive additions to the *Age of Louis XIV* and published the famous antiphysiocratic satire *The man of forty crowns*. In 1769 he composed his most comprehensive answer to the Physiocrats, the *Defence of Louis XIV against the author of the Éphémérides*. In addition, the topic plays a central role in his correspondence with Pierre Samuel Du Pont de Nemours, Abbé Baudeau and others. It should be pointed out that the official reception of the Physiocratic writings in this debate was much more positive than the reaction to Voltaire's contributions. The Physiocratic mouthpiece, *Éphémérides du citoyen* was, for instance, not only approved by the royal censor, but it was also praised for the 'solidity of its knowledge', 'truth of its inductions' and 'usefulness of its views'.[35] If the publication seemed 'most worthy of being printed' to the censor, Voltaire's antiphysiocratic *Man of forty crowns* was banned – as had been the *Age of Louis XIV* – and burned in public immediately after its publication in 1768. A 'grocery boy' who was caught selling the work along with other banned literature was pilloried for three days, branded and sent to serve time on a galley.[36]

As far as the terminology of the debate is concerned, it is noteworthy that the Physiocrats were the first opponents of Colbert to use the term 'industry' extensively. They used the term as prominently as Voltaire. However, as will emerge in the discussion, their understanding of industry was fundamentally different from Voltaire's in many respects.

Industry: source or consumer of riches

The fundamental question that divided Voltaire and the Physiocrats was what role industry played for economic progress and for the progress of civilisation. An authoritative statement of the Physiocratic view was given by Abbé Baudeau in the *Éphémérides*. In the *Explanation of the economic table for Madame de****** Baudeau explained to his anonymous pupil that it was fundamental to distinguish, 'the natural produce itself from the sorting, mixing, fashioning & decorations that it receives from art or industry.' As the Abbé seemed to fear that this level of abstraction might surpass the reader he added an example that he apparently deemed more within the reach of Madame de***: 'you perceive, Madame, when opening a hot pie that you must not confuse the pastry chef with the farmer'. It is well known, that this characterisation of industry as an activity that merely sorts, polishes, arranges and mixes the products of nature was of no little consequence in the Physiocratic paradigm. Du Pont de Nemours was categorical in his judgement. 'Industry', he wrote, was only an 'object of expenditure' but not a source of revenue.[37]

In this understanding, industry was classified among the sterile activities, that is, economic activities that were not 'really, efficiently, directly & immediately productive' and that were therefore not a source of wealth for the nation. In the light of the rise of this new condemnation of industry, Voltaire once again rallied to the defence of industry. In a letter to Du Pont of 1770, he affirmed his view that industry was one of the principal sources of wealth. From Ferney, he wrote to the economist who had proclaimed the sterility of industry: 'True riches reside here with us, they are in our industry.'[38]

It may be added that Voltaire not only believed in the productivity of industry, but that he also translated this belief into practical policies. At the time the project of taxing agriculture – the sole source of wealth – with a 'single tax' was widely discussed in France. However, Voltaire asked the ministry of finance for permission to share the tax burden of the region of Ferney between the local watchmakers and farmers. As Voltaire was well aware that his request did not fit with the prevalent views on political economy of the time, he prefaced it with a reference to Physiocracy. He wrote that it was quite appropriate that the rich agriculture in the regions of Paris, Milan and Naples ought to pay the bulk of taxes. But in the lands surrounding Ferney the situation was different. Voltaire's pleas were successful and taxation of the watch industry of Ferney – which had been created by Voltaire – was introduced. However much better founded Voltaire's views on taxation may have been than those of the Physiocrats, it must be said that his tax policy seems to have contributed considerably to the end of watch production in Ferney.[39]

The disagreement between Voltaire and the 'economists' – as the Physiocrats were called by many contemporaries – about whether or not industry was a source of revenue had further implications. As a result of this disagreement it was contentious what size the sector of industry should have in a nation. In a certain analogy to the position of Saint-Pierre, the Physiocrats condemned excessive expenses for the products of industry. However, while the principal reason for Saint-Pierre's rejection of industry had been moral doubts, the Physiocrats were more concerned with its negative economic effect. At the same time, they acknowledged that a certain amount of industry had to be tolerated in order to transform the raw products of nature. To fix the level of acceptable expenditure for industry was, in fact, an important concern for the Physiocrats. In an article in the *Éphémérides du citoyen* an anonymous author vigorously attacked Voltaire's belief in the positive effect of all expenditure on industry. In particular, the maxim from the poem *The Worldling* 'superfluity, a very necessary thing' was a thorn in the anonymous economist's side. As far as the author of the *Éphémérides* was concerned, Voltaire may have been an entertaining poet, but his maxim was hardly a sound principle. Indeed, he ironically praised Voltaire for his courage to utter a similar view.[40]

The Physiocratic definition of what was necessary in terms of expenditure for the products of industry, was not only less poetic, but, above all, more static. To define the acceptable level of expenditure was not an easy task in the Physiocratic paradigm since the solution had to integrate two contradictory principles. On the one hand, there was the imperative need to limit expenditure for industry because an increase in 'sterile expenses' necessarily diminished 'productive expenses' for the development of agriculture. On the other hand, however, there was a postulate that was so important to the Physiocrats that Du Pont de Nemours chose capital letters for it:

> THE SECURITY OF PROPERTY IS THE ESSENTIAL FOUNDATION OF THE ECONOMIC ORDER OF SOCIETY.[41]

The proposed solution to this dilemma is as bold as it is simple: the right level of sterile expenditure for industry was that of 1770. For to deprive men of the 'enjoyment' to which they were used was a crime or even 'the essence of injustice'. But the future was 'a different thing' altogether. To deny a future increase in 'enjoyment' was legitimate. There was not the same positive right to a future increase as there was to the present level of 'enjoyment'. Granting such an increase was not protected by justice. It was merely a matter of 'benevolence' (and could therefore be refused).[42]

However, it needs to be remembered that while this sophism theoretically contained the prospect of keeping the expenditure for industry eternally at the level of 1770, this would be an extreme case. As an increase of sterile expenditure was always possible as a 'benevolence', the thrust of the argument was that the expenditure for industry should grow in such a way that it did not interfere with the expenditure for agriculture. In other words, it was to be subordinate to the agricultural sector. This perspective differed fundamentally from that of Voltaire. In a way the priorities were inverted. For Voltaire industry was the locomotive of progress, for the Physiocrats it was a comfortable salon wagon that had to be prevented from slowing down the whole train.

It may be added that both sides in this debate carried their conviction to the most minute details of everyday life. In their preoccupation with the limitation of superfluous expenditure, the Physiocrats went so far as to promote a recipe for an 'economical rice dish' in the pages of the *Éphémérides*. The ingredients – rice, potatoes, bread, carrots, pumpkin, turnips, butter and salt – were to be mixed with water and cooked for over twelve hours. With this recipe the Physiocrat gave a practical meaning to an approach that can already be found in Fenélon's work. When the fictional kingdom of Salente is transformed into a Fenélonean agricultural state, the wise government of this utopia begins to regulate and control even the diet of the citizens in order to make sure that they renounce all luxuries. Considering that in the period when Quesnay and his followers promoted the 'economical rice dish' as the culinary manifestation of their economic theory Voltaire offered his guests 'a turkey with truffles from Ferney' which was 'tender as a young pigeon and as fat as the bishop of Geneva', one might be surprised that Physiocracy had any followers at all.[43]

Pro and contra *laissez-faire* in industry

If Voltaire and the Physiocrats disagreed over the size of the sector of industry vis-à-vis that of agriculture, they still agreed that a certain level of industry was important for the well being of society. Even the Physiocrats believed that some industry was required to sort, polish and transform the gifts of nature for human use and consumption. However, the agreement *that* at least some industry ought to be developed did not extend to the question of *how* it should be developed. This part of the controversy between Voltaire and the Physiocrats is to a certain extent reminiscent of his disagreement with Boisguilbert. Indeed, the Physiocrats claimed Boisguilbert and other writers of the late seventeenth century and early eighteenth century as their intellectual precursors.[44]

The Physiocratic idea of the best way to a flourishing industry was summed up by Quesnay himself: while the encouragement of agriculture was a suitable task for the government, the maxim for the sterile expenses was *laisser-aller*. Indeed, the Physiocratic literature is filled with appeals for *laisser-aller*. They were frequently illustrated with allegories from nature. The anonymous opponent of Voltaire in the *Éphémérides*, for instance, was convinced that the intervention of government was as useless, as 'ordering a river to flow'. Offences against the principle of rule of nature and *laisser-aller* were described with the same allegories. For example, Colbert's activism in the matters of industry was compared to the artificial water supplies of Versailles. Instead of leaving the river Seine to its natural flow, an enormous pump had been constructed in Marly in order to provide water for the fountains of the gardens of

Versailles. In a similar way, another interference with the work of nature was evoked by the author. He cited the forced shaving of beards under Peter the Great as another grave violation of the working of nature.[45]

Significantly, both examples for violations of the rule of nature were associated with heroes of Voltaire's historiography. In the *Age of Louis XIV* and the *History of the Russian empire under Peter the Great* Voltaire praised both monarchs for modernising their nations and guiding them to new heights of civilisation. In both accounts, their commitment to the development of industry is seen as crucial. Peter the Great was credited with the same benign use of his uncontested sovereignty as Louis XIV. Just as the French before Louis XIV were 'without industry, rotting in their misery', the Russians before Peter the Great were 'rotting in the absence of all arts', a state which 'suffocated all industry' in Russia. While the author of the *Éphémérides* deeply resented the Russian monarch's interference with the growth of beards, Voltaire praised the same monarch for single-handedly changing 'the face of his country'.[46]

The different judgements about Peter the Great illustrate how the two poles of *laisser-faire/laisser-aller* and sovereign authority that are familiar from the debate between Boisguilbert and Voltaire also informed the exchanges with the Physiocrats. The parallels were also acknowledged by the Physiocrats themselves. In particular, the Marquis de Mirabeau – father of Count de Mirabeau who travelled to Prussia – greatly admired Boisguilbert. The 'good man Guillebert', as he called him, was revered as an ancestor and as an early foe of Colbert. In particular, Mirabeau held it to Boisguilbert's credit that he had identified the rise of Colbert as the beginning of the ruin of France. Only through the lecture of 'our predecessor', affirms Mirabeau, had he overcome misleading interpretations that showed the reign of Louis XIV as 'the beautiful age of France'. He blamed nameless 'historians' for depicting this era as a great age. While it cannot be known what historian he had in mind, Voltaire was certainly the most prominent defender of the 'beautiful age' in Mirabeau's day.[47]

'A minister of the last century': industry, war and peace

The controversy about industry clearly reflected on the judgement of Voltaire and the Physiocrats about Colbert. Smith was mainly referring to the Physiocrats when he wrote in the *Wealth of Nations* about the widespread criticism against Colbert in France. And Voltaire complained in response to yet another critical article in the Physiocratic *Éphémérides* in 1769: 'For several years some people have not stopped criticising the administration of the famous Colbert.' The catalogue of Voltaire's library in Ferney lists one of the books to which he was probably referring: Du Pont's *Physiocracy*. In the editorial comments, Du Pont did not forget to mention which historical figure sinned most against the rules of Physiocracy. This was 'a minister of the last century who, dazzled by the commerce of the Dutch & the splendour of manufacturing of luxuries, threw his fatherland into a ... delirium'. This minister, he added, absurdly tried to create wealth from the 'the work of the skilled fingers'.[48]

Under the impression of the allegations that Colbert neglected agriculture, Voltaire added several examples of Colbert's achievements in agriculture to the 1768 Geneva edition of the *Age of Louis XIV*. To underline that these successes were the fruit of a conscious effort, he cited Colbert's memoranda to Louis XIV in which the minister named agriculture among the top priorities of his government.[49] However, Voltaire's main argument in favour of the minister remained the peak of civilisation that France had reached through the minister's system of encouragement of industry, arts, science and luxury. This was the main achievement with which Voltaire credited Colbert and it was also the very criterion that defined a great age for him.

While these achievements were the essence of a great age for Voltaire, they were merely vain splendour in the eyes of yet another anonymous author of the *Éphémérides* who wrote mockingly in 1769 that the glory of the 'great age, so cherished by our wits' had passed like the 'oakum that is burned in front of the pope at his coronation'.[50] It can only be speculated if this attack was directly aimed at Voltaire. His *Age of Louis XIV* was at that time certainly the most prominent defence of the great age. So much so, in fact, that the use of the term 'great age' must have been enough to make the contemporary reader think of Voltaire's work. Another indication that Voltaire was the target of this passage is that he himself understood it in this way. The 1769 article in the *Éphémérides* triggered a response from Voltaire in the form of the *Defence of Louis XIV against the author of the Éphémérides*. In his very personal response to the anonymous author, Voltaire wrote that he would consider himself 'false and low-minded' and 'without culture' and 'taste' if he did not admire the achievements of this great time. He thus affirmed his conviction that the ultimate end of all human efforts, of all 'human industry', was the perfection and refinement of arts, science, manners and government – in short, the progress of culture and civilisation.[51]

It was this notion of progress, of the continuous refinement of all aspects of life through human industriousness that set Voltaire apart from the Physiocratic project with its quest to uncover an already existing natural order. The notion that human effort and creativity – bundled into 'human industry' – could be the source of the progress of humanity was far removed from a doctrine that its founder Quesnay summed up in the motto: 'From nature, justice, order & laws. From man arbitrariness, rule & coercion.' Normative considerations about the goal of human progress were not at issue for the Physiocratic movement, since the natural laws clearly determined 'what use we must of necessity make of our faculties ... in order to be as happy as possible'.[52]

For Voltaire, in turn, man endowed with reason had the capacity to overcome the savage state of nature and bring about progress in arts, sciences and all other aspects of life. The development of arts and industry did not only form an inseparable combination because industry carried the progress of art and because art stimulated industry, but also because the perfection of art gave industry its purpose and orientation. It is through the industrious perfection of art that civilisation was progressing indefinitely (rather than trying to reach a naturally determined final point of perfection). This function of art was absent in the Physiocratic conception. A good illustration of the different perspectives might be seen in the different judgements about one particular writer of the age of Louis XIV: Molière. Voltaire considered him to be the best comic poet of all nations and Necker attributed a positive effect on French industry to the daily representations of his plays. Du Pont's perspective on the artist's work was quite different. 'Molière & and his highly witty comedies', Du Pont wrote, 'must be counted among the plagues that impoverished the nation'. The difference between Voltaire's and the Physiocratic conception of art is also apparent in Voltaire's reaction to one of the rare pieces of literary criticism by Du Pont de Nemours. In a review of Saint-Lambert's poem *The seasons*, Du Pont praised the poet for his romanticising hymn to the 'farmer' and his rustic life. Nevertheless, he criticised a verse of the poem that was not in line with the teachings of the Physiocratic party. In the incriminated verse Saint-Lambert referred to the peasant's abode as 'huts of the poor'. This was of course unacceptable for Du Pont. The farmer, the sole creator of wealth in the nation, could not possibly be described as living in misery. Despite the overall praise, this strophe of the poem was immediately branded by Du Pont as 'vulgar poetry'.[53]

When Voltaire read this, he apparently remembered seeing peasants living under less than luxurious roofs and pointed this out in a letter to Du Pont. The defence of Saint-Lambert offers a glimpse at an aspect of Voltaire's commitment to the progressive function of art, which was a function that it could only fulfil if it was not reduced to eulogising an ideal order. For Du Pont, however, it was crucial that art, poetry in this case, serve the cause of Physiocracy. Voltaire's support for the author of *The seasons* is all the more noteworthy since in the late 1740s the 'divine Émilie' had betrayed Voltaire's love (and of course that of her husband, the Marquis du Châtelet-Lomont) with the young Saint-Lambert.[54]

The Physiocrats did not only challenge Voltaire's notion of the association of progress and industry. For them industry and Colbert's policies were not associated to peacefully progress but to the almost uninterrupted chain of wars that had characterised the reign of Louis XIV. 'These wars', noted the Marquis de Mirabeau, 'that appeared so fatal to the economic plans of Colbert, were nevertheless his work and the consequence of his greed.' The thesis that Colbert's policies led to the wars of Louis XIV has remained topical in modern historiography and can be found in quasi identical form in Charles Coles's work on Colbert. In the conclusion he echoes Mirabeau – at least with regard to one of the wars of Louis XIV: 'Disastrous to his plans as it was, the Dutch war was of necessity approved by Colbert and sprang directly from the very core of his type of mercantilism'. Also Voltaire condemned the wars of Louis XIV. In particular he criticised the king for the sacking of the Palatinate in the Palatinate Succession War (1688–97) and for the Dutch war. However, while the critics of Colbert were eager to associate the wars with the policies of the minister of finance, Voltaire saw the responsibility for the wars with the powerful minister of war and enemy of Colbert, Louvois. In this view he is supported by Saint-Pierre. Also the Abbé who did generally not hesitate to criticise Colbert blamed the power hungry Louvois for the aggressive foreign policy of Louis XIV. Voltaire did not see a relation between Colbert's policies for the promotion of trade and industry and international conflict. Voltaire saw industry as a form of peaceful and productive existence that encouraged co-operation and exchange among those engaged in industry. Consequently any policy that supported the progress of industry also served these benign goals. The prosperous city of Geneva is cited by Voltaire as an example of the association of industry with peaceful prosperity: it was not only industry that made Geneva rich but its coupling with peace that created 'honest opulence' in this city. Similarly, the Quaker settlements of Pennsylvania are described as a realm of 'peace and industry'. Industry was thus frequently elevated beyond its function as a source of wealth. Voltaire speaks of 'honest industry' or 'praiseworthy industry', and even unites the pair 'industry' and 'peace' into one term: 'peaceful industry'. The notion of a peaceful, tolerant and prosperous coexistence is associated with industry. Much in the way that 'gentle commerce' has been emphasised as an eighteenth-century concept of the peaceful coexistence of nations, 'peaceful industry' is seen by Voltaire as the path that transcends internal discord. This observation is in line with the argument of Stedman Jones who sees a similar notion associated with industry in the early nineteenth-century writings of Say. As is well known, Voltaire saw the main source of discord in religious quarrels and a lack of tolerance. He specifically points to industry as a way of life that overcomes the eternal source of hatred and violence: 'gold, silver, industry, and talents do not belong to any religion'. This view is also well illustrated by a remark of Voltaire about France's history in the fifteenth century. He writes that the industry of the Norman merchant Jacques Cœur had been of more use to his country in peace time than had been Joan of Arc's bravery in wartime.[55]

The contrast between violence and intolerance and 'peaceful industry' is also apparent in the context of a campaign that Voltaire undertook in the 1760s. On 10 March 1762 the Huguenot Jean Calas was tortured, broken on the wheel, strangled and finally burned at the stake for having killed his son who had allegedly converted to Catholicism. While the exact circumstances of the son's death remain unclear to this day, Calas's condemnation rested on a rather sketchy case. After some hesitation Voltaire took up the fight to clear the name of Jean Calas whom he saw as yet another victim of intolerance and brutality. It is in one of the writings of this campaign that Voltaire contrasts the 'tyranny that the courts exercise on the souls' by the courts of Toulouse with the 'peaceful industry' of Jean Calas (who was a textile merchant). In 1764, after a long campaign, the sentence against Calas was revoked. In the following year the case was tried again and Calas's name was cleared.[56]

The debate about the Compagnie des Indes

The Physiocrats and Voltaire disagreed not only about Colbert's role in the past. They also disagreed about the future of one of Colbert's most prominent projects, the Compagnie des Indes. In innumerable pamphlets all aspects of what Voltaire called 'refined merchant industry' were heatedly discussed in the 1760s. At the origin of the debate were the financial difficulties that the crisis-ridden company had to face in this period. The Compagnie had, indeed, not been very fortunate in its undertakings. If Voltaire is to be believed, it was the only commercial company in the 'universe' that had traded for prolonged periods without producing even the slightest profit.[57] As with the Prussian trade company, Voltaire had a well-informed opinion about the French company. For some time he had considerable financial interests in the enterprise. The table of his revenues for the years from 1749 to 1754 mentions several 'incomes' from the Compagnie des Indes. The investment yielded a total profit of 52,532 *livres* during the period. Voltaire's not always reliable secretary Longchamp also reported that Voltaire had earned considerable sums in the trade between Cadiz and America in the 1740s. Luckily, the secretary writes, only one of the ships in which Voltaire had invested was captured by the English during the war of 1746. In the light of these investments and his observations in Prussia, Voltaire must be seen as a well-informed commentator on the East India trade.[58]

On 13 August 1769, the long agony of the Compagnie des Indes was over. A decree, issued in the royal retreat of Compiègne, took away its exclusive trade privilege. Before and after this decision the advantages and disadvantages of trading companies and especially the complex relationship between the 'refined merchant industry', the 'sovereign authority' and monopolies were the subject of pamphlets, treatises and controversial debates. The arguments in this controversy cited events from Pondicherry and Madras, and experiences from Paris, London, Amsterdam and Emden. The range of contributors included the political elite, frustrated stock holders, sectarian theorists as well as wealthy poets. Some of the period's most prominent thinkers in matters of political economy such as Morellet, Necker, or Du Pont de Nemours took part in this fight over the fate of the Compagnie. Among the heterogeneous participants in this debate was also Voltaire. He felt strongly about the fate of the Compagnie. In his *Secret memoirs for the history of the republic of letters in France* Bachaumont expressed his surprise about the 'triumphal eloquence' with which Voltaire supported 'a cause of this kind'.[59]

Voltaire's principal adversary in this debate was once again an anonymous author of the *Éphémérides*. In an article entitled 'Of commerce & of the Compagnie des Indes' the readers of the *Éphémérides* – among them Voltaire – were not only informed about the end of the Compagnie's monopoly, but the anonymous author also seized the opportunity to make a few remarks about the nature and the history of 'commerce with the Indies'. The result of the efforts of this anonymous economist is an article that stretches over three volumes and roughly 150 pages of the *Éphémérides* and examines the subject from a solid Physiocratic position. Voltaire – by his own account an avid reader of the *Éphémérides* – must have read this article in his château in Ferney. There, he stumbled over the harsh criticism that the article contained about Colbert, his company, and his policies in general. Saddened to see the age of Louis XIV disparaged 'in these *Éphémérides*', Voltaire decided to publicise a letter to the editor. He did so in the form of the *Defence of Louis XIV against the author of the Éphémérides* of which some parts have already been cited. But he did not only respond publicly. When he wrote the *Defence* for publication he also wrote a private letter to Du Pont de Nemours who he rightly believed to be the anonymous author. Du Pont was not only the author of this long article about the East India trade. He had also become the editor of the *Éphémérides* in 1768 after his predecessor Abbé Baudeau had been given an ecclesiastical position in Poland. Dupont's biographer Gustav Schelle has suggested that Du Pont's article against the Compagnie des Indes was inspired by the comptroller general Maynon d'Invau who did not want to give further financial support to the company.[60] Whether the attack was officially inspired or not Voltaire expressed his support for the Compagnie in both a public and a private letter. In order to make his reply intelligible it is necessary to first take a brief look at the Physiocratic critique of the Compagnie.

The critique in the article was based on the Physiocratic notions that have been discussed earlier. Commerce was seen as a sterile activity which did not generate practically any revenue for the country. This insight alone may have been enough to deter anybody from engaging in the Compagnie. It was, however, burdened with another weight. The way it undertook its commerce forced it to maintain establishments in Pondicherry and elsewhere, which in turn prompted her to maintain 'a civil & military power in order to administer & defend [these] establishments'. Burdened with the enormous 'expenses of war & sovereignty', the already sterile industry was of course doomed from the very beginning. The anonymous economist of the *Éphémérides* thus argued that the reason for the company's failure lay in the fact that it was at the same time 'commercial & sovereign'. The recipe that he proposed was straightforward and did not hold any surprises. All trade monopolies should be abolished and the commerce should be undertaken either by individual French merchants or by merchants of other nations. Any regulation was to be left to the eternal laws of nature.[61]

Voltaire was only partially of the same opinion. He had already defended Colbert against Saint-Pierre's allegation that the minister had neglected the Compagnie des Indes. Now, he justified the decision to establish the Compagnie in the first place. Voltaire did not believe in the sterility of the 'merchant industry'. For him, the choice of Colbert had been to either be 'tributary' to 'Dutch industry' or become one of its rivals by creating a French trading company.[62]

Voltaire was, however, just as clear about the failure of the company as he was on its necessity. Surprisingly, Voltaire's analysis of the reasons for this failure was, up to a certain point, rather close to that of the author of the *Éphémérides*. According to Voltaire, the first reason for the failure of the company was simply France's defeat in war. These defeats of the nation fell back on the company which was left without the strong military protection that made the English company so successful. However, the defeats only formed the general background of the failure of the company. The main reason lay in the structure of the company which Voltaire calls a 'corpse with two heads'. The conflict between these two heads of the company was seen by Voltaire at the root of its failure. The constant revolt of the 'council' of Pondicherry, which represented the commercial 'head' of the enterprise, against General Lally, the representative of 'sovereign power', had led to the French defeat in India and the subsequent disaster of the company.[63] Like the anonymous author of the *Éphémérides*, Voltaire blamed the double nature of the company for its failure. The difference was, however, that Voltaire saw the reason for the lack of success in the weakness of 'sovereign power', rather than in excessive 'expenses of sovereignty'. The story of the Compagnie was for Voltaire an example of 'merchant industry' that failed because 'sovereign authority' was too weak to guide, control and protect it. He saw this protection and guidance as crucial and was therefore sceptical about the future chances of individual French merchants to engage in the commerce with India after the abolition of the company's monopoly. To Du Pont he wrote: 'I doubt strongly that this commerce can ever flourish in the hands of individuals.' In order to underline this view, he described the success of the British, Dutch and Danish companies in his response to the *Éphémérides*. Their success demonstrated in Voltaire's eyes that it was not the concept of the commercial company that was flawed. In particular, the example of the Dutch company proved that the 'expenses of sovereignty' did not necessarily lead to failure. This company – 'a great sovereign power', as he emphasised – had already shared profits of 150 per cent among its shareholders despite huge expenses for its oversees establishments.[64]

Voltaire and the Hercule

Voltaire's prediction that individual French merchants would not be very successful in the East India trade was to be confirmed by his personal experience. While he was still intensely debating the pros and cons of trade companies in 1772 he invested in a venture of the newly founded merchant house Bérard Brothers. The three Bérard brothers had established themselves in 1765 in Honfleur in Brittany and were now preparing to step into the void that the end of the Compagnie had created in the East India trade. Voltaire – sitting in his retreat in Ferney but always on the look out for a lucrative business venture – joined investors from Geneva, Lyon, Hamburg and Paris in equipping the first ship belonging to an individual merchant that was to sail from Lorient to Bengal after the abolition of the Compagnie's monopoly. Voltaire invested the considerable sum of 40,000 *livres* in this premier. On top of that he paid 962 *livres* and 13 *sols* towards the ship's insurance policy that was taken out in London.[65]

The vessel that was equipped partly with Voltaire's money was the *Hercule*. Under the able guidance of Captain Clemansin du Maine and of the supercargo Thomas-Simon Bérard the ship left the harbour of Lorient on 7 March 1772. It may be mentioned *en passant* that the infrastructure used by the newly founded merchant house Bérard was a creation of Colbert. The port of Lorient had been founded in 1666 as the hub of the Compagnie des Indes Orientales.[66] In a lucky coincidence, Thomas-Simon Bérard did not only take it upon himself to personally supervise the 400 tons of cargo on his ship's voyage to Bengal but he also kept a diary of this voyage that has been preserved by his family. The historian is thus better informed about the events aboard the *Hercule*, than Voltaire who could only speculate about the fate of his ship. In September 1773, while anxiously awaiting the return of the vessel, he joked in a letter to Suzanne Necker that the crew of the *Hercule* might already have run off (or rather sailed off) with his money.[67] The concerns aboard the vessel were, however, quite different. The desire to maximise profit had led to a cargo that considerably exceeded the capacity of the vessel. Several large waves engulfed the bridge and the slowness of the *Hercule* ('only five knots') called for drastic measures. Thus, having reached the latitude of Sierra Leone, Bérard decided not only to get rid of the cow and several sheep but also of some of the ship's cabins. This decision of Bérard encountered strong opposition from Captain Clemansin who happened to occupy one of the cabins in question. In order to guarantee the success of his business venture Bérard found himself forced to offer his own cabin to the captain. While he noted in his diary that he was happy to make this sacrifice, he found other inconveniences much harder to bear. Not only did the ship's baker turn out to be 'an imbecile incapable of making bread' but Bérard also had to endure climatic conditions which made it impossible for him to wear stockings. The scenario was completed by the cook suffering an attack of gout resulting in a 'standstill of sauces' at the most unfortunate juncture. As Bérard pointed out, the cook's sickness struck when the ship's sow had produced 'an ample progeny'.[68]

Voltaire's fears that his money might be wasted by the Huguenot Bérard, however, were entirely unfounded. The only distraction on the long voyage seems to have been a dinner on the island of Anjouan. The *Hercule* had stopped there to stock up its provisions and Bérard was invited for dinner by the island's king together with the captain of a British vessel and some of his female passengers. Bérard was not impressed with the local cuisine ('badly seasoned') and regretted the absence of local women at the dinner ('grotesque'). However, even during this one and only extravaganza of the voyage, expenses were tightly controlled. Among the presents for his host, Bérard lists 'ten or so empty bottles' and a 'barrel of rancid flour'. After this intermezzo the *Hercule* continued her voyage and arrived in Pondicherry in September 1772, six months after the departure from Lorient.[69]

The trouble for Voltaire and his money was still to come. While the ship's supercargo and co-owner, Thomas-Simon Bérard, stayed in Pondicherry until 1774 in order to open up a branch of his business, the *Hercule* returned to France in September 1773. Voltaire, however, was not informed about this fact by his associates who were not keen on paying him his share of the profit. From Ferney he complained bitterly to his banker in Lyon: 'The booty has been divided. I will not suffer this injustice.'[70] His complaints finally resulted in the visit of one of the associates to Ferney where they came to some form of 'arrangement'.[71] The details remain obscure. It seems, however, that Voltaire received only a small sum and continued to hold a considerable stake in the enterprises of the Bérard brothers. This continued involvement was soon to prove fatal. On one of her subsequent voyages the *Hercule* sank with a cargo of Bengali saltpetre in the seas surrounding the Cape of Good Hope. Voltaire was greatly disappointed. Ironically he wrote to d'Alembert that he had hoped to win a prize from the Académie des Sciences with this saltpetre. While he communicated his disappointment to d'Alembert, he wrote to another correspondent that this misfortune would not result in a financial loss.[72] His outlook changed radically, however, when it turned out that Thomas-Simon Bérard, who had returned on another vessel to Lorient, had no intention of paying back his investors. Instead, Voltaire reports, he turned on his heel and went back to Bengal where he was out of the reach of his creditors. Even after this new voyage, Bérard was still unable or unwilling to pay back his creditors. In June 1777 Voltaire speaks of an initiative of the investors to recuperate at least some of their money. This initiative – the outcome is not known – concluded

Voltaire's engagement in the East India trade. In a letter to the Marquis de Florian – the husband of one of Voltaire's nieces – he estimated his loss on this investment at 90 per cent. This was a painful confirmation of his prediction regarding the prospects of individual merchants and the East India trade.[73]

For Bérard, however, these events were not the end of his involvement in the East India trade. Despite his limited success in the East India trade he was to become a founder and even general director of a new but ephemeral Compagnie des Indes in 1785. The new monopoly lasted until 1790 when the republic established freedom in the trade with India. Bérard himself was executed on the '14 floréal an II' (4 May 1794) for supporting the 'liberticide plots of the tyrant Capet'.[74]

Looking back on the events, it is remarkable that for Voltaire a business venture that spanned from Geneva to Brittany and Bengal seems to have been a natural form of investment. No less remarkable is the effortlessness with which opponents in the debate about the 'refined merchant industry' spoke about news, events and personalities from places as distant as Pondicherry and Paris. Their arguments were based on experiences and examples from Amsterdam, London, Madras and Lorient. The fall of Pondicherry led to further consequences in Paris. The unfortunate General Lally who surrendered to the British in India was tried and executed in Paris and the fall of the Compagnie des Indes was discussed in the light of the latest French defeats in India. The close-knit relations between distant regions of the world also aroused Voltaire's interest. 'It is quite remarkable', he wrote in a letter in 1773, 'that I am preoccupied with what happens in India here in Switzerland'.[75] Indeed, it is noteworthy that the issue of industry was discussed in a wide geographical context from early on. Considering that developments in Pondicherry or Madras played an important role in these debates, it appears that even the label 'European' is not sufficient to characterise the eighteenth-century perspective of the rise of industry. Economic change was already at this time discussed as a development that transcended political and geographical boundaries.

Jacques Necker's defence of Colbert

An active involvement in the East India trade and in the debate about the Compagnie des Indes was a quality that Voltaire shared with another admirer of Colbert: Jacques Necker. A successful banker from Geneva who later became the last finance minister of the Ancien Régime, Necker was also an important protagonist of the debates about the company. He was a stockholder of the Compagnie and held various offices in its hierarchy during the 1760s. However, it was mainly his eloquence and combativeness that made him the foremost defender of the Compagnie against the sharp attacks of Morellet and others. Against the arguments that were brought forward by Morellet or the anonymous author of the *Éphémérides*, Necker maintained that a trading company with a monopoly was necessary to compete successfully in the East India trade. The outcome has already been revealed: Necker's proposals for a restructuring of the Compagnie without giving up its monopoly fell through and the monopoly was abolished.

Even if Necker's defence of Colbert's trading company proved to be futile, he did not give up his admiration for Colbert himself. In 1773, a prize competition of the Académie Française gave him the opportunity for an elaborate defence of Colbert and his œuvre: for the 1773 'Prize for Eloquence' the academy had chosen the topic 'A Eulogy of Colbert'. The tradition to ask for a eulogy of a great man as the prize topic had been started by the academy in 1755. In the Paris of 1773 it was certainly not uncontroversial to propose as a topic the best eulogy of Colbert or any eulogy of Colbert, for that matter. In fact, later the academy felt the need to preface the publication of the prize-winning essay with a disclaimer. The academicians announced that they endorsed 'neither all the ideas, nor all the expressions' of the *Eulogy* and that they were fully aware that the minister's principles had become controversial. The disclaimer illustrates the effect of two decades of relentless Physiocratic attacks on Colbert's policies which – as has been seen – fit into a tradition of criticism that spans the entire eighteenth century. While the disclaimer illustrates that Voltaire's and Necker's views had become highly controversial, the choice of topic indicates at the same time that there was still significant support for Colbert's ideas in the establishment of the academy.[76]

At the end of the competition it was Necker's eulogy that was picked by the Académie as the most eloquent praise of Colbert. The essay had been submitted and published anonymously but Voltaire – himself an academician – had no doubt about its authorship. In the same letter of September 1773 in which he told Suzanne Necker about his adventures in the East India trade, he also sent his congratulations to the author of the *Eulogy*. He thanked Jacques Necker for 'preaching' the merits of Colbert to the 'economists'. He also suggested the possibility that the author of the *Eulogy* might follow in the footprints of the eulogised minister. In the same spirit, he had affirmed one day previously to La Harpe that he was delighted that somebody had finally blamed the 'economists' for their continued attacks against Colbert.[77] However, when the Marquise du Deffant pressed him for a more detailed comment on the work, Voltaire was evasive. In general terms he complained once again that the fashion of the day was to criticise Colbert and he expressed his delight that somebody had taken up the minister's defence. His comments on the work itself were, however, less enthusiastic: according to Voltaire, the *Eulogy* was written with 'arithmetic' and its author was an excellent banker. When the marquise insisted on a more substantial comment ('Answer the questions that I ask you!'), Voltaire reacted with slight annoyance. Nevertheless, he gave a small insight into the source of his discontent: 'there is in the [Eulogy of Jean-Baptiste Colbert] as much bad as there is good, there are as many improper words as right expressions, as many exaggerations as truths'. Faced with Voltaire's ambiguous comments it may be useful take a brief look at the work in question.[78] The most striking feature of Necker's eulogy is without any doubt that the flourishing of industry under Colbert features in it just as prominently as in Voltaire's writings. According to Necker, the great achievements of Colbert's administration were the 'new objects of industry' that were created everywhere. Colbert's laws and regulations were far from being a burden on the nation's industry. On the contrary: 'they were the institutions of a loving father who [knew] the industry of his children'. Like Voltaire, Necker saw Colbert in the role of a father who guided the 'industry of his children' to the full use of their talent and strength. If Voltaire spoke of a 'mind that guides the work', Necker saw in Colbert a 'mind that creates order'.[79]

The notion that order – in cosmology as much as in political economy – was not spontaneous but emanated from an intelligent creator was as much present in Necker's thought as it was in Voltaire's. In the chapter about Boisguilbert, Necker's comparison between the financial administrator of a state and the creator of the universe has already been mentioned. However, the administrator was not only the human being who most resembled the divine creator. His function also made the administrator the firmest believer in the existence of a supreme being. Because he saw how his own intelligence harmoniously linked all the elements of society, he understood that the harmony of the universe must have been established in the same way by a supreme intelligence. In a noteworthy turn, Necker thus inverted the allegory in the course of the *Eulogy*. On page eight the idea that a supreme intelligence created the order of the universe legitimises the role of the administrator, while on page 66 the earthly order created by the administrator confirms the existence of an intelligent creator of the universe. By stressing the particular relationship of the administrator to the creator, Necker constructed, in fact, a religious legitimisation for the administrator's authority.[80]

Considering the congruency of Necker's and Voltaire's fundamental arguments, the latter's restrained reaction to the former's treatise remains puzzling. Since Voltaire did not elaborate on the reasons one can only speculate about the origins of his discontent. The fact that Necker's piety was so clearly apparent in his eulogy of Colbert might have been too much for Voltaire. He agreed that there were certain parallels between the administrator and the divine creator. However, Necker's implicit religious legitimisation for the administrator's authority differed from Voltaire's worldly perspective on these matters. It might also be that he agreed with the substance of Necker's treatise but could not live with its stylistic faults. Necker would thus have shared the fate of another political economist, François Melon, about whom Voltaire had written: 'The importance of the matter must not cause the style to be forgotten.' Whatever Voltaire's doubts about Necker's *Eulogy* might have been in 1773 they took second rank in 1777. When the Genevese was called to Paris to serve as the minister of finance, Voltaire sent a poem to Suzanne Necker. In what seems to be the last time that Voltaire mentioned Colbert, he reminded the newly appointed minister of the role-model whom he had eulogised four years earlier.[81]

The positions that were expressed by Voltaire, Necker, Saint-Pierre and the Physiocrats in the mid-eighteenth-century debates about industry could hardly have been more controversial. Voltaire, Boisguilbert and La Beaumelle had mainly been at odds over the relation between the 'sovereign authority' and industry. The topic remained controversial between Voltaire and the Physiocrats. But another question emerged that was of even greater concern for Saint-Pierre and the Physiocrats. Both were in their own way concerned with the issue of how much industry a nation needed. Saint-Pierre wanted limitations that would exclude forms of industry which he saw as morally questionable. The Physiocratic position, with its condemnation of luxury, also contained some elements of such a moral approach. However, their main argument was that the growth of sterile industry should be limited in order to give preference to productive agriculture. In contrast to these positions, Voltaire advocated a limitless growth of industry. For him, the progress of industry would not only ensure the material progress of humanity, it would also serve the progress of culture. By declaring that all forms of industry contributed in one form or another to the progress of humanity, Voltaire freed the concept of industry from the limitations that moral or economic considerations might impose on it. He assured his readers that industry not only brought prosperity but that it was also a morally acceptable way of living which contributed to the progress of humanity.

However, despite the fundamental controversies a surprising point of agreement also emerges from these debates: the association of the term industry with the minister Colbert and his policies. Irrespective of whether industry was seen as something damnable or as a source of progress, the authors who used the term in these debates regarded it as a concept that was closely linked to the policies of Colbert. Voltaire and Necker admired Colbert for the creation of France's industry while the Physiocrats condemned him for neglecting agriculture over his encouragement of industry. The Physiocrats radically rejected Colbert's policies for the promotion of industry. Nevertheless they saw the origins of French industry as associated with these policies. In these early controversies about industry, debaters on all sides agreed that the growth of industry in France was closely related to the minister's policies.

The concern of the contemporaries with the relative sizes of industrial and agricultural sectors – whether discussed in economic terms or in moral terms – needs to be seen in the context of the disproportionate and rapid growth of industry in the period. Overall manufacturing grew faster than agriculture and in many regions dramatically so. This development announced the 'industrial revolution' in which industry eventually became the dominant economic sector in much of Europe. As de Vries points out, the fast growth of industry manifested itself in the eighteenth century mainly by a shift of labour from agriculture and the production of 'goods and services for direct consumption' to industry and the production of 'marketed goods'.[82] As the observations of Voltaire, Saint-Pierre and the Physiocrats show this structural change was widely discussed at the time. Many authors perceived it as a threat. Economic and moral arguments were fielded against the expansion of industry at the cost of agriculture. These eighteenth-century arguments drew on a long-standing tradition of opposition against manufacturing, luxury and the allegedly associated moral and economic decay. In France this tradition was most strongly associated with Fénelon and rose to new prominence in the debates of the eighteenth century. Against this 'agrarian' tradition contemporaries like Voltaire and Necker defended the growth of industry. They did not see a conflict of the growth of industry with the moral or economic well-being of a nation. However, Voltaire did see many instances in which the growth of industry conflicted with the economic, social and political institutions of the Ancien Régime. It was typical for Voltaire and for the debates of the period that he did not only observe these conflicts and discuss them in his writings but that he set out to change the institutions that hampered the progress of industry. The next chapter will explore the political campaign that Voltaire and others led in the 1760s and 1770s to promote industry and abolish some of the institutional obstacles against its growth.

5
A Political Campaign for Industry

While Voltaire was debating Jean Baptiste Colbert's policies for the promotion of industry, he was no less concerned about the ways in which the ministers of his time should contribute to the further development of industry. Debates about industry were in the eighteenth century – just as in later periods – often directly linked to projects of political and economic reform. Voltaire and many of his contemporaries were engaged in political campaigns to change specific institutions which they saw as obstacles to industry. One of the most prominent campaigns of this kind was Voltaire's campaign against serfdom in France and Russia during the late 1760s and 1770s. The campaign against serfdom was closely associated to the reform projects of Anne Robert Jacques Turgot's ministry from 1774 to 1776. Voltaire and Turgot both wanted to change the feudal rules which governed many aspects of economic and social interaction. The abolition of obsolete feudal rules was seen by Turgot and Voltaire as a precondition for the further development of industry. They argued that the institutional order and the legal condition of the individual had to be adapted to facilitate the further growth of industry. Voltaire saw in the rules of serfdom a particularly oppressive institution which posed a strong obstacle to the development of industry.

Voltaire's campaign concentrated on some of the last remaining serfs of France who lived in Saint-Claude in the French Jura. Saint-Claude was located a mere 60 kilometres from Voltaire's doorstep in Ferney. As if this was not enough to upset Voltaire, the serfs belonged to the canons of Saint-Claude. The fight against an obstacle to the growth of industry thus became inseparably associated with Voltaire's anticlerical views. Throughout the late 1760s and 1770s, Voltaire castigated the servitude of the inhabitants of Saint-Claude as an oppressive institution that made the progress of industry impossible.[1]

Voltaire's campaign against serfdom was a prominent topic of public debate in the period. The abolition of serfdom was controversial in particular during the ministry of Turgot. Voltaire's campaign was even mentioned in the *Encyclopaedia*. The article 'Saint-Claude' in the 1776 *Supplement to the Encyclopaedia* described Voltaire's ongoing fight for the serfs at length.[2] The contemporary prominence of Voltaire's campaign is also well illustrated by a prize competition that the Académie Française held in the year after Voltaire's death. The 1779 competition of the academy called for the best poem on the topic of the abolition of serfdom. It was won by a poem entitled *Voltaire and the serf of the Jura* by Jean-Pierre de Claris, marquis de Florian. The author – a writer of some note at the time – was the nephew of the Marquis de Florian who was the husband of one of Voltaire's nieces and who lived in Ferney for much of his life. The younger Marquis de Florian also grew up in Ferney where he was known as 'Florianet'. The topic of the prize competition was proposed by the academy because Jacques Necker had decided to free the serfs on the royal domains in 1779. However, while the Académie Française crowned a poem about Voltaire's campaign for the liberation of the serfs of Saint-Claude, the serfs themselves had to wait until the revolution to be freed. They did not live on a royal domain and their status was therefore not affected by Necker's edict.[3]

The importance that contemporaries attached to the issue of serfdom may seem surprising. Only about 140,000 peasants were subject to forms of serfdom in 1789. The institution persisted mainly in the regions of Marche, Auvergne, Bourbonnais, Nivernais, Bourgogne and Franche-Comté where Saint-Claude is located. Voltaire estimated the number of serfs in Saint-Claude at 12,000. If the estimates are correct, Voltaire was fighting for the freedom of just under one tenth of France's serfs.[4] Despite the relatively small number of individuals who were submitted to serfdom the issue was one of the most prominent topics of political controversy of the time. Partly, this was due to the symbolic function of serfdom. The institution stood for feudal institutions that were at the centre of widespread discontent. The feudalism as a coherent social system had long disappeared in the eighteenth century and only remnants – such as some forms of serfdom – continued to exist. However, the contemporary concept of feudalism was broader than today's. Many aspects of feudalism had disappeared but at the same time a great number of institutions that derived from feudal rules remained intact. 'As happened so often under the ancien régime', J. Mackrell comments on feudalism in the eighteenth century, 'a partial collapse of the system did not lead to its replacement.'[5] Many feudal privileges simply took on the form of contractual arrangements or continued to exist as customs and unwritten privileges and obligations. Also, the vexations that resulted from serfdom extended beyond those who were immediately submitted to it. Its rules affected also those who had any form of economic or other interaction with a serf or a feudal lord. The campaign against serfdom thus fits into the context of the enlightenment's mission to abolish rules and institutions that were vexatious and did not hold up to rational scrutiny. Just as religious, social and political life were scrutinised and often changed, the rule of the enlightenment was also applied to the sphere of the production and distribution of goods.

At the same time the campaign against serfdom fits into the context of the political conflict between centralised royal authority and the interests of the aristocracy. This confrontation was part of the process of state building which dominates the political history of the period. This political conflict was reflected in antagonistic intellectual tendencies. Voltaire was a staunch defender of the unmitigated royal authority against authors like Montesquieu and La Beaumelle who saw the independent power of the aristocracy as a counterbalance that prevented royal authority from degenerating into despotism. The difference is illustrated most prominently by the diverging views of the Frankish aristocracy. Its rule was celebrated by Montesquieu as an original and benign order while it was condemned as a 'gothic' obstacle to progress by Voltaire. The development of industry was a crucial part of this progress which was held up by archaic rules and feudal privileges.

The fate of the inhabitants of Saint-Claude and other French serfs was not only a prominent subject of public debate. It was also the last debate in which Voltaire was involved and in which his views about industry played an important role. However, Voltaire's most complex treatise on the relation between serfdom and industry was not written with regard to France's serfs but about the serfs of Russia. This text is fundamental for the understanding of Voltaire's involvement in the French debates. It will therefore be useful to consider Voltaire's arguments for the liberation of Russia's serfs before discussing his campaign for the abolition of serfdom in France.

The essay competition of the Société Œconomique in Petersburg

In 1766, the Société Œconomique of Saint Petersburg held one of the many essay competitions of the eighteenth century. The contestants were asked to answer the question of whether peasants should have the right to own land or only moveable property. The society was close to the new Empress who ruled Russia since 1762. The essay competition was thus associated to Catherine's reform efforts of the period. Voltaire's participation in the competition is to be seen in the context of the attempts of a number of French thinkers to influence Catherine's reforms. Voltaire – a largely uncritical admirer of the empress – was trying to convey his views in his numerous letters to Saint Petersburg. His interest in the affairs of Russia is also documented in a number of his writings such as the *History of Russia under Peter the Great* (1768) or his *A Russian in Paris* (1760). The former work was a substantial treatise about the progress of Russia under Peter the Great. Voltaire's perspective on Peter's reign is in many instances similar to his views about the reign of Louis XIV. The work was clearly intended to convince the readers – including contemporary and future monarchs of Russia – of the merits of Peter's policies. In the short pamphlet *A Russian in Paris* a fictional Russian visits Paris in order to learn from the French example. In particular, the Russian admired the achievements of the ubiquitous Colbert who encouraged 'industry' and 'arts'. The pamphlet was published for the first time in 1770. However, it circulated across Europe much earlier. In the Prussian archives a handwritten copy of the pamphlet can be found. In 1760 Jacob Friedrich von Bielfeld had sent it to Frederick II 'for his entertainment'. Besides being a correspondent of the king, Bielfeld was one of the most prominent Prussian writers on the matters of political economy. His most important writing was the 1760 work *Political institutions*. The circulation of Voltaire's political poem in Prussia in 1760 illustrates his continued links with Prussia and the importance of the Prussian context for the present debates even after Voltaire's departure from Berlin in 1753.[6] Voltaire was not the only French author who sought influence in Russian politics. The 'political tourism' to Petersburg was only rivalled by the attraction that Berlin exercised on visitors from all parts of Europe at the time. Lemercier de la Rivière – one of the most prominent Physiocrats – travelled to Saint Petersburg in 1767. He was followed in 1773 by Diderot. While Diderot wanted to promote his views on education, Lemercier travelled to Russia in order to convince Catherine of the Physiocratic teachings. Lemercier's travel was celebrated as an important success for the Physiocratic movement. Voltaire, however, did everything to discredit the Physiocrats and to promote his own views on political economy in Saint Petersburg. He wrote to Catherine and ridiculed La Rivière as 'this poor Solon, called La Rivière'. Moreover, Voltaire wrote a long letter to a favourite of Catherine, Count Shouvalov. In the letter he exposed once more the great merits of two monarchs who were among the most prominent targets of Physiocratic criticism: Louis XIV and Peter the Great. As an antidote to the Physiocratic teachings that Lemercier was promoting, Voltaire reminded the count in the closing paragraph of the letter that 'the west has only come to be something through the strength of industry'. The controversy between Voltaire and the Physiocrats about the benefits of industry that had already reached Prussia before was thus also carried to Russia.[7] Given the competition among French thinkers to influence Catherine's policies, it is not surprising that Voltaire seized the opportunity to participate in the essay competition of the Société Œconomique. The competition was announced in French newspapers, among them the *Éphémérides du Citoyen*. As may be remembered from the discussion of the controversy about the Compagnie des Indes, Voltaire was a regular reader of the *Éphémérides* and might have read the announcement in the columns of the Physiocratic publication which he received in Ferney. After hearing about the competition, Voltaire wrote – or rather dictated, since the manuscript is in the hand of his secretary Jean Louis Wagnière – the text that he sent to Saint Petersburg.[8]

Curiously, he did not compose one but two entries for the competition. He sent a French and a Latin text with largely identical contents. The editor of the manuscripts suggests that Voltaire may have written one of the essays for somebody else. It can no longer be verified under what name the two essays were submitted, for the reason that the manuscripts themselves were anonymous and only identified by numbers and a motto. The corresponding sealed envelopes with the names of the authors have not been preserved.[9]

It is possible that Voltaire submitted the second entry for his friend and collaborator Charles Frédéric Gabriel Christin (1741–99). The young lawyer worked together with Voltaire in the campaign against serfdom. They co-wrote several texts. Together they worked, for example, on Voltaire's 1766 comment on Cesare Beccaria's *Essay on crimes and punishments*. On the matter of serfdom they wrote the article 'Property' in the *Questions about the Encyclopaedia* of 1771 and the *Dissertation on the establishment of the Abbey of Saint-Claude* of 1772. Both texts contain passages from the essay that was submitted in the Petersburg competition. Therefore, it seems likely that the Petersburg essay, too, was the result of a co-operation between Voltaire and Christin. The double entry in the competition may have been Voltaire's way to take this co-operation into account. While it is plausible that Voltaire submitted the second entry for Christin it cannot be excluded that the philosopher decided to submit two entries in order to increase his chances of winning the competition.

If that was his intention, however, it was futile. Voltaire, who in 1767 was without any doubt the most prominent European author alive, only made it to sixth place in the competition of the Société Œconomique. His disappointment was so great that he never mentioned the competition again. Consequently, the essays that he submitted were never published in his lifetime. The two texts were discovered in 2001 by V.A. Somov in a Russian archive.[10]

It might perhaps have consoled Voltaire if he had known about the dubious proceedings of the competition. The deadline of the competition was repeatedly extended because the entries were not to the liking of the Société. The reason was that the majority of the entries radically called for a liberation of the Russian serfs. This, apparently, was not acceptable for Catherine and her Société. The essay that finally won the competition was by far the most cautious entry in the whole competition.[11] It may be added that serfdom was not abolished in Russia until 1861.

Voltaire's essay: serfdom as an institutional obstacle to industry

Although the jurors of the Société Œconomique did not find Voltaire's entries worthy of the first prize, they are still among the most important contributions to contemporary debates about industry. In the essays Voltaire explains how the fate of the Russian serfs, their right to own property and the progress of Russian industry were intimately related.

Two reasons, he wrote, speak for the property rights of the labourer in the land that he worked. First, men were born with the right to property in the land that they worked and above all with the right to property in their own labour. The great mass of Russian labourers was denied this right and lived in miserable conditions. Freeing the serfs would give them their innate right and liberate their 'brutalised soul'. But it would equally serve the 'general good'. For, under the status quo, the industry of the labourer was 'suffocated'. Serfdom, Voltaire argued, created men who were both mindless and lazy. The freed serf, by contrast, was the herald of a brighter future for the sovereign, the serf himself and the whole nation. The peasant would work his own land much harder and better than he had previously worked his master's. The freed serf would have more children since he would be more prosperous and his children would be born free. Aside from producing more soldiers for the sovereign and prosperity for the population, this situation would also lead to fundamental transformations in the long run.[12]

As free labourers produce more and procreate faster, all arable land would soon be cultivated producing more than enough to feed the nation. An overpopulation of peasants would be the result. The problem is solved as follows: 'The excess of agricultural workers spreads to the cities, to the sea ports, to the artisans' workshops, to the army.' The effect of the surplus of labour moving from the countryside into the workshops is benign. Commerce develops everywhere, the merchant marine and navy flourish and commercial companies spring up. In short, the result is the 'progress of industry and commerce' within the whole nation.[13]

Since the 'progress of industry' is made possible through the 'excess of agricultural workers' it is worth taking a closer look at the qualities that Voltaire associates with this group of individuals. Above all, Voltaire points out, the end of serfdom will mean that they will be free to sell their labour to whoever pays the highest price. However, according to Voltaire these people have a second important quality. They have the freedom to sell their labour and this is all that they have: 'This liberty replaces property for them.' The lack of property is by no means a coincidental quality. It is crucial for Voltaire. Society needs men who have only 'their muscle and their good will'. This argument is a recurrent theme in his writings. Fifteen years earlier Voltaire had made a similar observation in the *Age of Louis XIV*. The language is more explicit there: 'The farm labourer and the worker need to be kept in a state of necessity in order to work.'[14] Voltaire calls for a situation in which the worker is not only free to sell his labour but also obliged to do so because of his poverty. Only if an 'excess of agricultural workers' exists, free of the limitations of serfdom and free of property, can the industry of the nation progress.

The condition of the individual that Voltaire declares to be a precondition for the development of industry in 1766 bears a striking resemblance to Karl Marx's 1867 description of the condition of the industrial worker. In a famous passage from volume one of *Capital*, Marx describes the worker of his century as 'free in the double sense that as a free individual he can dispose of his labour-power as his own commodity, and that, on the other hand, he has no other commodity for sale'.[15] The difference is of course, that Voltaire's words of 1766 were uttered in a very different context. Voltaire described a situation that according to him needed to be *created* in order to facilitate the development of Russia's industry while Marx's passage is an analysis of the *status quo* in the industrialised nations in 1867. If Marx's is a lucid analysis, Voltaire's statement is in many ways even more remarkable since he recognised the crucial association of personal freedom and industry as a condition for the future development of industry at a very early stage. This relation between the individual's condition, individual industry and the sector of industry is at the heart of Voltaire's argument.

Voltaire uses the term 'industry' in two different connotations at the beginning and at the end of his argument. At the beginning he is concerned with the peasant's condition. The individual is 'suffocated' by the burden of serfdom. However, freedom means for the serf not only the end of the oppression of his soul and his natural rights. The end of servitude frees also his industry. Clearly, the term is used here in the sense of a personal quality. The oppression of the serf's industry is an oppression of an aspect of his personality. The inventiveness, the industriousness and the dexterity of the peasant are crushed by servitude. In his argument, Voltaire then links the personal freedom of the serf, his personal industry and the 'progress of industry and commerce'. By using the pair 'industry and commerce' Voltaire leaves no doubt as to the meaning of 'industry' in the latter case. Here, he is concerned with 'industry' in the sectoral meaning. The argument thus links the two semantic dimensions of industry and verbalises their complex interdependence.

The social implications of the rise of industry

However, the rise of industry was not only a benign phenomenon for Voltaire. In the essay he also foresees a potential threat to the exiting social order associated to this new phenomenon. Interestingly, Voltaire was not worried about the fate of the property-less workers – 'this class of people so contemptible in the eyes of the powerful'.[16] They would, he predicted, participate indirectly in the prosperity of those who become wealthy through industry. This argument of Voltaire is already familiar from his writings about luxury. Albeit property-less, 'this class of people' had at least been freed from the misery and the oppression of serfdom. For Voltaire, industry was a means of liberation rather than a mode of exploitation as many later authors saw it.

It was not the liberation of the serfs in itself which posed a potential threat to the social and political order for Voltaire. Instead, this order had to be protected from those who acquired wealth through industry. In more than one kingdom, warns Voltaire, it had happened that the liberated serf became rich 'through his industry'. Enriched by industry the former serf would eventually put himself in the place of his old master. Such a confusion of ranks would inevitably lead to the decadence of the nation. In the last paragraph of the essay, Voltaire suggested that society should be protected against the social climbers by laws limiting their ascent to political power. In particular he proposed to conserve the social order by putting limits on the sale of 'noble estates' in order to prevent newcomers from acquiring social status and political power.[17] Quite clearly Voltaire realised that the rise of industry would have an impact on the social structure of society. However, he also underestimated the power of this development when he suggested protecting the existing social order with similar rules.

However, Voltaire's suggestions for the protection of society against social climbers may have to be taken with a pinch of salt. After all this was written by a man whose name on the day of his christening had been François Marie Arouet and who, in 1766, had become 'My lord François Marie Arouet de Voltaire, knight, ordinary gentleman of the chamber of the king, count of Tourney, Prégny and Chambésy, lord of Ferney.'[18] Despite what many of his critics have said, hypocrisy was generally not one of Voltaire's character faults. He insisted throughout his life on controversial opinions that landed him in prison and in exile. However, the notion of restricting the acquisition of 'noble estates' is difficult to reconcile with Voltaire's own experience. He was certainly aware that he had to minimise the potential for social change in the description of his proposal to free the Russian serfs in order to make it acceptable in Russia.

Voltaire discussed the social implications of the rise of industry in other writings, too. Already in the *Age of Louis XIV* he had written about the effects that the new phenomenon of industry had had on different social groups in seventeenth-century France. In this period, Voltaire pointed out, the 'middling order' grew rich 'through industry'. At the same time the real income of the 'ministers and courtiers' decreased due to a rise in prices and the constant nominal values of their pensions and other revenues.[19] Such a development was a threatening outlook for Voltaire. It undermined the very foundations of the social order of his time.

Voltaire's essay for the Petersburg competition is an important text in more than one respect. On one level it is a passionate call to free the enslaved peasants of Russia. It is a call on the government of Russia to free their 'brutalised soul' and give them the natural rights that belong to every man. Nevertheless, it is also the outline of a project for the development of Russian industry. For as Voltaire wrote elsewhere in 1767, what Russia needed were men, laws, arts and industry.[20] The Saint Petersburg essay contains Voltaire's clearest articulation of the link between individual industry and the industry of the nation, or, in other words, the qualitative and sectoral dimension of the term industry. Here, Voltaire explained how out of the industry of the freed serfs something new would grow that was bigger than the sum of its parts: the industry of the nation. This new sector of activities was incompatible with the old feudal law and rules. Industry needed its own new rules that determined the status of the individual and the relations between those who were engaged in industry and who might today be called economic agents. Free individuals with full property rights in their labour, the freedom to move and the freedom to buy and sell labour were the elements of which the nation's industry could be built. It was the task of governments in Russia and elsewhere to create new laws and free individuals if they wanted to participate in the prosperity that industry could bring about. Finally, the essay raised some farsighted questions about the effects that the rise of industry would have on different social groups and the social order as a whole. Would not, asked Voltaire in 1766, those who became rich through industry ask for more political rights and thus undermine the existing social order? The answer to this question, however, was much less farsighted than the question. Like many of his contemporaries he believed that the political and social changes associated with the rise of industry could be implemented in the framework of the existing social order. However, the failure of his own campaign and many other attempts to modernise the Ancien Régime announced the inability of the existing institutions to evolve sufficiently.

Voltaire's campaign against serfdom in France

Voltaire did not only see serfdom as an obstacle to Russian industry. With the same arguments that he used in his Petersburg essay he fought for the complete abolition of servitude in France. His views were, however, highly controversial in France. Many of his contemporaries saw the abolition of the old feudal rules as the first step to social unrest. Mainly, the opponents of the abolition of all forms of serfdom were less optimistic than Voltaire about the consequences. He expected that the freed serfs would move to the cities and contribute to an increase in the nation's industry. The sceptics, however, predicted that the former serfs would not find employment in the cities. Instead, they would form a potential for revolt, misery and crime. In the tension between these two opposite scenarios the French debate about serfdom unfolded in the 1770s and became one of the principal political controversies of the time.

Voltaire took on his adversary – serfdom in the abstract, the canons of Saint-Claude in the concrete – with his usual weapon: the pen. He composed more than a dozen pamphlets and petitions. On this matter, Voltaire wrote letters and memoirs to two kings and three ministers. The campaign began under Louis XV and the minister Choiseul and lasted until Voltaire's death under Louis XVI and the ministry of Necker. In between lay the ministry of Turgot whose rise and fall was crucial not only for France but also for Voltaire and the serfs of Saint-Claude.

The origins of Voltaire's concern with the case of the serfs of Saint-Claude are obscure. He began to write about their situation, their limited property rights and the impact of these limitations on industry in the 1760s. It seems that the young lawyer Christin of Saint-Claude drew Voltaire's attention to the fate of the local serfs in 1764. Christin – Voltaire affectionately called him 'my beloved little philosopher' – wrote the first memorandum that was sent to the king on behalf of the serfs in 1770. Voltaire edited the text that was entitled *To the king in his counsel* and forwarded a copy to the wife of the minister Choiseul. In a letter of the period, Voltaire insisted that the memorandum was originally by Christin and that he had only slightly revised it. He was concerned not to appear among the authors. 'My name', he wrote, 'is fatal in ecclesiastical matters'.[21] Soon, however, Voltaire abandoned his anonymity and pursued the case more openly. A short *New request to the king in his counsel* of 1770 was followed by Voltaire's main writing in this affair, the six page pamphlet *Customs of Franche Comté* of 1771.

The *Customs of Franche Comté* is a passionate attack on the many 'vexations' that were imposed on the serfs and that crushed 'their heart, their industry, and the future'.[22] Voltaire described these hardships vividly. It needs to be noted that Voltaire and Christin called the inhabitants of Saint-Claude 'serfs' despite the fact that their precise status was that of *mainmortables*. As opposed to serfs *mainmortables* were allowed limited ownership of property. Since the term 'serf' was used in the contemporary debates to describe the inhabitants of Saint-Claude, it will also be used here to avoid confusion.

The property rights of the serfs were curtailed in many ways. These limitations resulted in a great number of problems for the serfs and others and were perceived as strong obstacles to the development of industry. The canons were, for example, to inherit all possessions of a serf if his children – serfs themselves – did not live in his house until his death. A child could thus not think of any 'establishment' or 'function' that would require him or her to leave the family's house. The children were condemned to remain in their father's house. This 'vexation', concludes

Voltaire in the *Customs*, was one of the reasons for the lack of industry of the people of Saint-Claude. The importance that Voltaire attached to this vexatious rule becomes intelligible in the context of his perspective on the economic development of France. Looking back on the previous two centuries in 1767, he observed that a shortage of labour started to occur in his time in agriculture because an increasing number of workers took their industry to the professions of 'embroiderer, engraver, watch-maker, silk maker, prosecutor and theologian'. While the last two professions named are a good illustration of how political and economic thought was intertwined with political and religious commentary the observation as a whole is indicative of the importance that changes in individual economic behaviour, namely individual industry, had in the eyes of the contemporaries for the overall economic development. In this passage Voltaire describes the disproportional growth of manufacturing in terms of changes in individual economic behaviour: many individuals left their agricultural work in order to engage in manufacturing. Any rules that prevented such a change were clearly insurmountable obstacles to the development of industry. This perspective is of particular interest in the context of de Vries interpretation of the rise of industry. The change of economic behaviour and the increase of labour time devoted to the manufacturing of refined goods that is at the heart of de Vries argument was not lost on the contemporaries. Voltaire is describing exactly this development. However, contemporaries such as Voltaire and Turgot also clearly saw that the change in economic behaviour depended crucially on the institutional framework. While the importance of the institutional context and of political decisions was widely discussed by the contemporaries it is, unfortunately, often missing in today's approaches to the economic transformation of the period.[23]

For Voltaire the rules of serfdom were obstacles to industry and were also the cause for the inertia and backwardness of the inhabitants of Saint-Claude. The 'pestilence of slavery' led them to vegetate in a state of uselessness to themselves, their children and the nation. Their dignity was taken away and they were degraded to a state similar to that of their own cattle or even to that of 'human vegetables'.[24] Serfdom with its limitations on the property rights of the serfs had many degrading consequences for the inhabitants of Saint-Claude. One of the examples that Voltaire cited was that if a young man found a way to gain personal freedom he would be punished by losing all his rights to his father's inheritance. Another example was that of a young man who marries, and decides to live with his wife's family. He, too, would completely lose his inheritance. In another pamphlet of 1772 Voltaire illustrated the injustice of the inheritance laws with the case of the serf Jeanne-Marie Mermot. She had not spent her wedding night in her father's house. Since this was against the rules of serfdom the canons took her inheritance when her father died. She was thrown out of her house, became a beggar and her four children lived in misery. Voltaire emphasises a particularly cruel detail of this story: as the canons took the woman's property they did not even leave her the milk that she had set aside for her youngest child.[25] In his pamphlets against serfdom, Voltaire used all his writing skills to bring out the cruelty of the inheritance laws to which the serfs were submitted. Whether the episodes used to illustrate the cruelty of serfdom were factually accurate remains difficult to ascertain. Voltaire was very precise in bringing out the specific aspects of serfdom that were obstacles to industry. However, when he condemned these aspects he did so with touching episodes about the serfs' lives rather than with arguments about political economy.

The 'vexations' of serfdom were not limited to the serfs but extended to free individuals, too. To illustrate the consequences of the limitations to inheritance, Voltaire described the hypothetical case of a serf who died suddenly without inheritors. The lord was then allowed to confiscate the property without repaying any loans that the serf had taken out. The serf's creditors would go unpaid. As a result, serfdom turns even a 'solvent and well-intended debtor' into a risk for the creditor.[26] The burden of serfdom was thus not limited to those who were immediately subjected to it but it extended also to the free members of society. Seen in this way, the ancient rules of serfdom were, in fact, a source of insecurity. This aspect is frequently emphasised. Because of the antiquity and complexity of feudal rights, they led to constant litigation between lords and serfs as well as between lords. The result was not only a huge cost but also a considerable insecurity that burdened economic activity.

Besides the limitations that pertained to the person of the serf, his property was submitted to a number of further constraints. The first among the rules denounced by Voltaire was the prohibition to sell or exchange goods. In a decade in which a Scottish admirer of Voltaire declared 'truck, barter and exchange' to be a 'propensity in human nature', many perceived this rule as a severe infringement of individual rights. Other limitations of property rights were perceived as equally unjust. The serf could not, for instance, take out a 'mortgage' on any of his goods without the agreement of the lord. In both cases the permission could be obtained for the price of one-third of the sum in question. Quite clearly such rules were strong obstacles to the serf founding any 'establishment' or taking up any function other than that of peasant-serf. Again, Voltaire looked for a touching example to denounce the rules against buying, selling and exchanging. An old sick man, he writes, would be barred from selling his property or borrowing money in order to survive. Finally, Voltaire also denounced a non-material aspect of serfdom. In a memorandum to the king, Voltaire writes about several children who had become the prey of wild animals because their parents were barred from carrying weapons to defend them.[27] Already in the context of the rules of inheritance Voltaire had compared the situation of the serfs to that of their cattle. Here, he repeats the analogy and adds another cruel consequence of feudal rule.

It is noteworthy that this last grievance is the only one that does not regard the material aspects of serfdom. Voltaire's concern with the freedom of the serfs of Saint-Claude was, in fact, largely a concern with their freedom to exchange and sell goods and labour, and to borrow money. In short it is a concern with their freedom to develop industry. It is thus not surprising that the pair of freedom and industry appears several times in the writings about Saint-Claude. Voltaire argued that the limitations of serfdom strangle the individual industry of the serfs. But there was hope for the future. Together with their freedom, Voltaire predicted, the serfs would gain the same industry and prosperity that the rest of France was enjoying since the time in which serfdom had been abolished there. To illustrate the future of Saint-Claude, he briefly discussed the effects that the abolition of serfdom had had on the rest of France: 'Together with freedom [our sovereigns] gave industry and prosperity to the subjects within their domains. All of France, whose name, appearance, industry and happiness provoke the jealousy of other nations, has only enjoyed these advantages since its days of freedom.'[28] Note that the term 'industry' has two connotations in this passage. In the first part, the French monarchs give industry to their subjects. Here, Voltaire is concerned with individuals who are given the right and possibility to exercise their industry. However, the result of this change at the individual level is associated to the development of the sector of industry. In the second part of the passage it is described how the freedom of the individual to be industrious leads to the development of France's industry. Here, the concern is with industry as a sector of activities within the nation. However, in 1771 when Voltaire was expressing the hope that freedom and industry would soon be brought to Saint-Claude the moment of liberation was still a long way off for its serfs.

The campaign against serfdom under the ministry of Turgot

Voltaire's campaign began under the ministry of his close friend Choiseul, but the controversy escalated under the ministry of Turgot. Choiseul who supported many reforms of the time was ousted in 1770. However, Voltaire had vowed to work for the serfs until their freedom was achieved and he continued his epistolary campaign with the new administrators. Soon, however, a major change occurred in French politics: in 1774 Louis XV died and his nineteen-year-old grandson became Louis XVI. Voltaire and many of his contemporaries pinned their hopes for a 'wiser and happier' age on the new monarch.[29]

At one point, in February 1776 shortly before the fall of Turgot, Louis XVI even inspired a poem by Voltaire. One evening Sésostris, young prince of Egypt, strolls in a leisurely way down the banks of the Nile in Memphis. In the twilight he sees two goddesses. The first represents sensual pleasure. She is beautiful, her smile is sweet and her demeanour seductive. Behind her, however, Sésostris notices three spectres: 'Disgust, Boredom and Remorse'. The other goddess – less beautiful, as Voltaire points out – is busy with manuscripts and scientific instruments. Her name is Wisdom. Torn between the two goddesses, the prince gives 'two kisses in passing' to the first but ends up giving his heart to Wisdom. Responsible for this somewhat surprising outcome is the nameless 'loyal guide' who is accompanying the prince on his walk. This 'angel' helps the prince in his decisions and is there to guide his steps. Quite clearly, the poem had not much to do with Egypt. Young Sésostris was in reality strolling along the Seine and the 'loyal guide' was nobody else than the minister Turgot.[30]

The appointment of Turgot first as the minister of the navy then as finance minister was warmly welcomed by Voltaire. In his letters of the time, he recalled two weeks that Turgot had spent at his house in Geneva many years ago. He also praised Turgot's administration in Limoges and compared Turgot to the great Colbert and the great Sully in the same letter. Enthusiastic for the new era, he even went so far as to hope for an 'age of Louis XVI' superior to that of Louis XIV. Voltaire eagerly followed the events of Turgot's ministry. From his remote retreat, he intervened more than once in support of the minister. It is not possible here to analyse the events of Turgot's ministry or even Voltaire's support of Turgot comprehensively. Instead, the focus will be on the development of Voltaire's campaign for the serfs of Saint-Claude under the ministry of Turgot.[31]

Voltaire was certainly not mistaken to pin great hopes on the ministry of Turgot with regard to the fight against the limitations of serfdom. It has been pointed out that Turgot's reform edicts invite the listeners to 'think themselves into, or sympathise with, the sentiments of the cultivator oppressed by subaltern officials of the administration of roads, the seamstress excluded from joining a corporation, the independent flower seller, the carrier who is forbidden to untie his sacks of grain in the street, the trader whose house is searched by magistrates'.[32] The spirit of Turgot's concerns is quite close to that of Voltaire's preoccupation with the oppressive feudal rules of Saint-Claude. Voltaire's many descriptions of the vexations caused by feudal rules were written to make the reader feel the injustice that the serfs were submitted to. His pamphlets were intended to make the reader understand how these unjust laws were shackles to the industry of the oppressed. However, Voltaire did not appeal to the reason of the reader or try to convince him with abstract principles of political economy. His arguments about industry appeal to the compassion of the reader by vividly describing the burdens of serfdom.

Voltaire argued abstractly in his Petersburg essay, and concretely in the case of Saint-Claude, that the 'difficulties' of feudal law were, at the same time, hurting the natural rights of the individual and the development of the nation's industry. A similar line of argument concerning industry and individual rights can be found in Turgot's reform edicts promulgated by Louis XVI in a *lit de justice* on 12 March 1776. This act of legislation complemented earlier reforms such as the liberalisation of the grain trade.[33] The two edicts that were most important in the context of Voltaire's campaign against serfdom were the abolition of the *jurandes* and the *corvée*.

The *jurandes* or corporations regulated all aspects of a trade from wages to the quality of products. In particular they provided a high entry-barrier against anyone who wanted to obtain the permission to be engaged in a trade. By creating various obstacles to obtaining permission the corporations strengthened the position of the established masters. These rules, the minister wrote in the preamble of the edict, were nothing less than 'bizarre, tyrannical, contrary to good conduct'. In particular, they prevented individuals who – by 'taste' or 'necessity' – wanted to take up a trade from doing so or from being employed by a master. At the same time, the rules limited the rights of the employers. A 'citizen' could not simply hire who he wanted or pay a freely negotiated wage. He was bound by the rules of the corporation. This situation was characterised by Turgot as an 'enormous hindrance ... to industry' and as an infringement of the natural rights of the individual.[34]

The other principal object of Turgot's reform was the abolition of the *corvée*. This institutions required most peasants to contribute a certain number of working days to the maintenance of existing roads and the construction of new ones in their region. Following Turgot's edict this labour obligation was to be replaced by a tax. This, he argued, would bring several improvements. It would free the peasants from a great burden. To be called away from work on his own farm was always a great inconvenience for the peasant. It could even threaten his existence when the *corvée* was requested during crucial periods of the agricultural production cycle. Two or three days of feudal labour service during harvest or sowing could severely affect the work of a whole year. This vexation and possible loss of production through the *corvée* was not balanced by a gain for society as a whole. Because the peasant was forced to work on the roads he lacked the necessary motivation and skill. The work was done 'without intelligence'. Accordingly, the quality of the roads built under this regime was poor. Finally, the burden of road building and maintenance was not divided justly. Only small farmers were subject to the *corvée* while the roads that were built benefited mostly the wealthy land-owners who were engaged in trade.[35] These shortcomings were to be remedied by Turgot's reform which replaced the labour obligations by a tax that was to be levied not only on those submitted to the *corvée* but on a broader basis of tax payers. The burden was thus to be shared more evenly. Out of the tax revenue qualified workers and entrepreneurs would be paid to build and maintain the roads of the kingdom.

The reform projects of Turgot were intimately linked with Voltaire's fight for the abolition of serfdom. They shared a common concern with the freedom of the individual and the development of industry. But the projects of Turgot and Voltaire were also linked by a common enemy and by an event that took place days before Turgot's edicts were promulgated. A detailed look at the chronology of the debate will demonstrate the close connection between Voltaire's and Turgot's projects.

'Industry will be harmed even more'

When Turgot sent his reform edicts – among them the new rules concerning corporations and *corvée* – to *parlement* on 2 February 1776 they met with stiff opposition. Pamphlets against the abolition of the corporations were circulating on the streets of Paris. Two themes emerge from the arguments against the abolition of the corporations: first, the fear of negative effects on the development of industry and, second, the fear of the social consequences that such an institutional change would engender.

In one of the more prominent pamphlets against Turgot's projects an anonymous author warned of the grave consequences for the 'development of industry' if Turgot's projects were to be implemented. 'Industry would be harmed even more', writes the author, '[and] even more submitted to tyranny by liberty itself than it ever could have been by any regulation.' The quality of industry would decrease because of the lack of quality standards and the influx of unskilled workers. Holland or Switzerland may be models for freedom of industry, he wrote, but they were not models for the 'perfection of arts'. Swiss watches were produced in freedom but they could simply not match the quality of the French produce. All great and prosperous nations, the author maintained, had guilds. The only exception to this rule was Holland. This country, however, could hardly serve as an example. The Dutch were a people of continuously travelling merchants and therefore regarded their fatherland as a mere 'inn'. To the author, it was therefore hardly surprising that they had never taken the time to give proper laws to their nation.[36]

The second concern that was voiced by the anonymous critic of Turgot had to do with the social consequences of the proposed legislation. If the rules of the guilds were abolished in France, the unrestricted influx of workers into the 'refuges of industry' of the cities would have grave social consequences. In his Petersburg essay, Voltaire had described how the migration of the freed rural population into the workshops, cities and ports of Russia would bring prosperity to that country. The defenders of France's corporations foresaw a strikingly different scenario. In France the migration into the 'refuges of industry' was not limited by serfdom – with the exception of Saint-Claude – but by the rules of the corporations. Rather than being tied to the land, the population was barred from the cities. If the rural population was to find the 'barrier that terrifies their imagination' abolished, the consequences would be disastrous. Despite their loutish manners and their clumsiness they would flood into the cities in the hope of finding employment. However, their lack of skill and the limits to the 'consumption of the ... products of industry' would not allow them to survive in the city. In fact, the description of the migrant worker's fate in the city is not less vivid than Voltaire's description of the limitations of serfdom: unable to find employment in the city the worker is degraded and humiliated. He is drawn into 'shameful distractions' and crime. The worker's misery and grief end only with his lonely death in a hospital. Not only would the workers suffer but the social order of the whole nation would fall into decay. After the abolition of the corporations the workers would be free from the hierarchy of the corporations in which the master exercised 'a preliminary police'. Without the help of the masters, the magistrates would be unable to maintain public order. 'Anarchic independence' in matters of work would quickly spread and lead to complete disorder.

The corporations were defended as an element that 'held everything in balance'.[37]

It should be noted that the social instability which is predicted to follow the abolition of the corporations is different from the disorder that Voltaire saw as a potential consequence of the end of serfdom in Russia. In both scenarios a great number of property-less labourers flock into the cities to work. The difference lies in the expectations about the further development of industry. Voltaire expected that the growth of industry would readily absorb all additional workers. The more pessimistic observers saw limits to the demand for the products of industry. Consequently they foresaw a great number of unemployed and miserable workers. These different scenarios also informed the opposite fears about social instability that both sides voiced. Voltaire saw the existing social order threatened by the slow ascent of those who grew rich through industry. His opponents saw the principal danger in the violent revolts of those who would not find employment in the 'refuges of industry'. Turgot was clearly not convinced by either of the arguments against the abolition of the corporations. However, he apparently feared that others could have been less resistant to the subversive propaganda. On his initiative, the above pamphlet and three others were censored on 22 February 1776.[38] This was not the first occasion on which Turgot used oppressive means against the opponents of his legislative projects. At the beginning of Turgot's ministry, the liberalisation of the grain trade had resulted in the popular uprisings of the 'flour wars'. Turgot – applauded by Voltaire – had suppressed the revolt successfully. Where necessary, the new economic institutions were imposed with force on the population.[39]

Vexatious feudal privileges

In 1776 the opponents of Turgot responded swiftly with an act of censorship of their own. On 24 February *parlement* decided that a brochure written by Pierre François de Boncerf, a young official in Turgot's administration was to be burned 'at the foot of the great stairway of the Palais'.[40] The pamphlet is of particular interest because of the example that the author used to illustrate the vexations or 'inconveniences' of feudal law. He repeatedly cited the example of the serfs of 'St. Cl'. While Boncerf also denounced the 'feudal tyranny' in Russia and Poland, he takes most of his concrete examples from the Franche-Comté. In the pamphlet the mother of four appears again whose fate had been described by Voltaire. However, Boncerf also gives many new examples of the vexations of the 'myriad' of feudal laws. Again the reader is confronted with upsetting cases of relatives who were denied their inheritance by the feudal lords. The pinnacle of oppression was reached for Boncerf in a case where the lords appropriated an inheritance but did not pay back a 'mortgage debt' of the deceased. As in Voltaire's examples economic insecurity plays the most important role among the vexations of feudal laws. The loss of time and constant quarrels over obscure laws are blamed as an obstacle to prosperity. Lords and serfs find themselves occupied with 'a thousand embarrassments & difficulties' that prevent them from engaging in useful activities. In fact, a good part of the nation's 'time, industry & activity' are absorbed by obsolete rules and regulations. For Boncerf, prosperity could only be reached by establishing the freedom of people, goods and actions. He cites the examples of Lorraine where serfdom had been abolished in 1771. Since that time, he writes, Lorraine had become one of the leading regions in Europe in 'industry', 'arts', 'agriculture', 'economy' and 'manufactories'. As a contrast to the flourishing region of Lorraine, Boncerf points to 'St. Claude' (he switched to using the full name after page nineteen). Everywhere else in France people were more 'commercial' and 'industrious'.[41] However, Boncerf did not only take up the case of Saint-Claude and repeat the arguments about the vexations of feudal laws and their impact on industry. He also offered a solution to the problem of liberating the serf without infringing on the property rights of the lord. Boncerf proposed that the serfs should be given the chance to buy their liberty from the lord. Voltaire had proposed a different solution. He suggested that the lords should be obliged to accept the transformation of their feudal rights into rent payments. In a letter of December 1775, Voltaire had tried to press the issue but with the conflict over Turgot's reform edicts escalating in 1776 the proposal from Ferney was apparently not any more discussed in Paris.[42] The *parlement* of Paris and in particular Turgot's powerful opponent, the *avocat-général* Antoine-Louis Séguier, vigorously opposed Boncerf's proposals. In the prosecutor's statement, Séguier justified reasons for the decision to burn the pamphlet. He explained that the seeming moderation of the plan was a mere cover. Once the serfs had gathered in front of the lord's château in order to buy their freedom, he argued, it would be impossible to refuse it. With the support of the minister the 'hot-blooded ... multitude' would eventually force the lord to give up the feudal rights against his will. This not entirely unrealistic scenario was perceived as a fundamental threat to society. If Boncerf's views were to take possession of the masses this would result in nothing less than a general uprising of the serfs against their lords and the whole people against the monarch. 'The cruellest anarchy' was to be expected. As in the pamphlets against Turgot's reforms, the abolition of even the most minute feudal law was understood as an attack on the established order as a whole.[43]

For Séguier, Boncerf's ideas were part of a larger current that he called a 'frenzy' stimulated by the love of liberty. He discerned a 'secret faction' or 'hidden agent' that was working against the nation's rules and order. Séguier summed up his scenario in a passage that compared the 'secret faction' to subterranean volcanoes. These volcanoes, he predicted, announced their existence by small earthquakes – such as Boncerf's pamphlet – and erupted eventually burying everything under a huge current of lava. 'How sublime this piece is!', Voltaire ironically commented on this apocalyptic vision.[44]

Despite the fact that Voltaire was far away from Paris he took great interest in the events in the city. They were, after all, immediately connected to his project of freeing the serfs of Saint-Claude. It seems to have been Condorcet – himself an associate in Turgot's ministry – who sent a copy of Boncerf's pamphlet to Ferney. Voltaire's first reaction was a short letter to Boncerf congratulating him on the brochure. After the letter started to circulate publicly in Paris it was censored like the work that it was praising. Curiously, it was not suppressed by the party of Séguier but by Turgot. It seems that the minister did not want to further escalate the conflict with *parlement*. He may also have thought that it would not be helpful to have Voltaire's name too closely associated with his projects. The minister thus simultaneously tried to silence Voltaire and to prevent Séguier from further pursuing Boncerf. Turgot did everything to avoid a further circulation of Voltaire's letter to Boncerf. In particular he was worried that the letter might be reprinted in Holland. Silencing Voltaire, however, was an impossible task even for his friends. Taking on the alias of 'Reverend Father Polycarpe, prior of the Bernadines of Chézery', Voltaire wrote an open letter to Séguier and congratulated him ironically on the condemnation of Boncerf's 'abominable and detestable brochure'. 'Father Polycarpe' called on the three orders of church, nobility and *noblesse de robe* to rally in defence of feudal laws. Voltaire thus described ironically what he saw as a reactionary coalition against Turgot's and his own reform proposals.[45]

The progress of industry: a common concern of Turgot and Voltaire

The legislative reform projects of Turgot and Voltaire, however, were not only joined together by their common enemies. They had a motive in common: the further development of industry. In a pamphlet that

Voltaire wrote shortly after the Boncerf affair, he stated more clearly than anywhere else the common motivations that underlay his fight against serfdom and Turgot's reforms of the corporations and the *corvée*. In the short text Voltaire poses yet again as a Benedictine monk who thanks Séguier for defending the feudal laws of serfdom and for fighting against a false maxim of modern philosophy. This maxim is given as a direct quotation by Voltaire: 'The right to work belongs to all men: this possession is the first, the holiest, and the most imprescriptible of all.' The passage is cited from Turgot's edict about the abolition of the corporations. As often, Voltaire was not concerned with giving the correct wording but he certainly reproduced the essence of Turgot's statement accurately.[46]

In the pamphlet Voltaire uses the words 'liberty for industry' to sum up the essence of his own and Turgot's concerns.[47] The rules of the corporations and the laws of serfdom were both obstacles to industry. They hindered the development of industry in different ways. While the laws of serfdom were attached to the person, the rules of the corporation were associated with the trade. In other words, serfdom prevented the poor from selling their industry while the rules of the corporations prevented it from being bought. Voltaire's concern was to turn the serfs of Russia and France into free men and free workers, while Turgot's concern was to protect the worker against the oppressive laws of the corporations. 'Above all we owe this protection' Turgot writes in introducing the edicts, 'to that class of men who have no other property than their industry and the work of their hands.'[48]

In particular, Turgot wanted to ensure that everybody could sell their labour and obtain a freely negotiated price for it.[49] Rules that were obstacles to the free buying and selling of labour were not only unjust but they also caused great harm to industry. Corporations and the *corvée* were such obstacles. The guilds protected the master's monopoly to exercise a trade. Frequently, the monopolists used their power to force apprentices to work without salary for years. The monopoly also resulted in wage controls that favoured the employers. In addition to that, other rules prevented the free buying and selling of labour: some guilds did not accept apprentices who were from another city or who were not children of a master. Marriage, too, was a reason to be excluded from an apprenticeship. These rules had in common either to prevent the buying and selling of labour altogether or to affect the price to the advantage of the buyer.[50]

The *corvée*, in turn, interfered with the freedom of the peasant to freely dispose of his labour power by requiring him to contribute a number of working days to road building. Substituting for this obligation by a tax did not only make the peasant free to sell his labour. It also gave the government the possibility to choose where to buy the labour for public works and thus obtain a better quality. Turgot denounced the rules of the corporations and the *corvée* as unjust because they favoured the rich over the poor. Condorcet, in his *Life of Voltaire*, even described the guilds as a form of servitude. Like serfdom, the guilds with their rules against the free selling and buying of labour were not only thought of as unjust; they were also considered a burden that put a great strain on industry and that would eventually destroy it.[51]

The concern that led Voltaire to oppose serfdom was quite similar. The rules of serfdom, like the rules of the corporations and the *corvée*, prevented the peasant from selling his labour freely and from freely disposing of his property. These rules went even further in that they prevented the serf from buying or selling any good without the consent of the lord. Again, these were rules made by the powerful in their own interest. Freeing the individual from this yoke, and freeing the individual's industry were closely connected for Voltaire. Since industry was for him a natural part of any individual's personality, freeing the person meant also freeing the person's industry.[52] Where Turgot argues that the guilds 'extinguish' the population's industry, Voltaire speaks of feudal laws 'suffocating' the peasant's industry. The intricate relation of the individual's industry and the nation's industry is one of the crucial elements of Voltaire's and Turgot's thought. The relation is of importance not only for the understanding of these debates but also for the understanding of the semantic breadth of the term industry. In the Petersburg essay, Voltaire offers a richly complex picture of the consequences of the abolition of serfdom for the individual's and the nation's industry. In this analytic chain a change in the condition of the individual leads to the creation of a new branch of activities that makes the nation flourish.

In a rather similar way, Turgot's argument associates the condition of the individual not only with the development of individual industry but also to that of the nation. Turgot is addressing the details of the individual condition of the worker, but he is also contemplating the effects of the reforms on the sector of industry. In his memorandum to Louis XVI, the minister explains the intention of his 1776 edits in the context of the 1774 liberalisation of the grain trade: 'This second undertaking will be for industry what the first will be for agriculture.' Here, Turgot places the effect of his reforms in the greater framework of the economic sectors of industry and agriculture. Just as the reform of the rules of the grain trade would result in a further development of agriculture, the changes in the condition of the individual worker would bring about a progress of industry. As a result, the 'wealth of the state' would increase considerably.[53] Turgot's perspective places the individual in the foreground. The institutions that prevent the worker from gaining a decent living by crushing his industry have to be abolished. However, in the background looms another industry. It is not the industry of the individual but it is the sector of industry that – together with the sector of agriculture – produces the wealth of the nation. It is fascinating to observe how the 'micro' and 'macro' perspectives on industry are associated in the understanding of Voltaire and Turgot. Significantly, their key concern is with the condition of the worker rather than with technical progress. The development of industry was perceived as depending on the creation of appropriate laws and a profound transformation of social relations. Equally noteworthy is that the insight into the intricate relationship between the individual condition and the sector of industry translated into concrete political campaigns to change specific laws that were seen as obstacles. Voltaire and Turgot attacked serfdom for a number of reasons. A very prominent motive for both was that the feudal institution was in the way of the further development of industry. The arguments of Voltaire target mostly the restrictions that serfdom imposes on the economic life of the peasants. However, while he argues against the institution on the basis of abstract principles of political economy in the Petersburg essay, he attacks it with concrete examples in the texts that were written for the public. In the fight for something as prosaic as industry Voltaire tried to touch the reader's heart rather than his reason.

The campaign against serfdom after the fall of Turgot

With the fall of Turgot in 1776, Voltaire's hopes of liberating the serfs of Saint-Claude practically ended. When Turgot was ousted, Voltaire commiserated with the minister in a poem. The people of Paris, he wrote, were ungrateful. They complained about Turgot's edicts in the morning and booed Voltaire's own plays in the evening. In the *Life of Voltaire*, Condorcet talks about the failed campaign against serfdom. The minister, he writes, was already so weakened and isolated that he could not help Voltaire's cause. It would be left to the revolution to bring about a government powerful and radical enough to free the serfs of Saint-Claude and the other French serfs.[54]

In fact, Alexis de Tocqueville has characterised the radical abolition of feudal institutions such as serfdom as the 'real objective' of the French revolution. The fight against serfdom was also seen as one of the principal achievements of Voltaire in the post-revolutionary period. When his body was moved to the Panthéon in 1791 the sarcophagus bore the inscription: 'He fought atheists and fanatics, he inspired tolerance, he demanded human rights against the servitude of feudalism.' In Tocqueville's analysis of the causes of the revolution great emphasis is put on the perception of the feudal rules of the Ancien Régime as oppressive and vexatious. In particular he saw them as conflicting with the emerging industry. 'Everybody found himself weakened according to his own condition, disturbed in his habits or hampered in his industry', Tocqueville wrote of the perception in the decades before the revolution. Among the institutions that were crippling industry most, Tocqueville points out the feudal laws – he specifically mentions the last serfs of France belonging to an ecclesiastical lord – alongside with the corporations and the unjust tax system. As industry developed further under Louis XVI the friction with the laws of the Ancien Régime increased. This constellation is seen by Tocqueville as one of the principal causes of the revolution.[55]

However, the conflict between the development of industry and feudal institutions is not only pointed out in Tocqueville's nineteenth-century analysis. The writings of Voltaire and his contemporaries demonstrate that this conflict was explicitly discussed in the debates of the 1770s. Voltaire clearly analysed the tension between many of the legal and social institutions of his time and the progress of industry. However, he did not only grasp in an abstract sense that a fundamental change in the legal and social condition of the individual was required to allow for a further growth of industry. In a personal crusade he set out to bring that change to one of the remotest parts of France. Moreover, both opponents and proponents of institutional reform agreed that the growth of industry would be associated with profound social change.

Voltaire's concern with the legal status of the serfs of Saint-Claude – and those of Russia – like Turgot's concern with the corporations and the *corvée* points to an important feature of eighteenth-century perspectives on industry. Increasingly, the term came to be associated with a specific legal condition of the individual and specific forms of interaction between economic agents: only free workers who owned their labour power and skill could fully develop industry. Turgot expressed this understanding when he wrote about the forced labour of the *corvée*: 'No work that requires an education, no individual industry can be carried out under the force of a *corvée*.'[56] Skill and labour that were exercised outside the framework of a free labour market – for example under the rules of serfdom or the control of a corporation – could not turn into a flourishing industry. The free exchange of labour came to be seen as a crucial characteristic of the developing sector of manufacturing. This view was also shared by observers who viewed the economic development of the time with suspicion. In *Émile* Rousseau pointed out that the main characteristic of the rapidly developing economic world around him were 'exchanges of industry'.[57] He was using the term in the sense of 'exchanges of industriousness' or 'exchanges of labour' in this context. It was clear to many contemporaries that the new phenomenon of industry was not merely the sum of many hard working individuals. Instead, industry was seen as a new economic sector that had its own logic and that required its own rules and institutions. The conflict of the growth of industry with the institutional order of the Ancien Régime thus emerged clearly in the debates of the eighteenth century.

Conclusion

Looking back at a quarter century of debates about industry in the middle of the eighteenth century it is remarkable that industry was so widely discussed at such an early time. Several decades before the period that came to be known as the 'industrial revolution' the phenomenon of industry had already become the subject of controversial public debate. In these debates the production and consumption of goods – just as many other aspects of social, political and religious life – were increasingly submitted to rational scrutiny by the thinkers of the enlightenment: rules, behaviours and production techniques in manufacturing that did not conform to rational principles had to be changed. The progress of industry in this period was thus in many ways associated to the progress of the enlightenment and the application of its rational principles to the sphere of manufacturing. However, the study of contemporary debates does not only illuminate the concern of many prominent enlightenment thinkers with the manufacturing and consumption of goods. Contemporary comments also suggest a fresh perspective on the rise of industry. The study of contemporary observations cautions us against an unbalanced concentration on technical change when we examine the causes of the rise of industry. Techniques and machinery used in industry have changed and continue to change; the individual conditions and dispositions which many eighteenth-century observers saw as the defining elements of industry have remained characteristics of this economic sector.

More specifically, four aspects of the controversies that have been discussed here stand out: first, the concentration of contemporary arguments about industry on the disposition and condition of the individual rather than on mechanisation; second, the widespread perception that the origins of industry were associated with the policies of Jean Baptiste Colbert and other administrators; third, the controversy over the question of whether and to what extent the growth of industry was desirable; fourth, the perception of industry as a phenomenon that transcended national borders.

The first and most noteworthy aspect of the debates is that the concern of contemporary observers with industry clearly preceded what came to be known as the 'industrial revolution'. It is therefore necessary to reconsider the idea of industry as closely associated or even virtually identical to large-scale mechanisation of labour. Eighteenth-century authors were concerned with the progress of industry as an economic sector but their interest for the mechanisation of production was marginal. Instead, the arguments concerning the growth of the sector of industry focus on the disposition and condition of the individual. This perspective is clearly reflected in the semantic transformation in which the sector of industry derived its name from a term that initially denoted a quality of an individual.

The contemporary understanding thus differs from the ways in which many later observers came to think of industry. Eighteenth-century debates about the subject are in many ways unfamiliar to the modern reader. However, early perceptions of industry should not be dismissed because they do not focus on mechanisation. Instead, it is possible to derive new insights about the rise of industry by considering the early debates about the subject.

The eighteenth-century authors and administrators who have been discussed here were fundamentally concerned with the individual and the interaction of individuals. When the writers of the time were considering industry they were mostly speaking about the dispositions and the conditions of those who were involved in industry. The debates about industry were about the growth of the sector of industry but the contemporary arguments focused on the individuals of whom this sector was composed. The origins of industry were associated to the disposition of the individual and the social and legal condition in which the individuals lived. On the one hand, the concentration was on dispositions such as skill, inventiveness and industriousness. On the other hand the legal and social conditions – for example of the men and women submitted to serfdom or to the rules of the guilds – were at the heart of contemporary concerns with industry.

Controversy focused on the question of how to further develop the individual qualities that were considered to be crucial for the growth of industry. Was the self-interest of the individual strong enough to make him or her industrious? Was it necessary to educate individuals to be industrious? Would inventions simply spring up or was it necessary to actively promote the acquisitions of skills and relevant knowledge? The contemporaries also debated the ways in which the development of these dispositions were interrelated with the legal and social condition of the individual. They asked how the legal status and the social position of the individual would affect his or her ability to be involved in industry and to develop the dispositions that the growth of industry required. Would the abolition of serfdom make the individual more industrious?

Would industry be harmed or fostered by the abolition of guilds? However, the growth of industry was not only considered as a consequence of the changes of the condition and disposition of the individual. The growth of the new sector was expected to affect the individual in many ways. The writers and administrators of the time were concerned with the effects that the growth of industry might have on the moral and social condition of the individual. Would those who engaged in some form of industry not become morally corrupted? And would they not attempt to change their social condition in a way that might threaten the social order?

While the answers that eighteenth-century observers found to these questions differed greatly, they still shared a prominent concern with the individual when they were reasoning about the growth of industry. This perspective is also reflected in the semantic development. The sector of industry derived its name from an individual quality. As has been demonstrated, the sectoral connotation grew out of the qualitative meaning in the course of the eighteenth century. However, the sectoral connotation did not substitute the qualitative in the period. They coexisted and frequently appeared in the context of the same argument. This close relation between the two meanings of industry is surprising only for the modern reader. In the light of the eighteenth-century approach to industry as a matter closely associated to the individual the semantic transformation becomes more intelligible.

The contemporary concern with the legal and social condition of the individual was closely related to the concern with the rules that governed the interaction between the individuals who were involved in industry. This concentration emerges particularly in Voltaire's writings. For him, the individual's industry – skill, industriousness and inventiveness – could only be turned into a sector of industry if the individuals involved could interact appropriately. Above all they needed unrestricted property rights in their labour. They had to be free to buy and sell from each other their labour and the products of their labour. Individual industry needed to be traded and moved from one place to another in order to be applied to new tasks and branches of industry.

In the early debates about industry, the term was associated with specific individual qualities and institutional arrangements rather than with any particular set of technologies or tools utilised. In particular in Voltaire's writings, the concentration on the individual as the constitutive element of the new sector of economic activities stands out. For Voltaire, the men of industry were hard working. However, they were not only exercising the traditional tasks of their trade. These individuals were inventive and ready to adopt a new technique or to make a new produce.

They were not bound by feudal rules to a certain location or a certain trade. They were free to move to another employment or another location where their skill was needed. Those who made up the sector of industry were also free to sell their labour to whoever would pay them most. But they were also free of other possessions. They were therefore obliged to sell their labour rather than being idle. The absence of other possessions such as a piece of land or a house also removed obstacles to them moving to another place where they might sell their skill. For those who used the term industry for the first time in the modern sense, the rise of industry was fundamentally about individuals with new qualities and about new institutions that governed their interaction. In this perspective on the rise of industry as a matter closely associated to changes in the disposition of the individual and to transformations of the institutional order might lie one of the lessons to be learned from eighteenth-century observers.

It is significant to note that Voltaire and other contemporary proponents of industry such as Turgot were keenly aware that the transformations which were required for the development of industry conflicted in many instances with the existing institutional framework of the Ancien Régime. In their view, this emphasised the urgent need for reform. Significantly, Voltaire and Turgot both worked for reforms 'from above'. Voltaire's pamphlets against serfdom were not written for the serfs of Saint-Claude. He tried to convince ministers and monarchs of his views. The necessary reforms were expected to be initiated and implemented by a wise minister. For Voltaire, the only authority strong enough to confront the vested interests that stood against the reforms was that of an uncontested royal government. However, Voltaire also witnessed the failure of his own and Turgot's reforms. Despite the great trust that Voltaire placed in the authority of government, Turgot had been unable to impose his projects. It was only after the revolution that the reforms proposed by Voltaire and Turgot could be implemented. That institutional obstacles to the development of industry under the Ancien Régime were perceived as one of the reasons for the revolution has been pointed out in Tocqueville's writings. The protection of industry remained a prominent concern in post-revolutionary politics. The 1793 draft of the *Solemn declaration of human rights*, for example, contained specific provisions to protect the freedom of industry and the property rights in the fruits of industry.[1]

The concentration of eighteenth-century arguments on the disposition and the condition of the individual supports recent re-evaluations of the process of industrialisation in Europe by economic historians.

One thing that we can learn from contemporary observations is that the nature of industry and the principal features of the rise of industry are associated to change in economic behaviour and economic institutions rather than to large-scale mechanisation. Jan de Vries has proposed an explanation for the rise of industry that concentrates on a profound change in the 'economic behaviour' of individuals. Two characteristic features of de Vries 'industrious revolution' are, first, the emergence of an 'industrious disposition' of the individual that manifests itself in a reduction of leisure time, and, second, a 'reallocation of labour from goods and services for direct consumption to marketed goods'.[2] These two concerns also emerge from the contemporary debates. The promotion of individual industry was seen by Voltaire and many others as crucial for the growth of industry. Equally, Voltaire was concerned with changing the feudal rules that formed the institutional framework. The goal was that individuals should be able to freely buy and sell their labour and the fruits of their labour. That labour could freely be bought and sold, was seen as a precondition for the development of industry. Where labour was appropriated through institutional arrangements other than a free labour marked – for example through the rules of serfdom – industry could not develop.

However, the contemporary perspective on how the 'industrious disposition' and the shift towards more marked, co-ordinated organisation of production came about differs to some extent from de Vries's. In his view changes in taste resulted in an increased demand for marked supplied goods. This is based on the assumption that these goods were of higher quality and therefore more desirable. In this paradigm, the choice to acquire goods on the market rather than to rely on self-sufficient production led to a reduction of leisure time. The buyers needed to sell increasing amounts of labour time in order to buy the desired products. Essentially, de Vries sees the 'industrious revolution' as a result of household decisions to consume more refined market supplied goods.[3]

This differs from eighteenth-century perspectives in four important respects. First, there was a strong contemporary concern with the association of an increased consumption of luxury goods and the development of industry. However, the increasing desire for market supplied luxury goods was seen as limited to certain segments of society. Madame du Châtelet wrote about rich and worldly people who stimulated industry with their consumption. In Voltaire's poem *The Worldling* it is at a 'bourgeois table' where the luxury goods are consumed. Throughout Voltaire's writings the monarch's consumption of luxury goods emerges as the strongest stimulus for industry. Similarly, expenses of the government for streets, buildings, fountains and canals play an important role in stimulating industry. All forms of expenditure were believed to increase industry. However, the political decisions – often associated to the ministry of Colbert – about public spending on projects that developed industry were at the centre of contemporary explanations for the rise of industry. De Vries's concentration on the consumption of private household might therefore be too narrow and too wide at the same time: too narrow because it does not sufficiently take into account public spending as a source of demand for the products of industry and as an investment in infrastructure needed for the development of that sector; too wide because the constraint on household income was such that in many cases the consumption of market supplied goods could not be significantly increased even if leisure time was reduced. Additional labour time was primarily used to increase domestic production of goods of first necessity and not to generate additional income for the purchase of market supplied luxury goods. Contemporaries did not consider the consumption of lower income households to be a noteworthy stimulus for industry.

The second difference between de Vries's and contemporary perspectives lies in the reasons that bring about the 'industrious disposition' of the individual. In de Vries's paradigm, households renounce their self-sufficiency and individuals sell more of their labour in order to buy goods of higher quality. In this view it is the choice to switch to a demand pattern of superior goods that makes the individual more industrious. It has been pointed out that Voltaire's outlook on the motives that made the individual more industrious was somewhat less blissful. In his view, the 'manoeuvres' of his time did not work because they wanted to substitute inferior consumption goods with products of higher quality. Rather, they had no alternative to selling their labour. Having their arms as their only asset they were forced to work in order to survive. While Voltaire emphasised that 'this class of people' should not be miserable, he generally approved of this condition as a reliable way to create an industrious workforce.

The third aspect of de Vries's interpretation which may be questioned in the light of contemporary debates is that he focuses exclusively on the reduction of the individual's leisure time. Eighteenth-century concerns with individual industry were more comprehensive. The increase of labour time was an important concern but Voltaire's view was that the acquisition of skill and the quality of inventiveness played a central role among the dispositions of the individual. These qualities would not be developed simply because the individual wanted to consume more but also because of the systematic efforts to help and improve the level of skill of the workforce. There was great concern with the 'invisible strings' through which cultural progress and the progress among eighteenth-century writers of industry were linked. Moreover, de Vries's concentration on the reduction of leisure time does not take into consideration the contemporary concern with population growth. A greater number of industrious workers was a concern at least as prominent as the increase of the individual's working time.

Fourth, and maybe most importantly, there was stronger awareness among contemporaries that many institutional obstacles prevented individuals from selling more of their labour time. The rules of serfdom and the regulations of the guilds prevented or at least impaired the individual's ability to buy or sell labour. Voltaire and Turgot emphasised the ways in which the existing institutions were incompatible with the growth of industry. While the importance of the institutional framework and the obstacles that it posed to the growth of industry were prominent concerns in the eighteenth century they do not play a significant role in de Vries's discussion. In his argument the shift from self-sufficiency to market supplied consumption is the result of a choice of the households and occurs as a gradual and continuous transition. However, in the period that the present study has been concerned with the institutional reforms that favoured this shift – such as Turgot's ephemeral abolition of the guilds or Necker's partial abolition of serfdom – were political decisions imposed by the government. And when corporations and serfdom were completely abolished by the revolution this was the consequence of a fundamental change in the political and social order. The institutional change was most likely welcomed by the serfs and journeymen but they did not bring it about by altering their consumption habits. Even if one agrees with de Vries's view that the eighteenth century saw a process of the 'absorption into the market economy' of spheres previously governed by feudal institutions it seems necessary to emphasise that this transformation was associated to political decisions and fundamental institutional change.

A second prominent feature of the eighteenth-century debates about industry – besides the widespread concern with individuals and their interaction – was the controversy over the policies of Colbert. Did his work and that of other government administrators help or harm industry? Despite the disagreement about this issue there emerges a consensus among the contemporary commentators who have been discussed here. With the exception of Turgot they agreed that for better or for worse the origins of French industry were closely associated with Colbert's policies and the expenditure of Louis XIV. Voltaire praised industry and the minister who created it and the Physiocrats condemned both rigorously. But independently of whether the minister was thought of as famous or notorious the origins of the phenomenon industry were associated with his policies. However, the agreement that industry had in the past grown under the control of a powerful government administration did not extend to the future of industry. Arguments to remove the sector of industry from the influences of government administration can be found prominently in the writings of Pierre le Pesant de Boisguilbert and the Physiocrats. Adam Smith and Turgot shared this view and less explicitly it was also present in Angliviel de La Beaumelle's thought. Among those who believed in the continued necessity of governmental guidance in matters of industry were Charles Irénée de Castel, Abbé de Saint-Pierre, Jacques Necker and most prominently Voltaire. The latter did not only find his beliefs confirmed by his observations in Prussia but he also saw the need for government action to further the development of industry in France. The abolition of serfdom and guilds were crucial for industry and could only be implemented by a minister with the common good in mind. It was hardly probable that guild masters and feudal lords would give up their privileges voluntarily. Against their vested interests only the minister who commanded the full authority of an uncontested royal government could implement the necessary reform.

This perspective on the minister as the protector of industry against the vested interests of specific individuals or groups also explains Voltaire's simultaneous admiration for Colbert and Turgot. Turgot himself did not think highly of Colbert and today the two ministers are frequently thought of as exponents of diametrically opposed approaches to political economy. However, Voltaire compared the two ministers repeatedly and praised both for their promotion of industry.[4] For him what they had in common was that they worked for the 'general good' and against vested interests. In the *Age of Louis XIV*, Voltaire described Colbert's confrontation with the stubborn and egoistic merchant Hazon. In situations like this one, the minister defended the interest of the nation as a whole against the 'individual interest' of a merchant, a company or a city.[5] In quite a similar way, Voltaire hailed Turgot as a minister who loved justice 'as much as others love their interests'.[6] The minister's oppression of the uprisings against the liberalisation of the grain trade was similarly seen as a fight against vested interest.[7] Turgot did not shy away from changing laws that favoured the interest of a small number of guild masters over the great number of workers. If the masters and feudal lords of the 1770s were just as indignant about Turgot's reforms as the merchants of the seventeenth century were about Colbert's new legislation, that was an honour for the ministers in the eyes of Voltaire.[8] That the two ministers worked for an ungrateful population is a favourite theme in Voltaire's writings about Colbert and Turgot. The former was much hated by the population when he died in 1683 and the latter was forced out of office in 1776 by the intrigues against him.

The understanding that emerges from Voltaire's writings is that industry needed to be protected against the many personal interests who only sought their individual advantage but might harm the overall progress of industry. It would therefore be misleading to read his writings in the light of modern contrasts between Colbert and Turgot along the lines of more or less government activity in the matters of industry. For Voltaire, the duty of the government to administer the affairs of a nation in order to ensure its well-being clearly extended over matters of industry. Consequently, he was mainly interested in the question of how a minister fulfilled his duty of guiding and developing industry. Seen from this perspective Colbert's legal reforms, tariffs, subsidies, monopolies, quality controls and his hiring of foreign workers were not fundamentally different from Turgot's attempts to make new laws in order to help the growth of industry. For Voltaire, both ministers simply promoted and protected industry in different ways and at different times. It may be worthwhile to reconsider Voltaire's pragmatic perspective in which the origins and the future of industry were inseparable from the conscious political efforts to develop that sector and in which the future of industry was seen as inseparable from the political decisions that accompanied it.

De Vries concentration on the unintended consequences of changing habits of consumption is perhaps the single most important difference between his approach and the perception of many eighteenth-century authors. The creation of industry was largely ascribed to the conscious efforts of Colbert, Frederick and other administrators rather than to the unintended consequences of changing habits of consumption. However, de Vries's focus on the far-reaching consequences of changing habits of consumption is at the same time reminiscent of a prominent late eighteenth-century explanation of the rise of commercial society. When Adam Smith set out to explain how the commercial society of his times emerged from the shadows of the feudal times his approach concentrated on changing habits of consumption among the feudal lords. The lords were fascinated with the 'trinkets and bubbles' of luxury and slowly granted commercial liberty to the growing cities in exchange for payments that enabled them to acquire the items they desired. A fascination with a changing and attractive world of goods and the need for a cash income in order to consume are at the centre of both approaches. Both approaches explain different but related phenomena by emphasising unintended consequences of changing habits of consumption. However, Smith's approach – like that of Voltaire and many other contemporaries – contained a strong political element. The changing consumption habits of the feudal lords led them to take a political decision about institutional change. The impact of the institutional and political framework of economic development does not factor in de Vries's and many other modern explanations of the rise of industry. For eighteenth-century commentators the importance of institutional change for the economic transition of the period was far too important to be neglected. It is perhaps useful to reconsider this contemporary perspective in order not to neglect an important factor in the economic transition of the period.

A third noteworthy characteristic of eighteenth-century debates was that the desirability of the growth of industry was contentious. Moral and economic arguments were brought forward to prove that industry as a whole or at least certain branches of it should not expand further. This perspective differs significantly from modern approaches. Today, growth rates of industry tend to cause concern only when they are considered to be too low.

The contemporary concerns with the growth of industry reflect the dramatically changing relative importance of industry and other economic sectors. Industry was growing fast and while the contemporaries did not anticipate that it would soon become the single most important economic sector their concern was with the rapid and disproportionate growth of this sector which heralded the structural change that the 'industrial revolution' eventually brought about.

This structural change was the source of many concerns which were voiced in moral and economic terms. One concern was that the growth of industry may impoverish a nation. Today the notion that a growing industry generates wealth is generally considered to be beyond doubt. However, between Voltaire and the Physiocrats, and to some extent also between Voltaire and Saint-Pierre the issue was contentious. Another contemporary perspective on industry is unfamiliar to the modern observer in a similar way. In particular Saint-Pierre opposed the growth of certain branches of industry on moral grounds. It is noteworthy that there were at least two different sets of contemporary arguments against this position. The first and most radical was that of the Physiocrats. They argued that the sector of industry should not be submitted to moral considerations at all. The second argument against Saint-Pierre, that of Voltaire, is less radical. In his view industry was to be judged according to ethical categories. In fact, his case for industry rested to a large extent on the benign effects on culture, prosperity and peaceful coexistence that he ascribed to the phenomenon. Consequently, any form of industry that might not have such benign effects would have been much less desirable in the context of his argument. However, Voltaire argued that virtually all forms of industry led eventually to some form of benign effect on the individual. His moral approach was thus one that de facto legitimised all forms of industry and freed the growth of industry from any limitations that moral considerations might impose on it. Voltaire's unparalleled prominence during the eighteenth century makes his defence of industry as a morally benign and economically sound way of life important. His views must be seen as a contribution to the process of producing a mind-set which allowed for the unimpeded progress of industry in his time and after.

A fourth characteristic feature of eighteenth-century perspectives on industry seems to be that it was perceived as a phenomenon that transcended national borders. In particular, Voltaire emphasised the way in which industry was a universal phenomenon that could bring cultural progress and prosperity to all parts of the world. Industry also plays an important role in the competition between nations. In the description of a nation the development of industry is considered an important feature. However, even the most sterile nation can develop industry if the right political steps are undertaken. In Voltaire's view there are no nations or regions that are predestined by certain endowments or by a 'national character' to be rich or poor in industry. He visited Prussia that had been a poor country and where industry was by that time in full development and he predicted that the industry-less French Jura would become prosperous and industrious as soon as serfdom would be abolished. Industry was also perceived as a global phenomenon in the sense that the development of industry in one country was in many ways interrelated with that of other nations. The knowledge and skill that was important for the growth of industry often travelled from one country to another in the shape of migrating workers and entrepreneurs. Prussia did not only adopt policies similar to those of Colbert in order to develop 'industries' but it also imported French immigrants who brought French experience and expertise with them.

This transfer happened on different levels. Small and larger groups of French Huguenots established themselves as hat and glove makers. Families who had already worked in the mulberry plantations of Louis XIV came to raise Prussia's mulberry trees. The Frenchman chevalier de la Touche was one of the many foreigners who proposed the establishment of a trading company in Emden to Frederick II. Finally, French thinkers such as Voltaire and Mirabeau, travelled to Prussia. With them they brought views on industry that had been formed in the French context.

In Ferney, Voltaire was not only writing about French industry but also about the progress of Russia's industry. From his château close to the Swiss border, he followed the development of an investment that he had made together with partners from Hamburg, Paris and Geneva and the outcome of which was decided by events in Pondicherry and Lorient. In Voltaire's own words: 'Since approximately two and a half centuries ago all parts of the world have been united by the industry of our fathers'.[9] The phenomenon of industry did thus not begin to transcend national borders at some point in its development. Rather, it was considered a global phenomenon from early on.

That the phenomenon transcended national borders is also illustrated by the fact that many European languages have borrowed the term industry from the French language. The leading European industrial nation of the eighteenth century exported not only economic policy models, knowledge, expertise and skilled workers. It also exported the term industry as the designation for a new sector of economic activities. The development of the German term industry has been briefly discussed. It would be rewarding to trace in more detail how the term entered other languages and how it evolved in these languages. Nineteenth-century debates about industry were not only informed by eighteenth-century perspectives but also formed the context in which the concept of industry continued to evolve.

The entering of the term into the technical jargon of economists would equally warrant a closer examination. In the time immediately following the period that has been examined here political economy established itself as an academic discipline with its own terminology. In the context of this development the term industry also became part of the language of economics. It would be necessary to examine how and when the term industry came to be associated with heavy machinery, namely the steam engine. Moreover, the rise of the term industry was associated with a host of related terms such as 'manufacture', 'fabric', 'industrial' and 'proletarian'. Together with the further growth of industry during the nineteenth century a whole language developed to conceptualise the transformations that were associated with the new economic sector. As in the case of industry, the study of these terms in their historical context helps to better understand the phenomena that they describe.

Notes

Introduction

1. 'Alors a commencé une révolution dans le commerce, dans la puissance des nations, dans les mœurs, l'industrie & le gouvernement de tous les peuples'. Abbé Raynal, *Histoire philosophique et politique des établissements & du commerce des Européens dans les deux Indes* (7 vols, Amsterdam, 1770), I, p. 1. 'La raison et l'industrie feront toujours de nouveaux progrès'. Voltaire, 'Conclusion et examen de ce tableau historique' (1763), in *M*, XXIV, p. 475.
2. The question of contemporary awareness of the rise of industry and the 'industrial revolution' has been widely discussed among historians. See for example: D. McCloskey, 'The industrial revolution 1780–1860: a survey', in Joel Mokyr, ed., *The econonomics of the industrial revolution* (London, 1985), pp. 53–74. Eric Hobsbawm, *Industry and empire* (London, 1999), pp. xi-12. Colin Jones, *The great nation* (London, 2002), pp. 159–70. Joel Mokyr, 'The industrial revolution and the new economic history', in idem, *The economics of the industrial revolution,* pp. 1–51. Gareth Stedman Jones, *'Industrie', Pauperism and the Hanoverian State: the genesis and political context of the original debate about the 'Industrial Revolution' in England and France, 1815–1840,* Working paper of the Centre for History and Economics (Cambridge, 1997).
3. 'Aufklärung ist der Ausgang des Menschen aus seiner selbstverschuldeten Unmündigkeit.' Immanuel Kant, 'Beantwortung der Frage: Was ist Aufklärung', in Horst Brandt, ed., *Was ist Aufklärung* (Hamburg, 1999), p. 20. (Transl.: *Foundations of the metaphysics of moral, What is enlightenment,* Lewis White Beck, transl. (Chicago, 1949), p. 286.) 'Den Menschen die Furcht zu nehmen und sie als Herren einzusetzen'. 'Der Praxis gebieten'. Theodor Wiesengrund Adorno and Max Horkheimer, *Dialektik der Aufklärung* (Frankfurt, 2004), pp. 9, 31. (Transl.: *Dialectic of enlightenment,* Edmund Jephcott, transl. (Stanford, CA: 2002), pp. 1, 19.)
4. 'Die Mitteilung der reinen Einsicht ist deswegen einer ruhigen Ausdehnung oder dem *Verbreiten* wie eines Duftes in der widerstandslosen Atmosphäre zu vergleichen.' Georg Wilhelm Friedrich Hegel, *Phaenomenologie des Geistes* (Leiden, 1907), p. 488. (Transl.: *Phenomenology of spirit,* A.V. Miller, transl. (Oxford, 1977), p. 331.) Johann Gottfried Herder, 'Auch eine Philosophie der Geschichte zur Bildung der Menschheit' (1774), in Wolfgang Pross, ed., *Herder Werke* (2 vols, Munich, 1984), I, p. 680. The examples of censorship of Voltaire's works are legion in the eighteenth century and after. The 1752 public burning of Voltaire's *Diatribe du docteur Akakia* in Berlin marked the rupture between him and Frederick II. René Pomeau, *Voltaire en son temps* (2 vols, Paris, 1995 edn), I, p. 703. For Voltaire's works and the Transylvanian censors see Icob Mârza, 'Une liste de livres interdits en Transylvanie (seconde moitié du XVIII siècle)', in *Revue des Études Sud-Est Européennes,* 21 (1983), 177–81. Voltaire to Jean Baptiste Nicolas de Lisle, 13 Oct. 1773. D 18583. Hegel uses 'Bautz! Baradautz!' in German. Miller translates this powerful onomatopoeic

language somewhat timidly as 'bang! crash!'. Hegel, *Phaenomenologie des Geistes*, p. 489. (Transl.: *Phenomenology of spirit*, p. 332.) Marie Jean Antoine Nicolas Caritat, marquis de Condorcet, 'Avertissement des editeurs', in *K*, VL, p. 3.

5. Franco Venturi, *Utopia and reform in the Enlightenment* (Cambridge, 1971), p. 2. Peter Gay, *Voltaire's politics* (Princeton, NJ: 1959). Nannerl Keohane, *Philosophie and the state in France: the Renaissance to the Enlightenment* (Princeton, 1980). Maxine Berg and Elizabeth Eger, eds, *Luxury in the eighteenth-century: debates desires and delectable goods* (Basingstoke, 2003). Maxine Berg and Helen Clifford, eds, *Consumers and luxury: consumer culture in Europe 1650–1850* (Manchester, 1999). Albert Hischman, *The passions and the interests* (Princeton, NJ: 1977). Gareth Stedman Jones, *An end to poverty* (London, 2004). Emma Rothschild, *Economic sentiments* (Cambridge, MA: 2001). Michael Sonenscher, *Work and wages: natural law, politics, and the eighteenth-century French trades* (Cambridge, 1989).
6. François Crouzet, *De la supériorité de l'Angleterre sur la France* (Paris, 1985), p. 30. Patrick O'Brien and Caglar Keyder, *Economic growth in Britain and France 1780–1914* (London, 1978), p. 192. Denis Woronoff, *Histoire de l'industrie en France* (Paris, 1998), p. 178.
7. Jean-Jacques Rousseau, *Les Rêveries du promeneur solitaire*, Henri Roddier, ed. (Paris, 1960), p. 101.
8. Hobsbawm, *Industry and empire*, p. xi. Mokyr, 'The industrial revolution and the new economic history', p. 1.
9. Mokyr, 'Demand vs. Supply in the industrial revolution', in idem, ed., *The economics of the industrial revolution*, pp. 97–118, p. 108.
10. D. McCloskey, 'The industrial revolution, 1780–1860: a survey', in Mokyr, ed., *The economics of the industrial revolution*, pp. 53–74, pp. 54, 74. Travellers are cited in almost all studies about the growth of industry cited here. See also David Landes, *The unbound Prometheus* (Cambridge, 1969), pp. 128–29. Patrick O'Brien and Caglar Keyder, *Economic growth in Britain and France 1780–1914* (London, 1978), pp. 186–90. Stedman Jones, *'Industrie', pauperism, and the Hanoverian state*, p. 39. Hobsbawm, *Industry and empire*, p. 1. Mokyr, 'Demand vs. supply', p. 107. Joseph Schumpeter, *The history of economic analysis* (London, 1954), p. 4.
11. Jan de Vries, 'The Industrial Revolution and the Industrious Revolution', *Journal of Economic History*, 54 (1994), 249–270, pp. 254, 262.
12. On the link between enlightenment thought and Watt and his circle see Peter Jones, 'Living the enlightenment and the French Revolution: James Watt, Matthew Boulton and their sons', *Historical Journal*, 1 (1999), 157–82. 'Chefs-d'oeuvre de l'industrie'. Jean-François Marmontel, *Mémoires* (1804) (2 vols, Clermont-Ferrand, 1972), II, p. 200.
13. Francis Bacon, 'In praise of knowledge', in idem, *The works of Francis Bacon*, Basil Montagu, ed. (16 vols, London, 1825), I, p. 254. 'La raison et l'industrie feront toujours de nouveaux progrès'. Voltaire, 'Conclusion et examen de ce tableau historique', p. 475.
14. Raymond Williams, *Keywords* (London, 1988 edn), p. 165.
15. 'Spectacle imposant de la nature', 'industrie humaine', 'Dictionnaire de l'industrie', 'Dictionnaire d'histoire naturelle'. Henri-Gabriel Duchesne, *Dictionnaire de l'industrie* (6 vols, Paris, 1795), I, pp. iii, xii.

16. Lorraine Daston, *Eine kurze Geschichte der wissenschaftlichen Aufmerksamkeit* (Munich, 2001), p. 11.
17. 'Die mannigfaltigen Affinitäten zwischen Seiendem werden von der einen Beziehung zwischen sinngebendem Subjekt und sinnlosem Gegenstand, zwischen rationaler Bedeutung und zufälligem Bedeutungssträger verdrängt.' 'Inkommensurable', 'sie macht Ungleichnahmiges komparabel, indem sie es auf abstrakte Größen reduziert'. Adorno and Horkheimer, *Dialektik der Aufklärung*, pp. 13–19. (Transl.: *Dialectic of the enlightenment*, pp. 4–9.)
18. Adorno and Horheimer, *Dialektik der Aufklärung*, p. 33. (Transl.: *Dialectic of enlightenment*, p. 20.) 'Elle fertilise tout, & répand par-tout l'abondance & la vie'. Louis de Jaucourt, 'Industrie', in Denis Diderot *et al.*, eds, *Encyclopédie de Diderot et D'Alembert sur CD-ROM (conforme aux 17 volumes de l'édition originale 1751–1765)*, REDON, publ., Version 1.0.0. The article is initialled 'D.J.' for 'Chevalier de Jaucourt'. However, in the introduction, Jaucourt mentions that the article (or possibly only parts of it) are by 'M. Quesnay'.
19. Christiane Mervaud, ed., *Le siècle de Voltaire – hommage à René Pomeau* (2 vols, Oxford, 1987). 'Voltairens großes Talent ... sich in jeder Form zu kommunizieren, machte ihn für eine gewisse Zeit zum unumschränkten geistigen Herrn seiner Nation. Was er ihr anbot, mußte sie aufnehmen; kein Widerstreben half'. Johann Wolfgang von Goethe, 'Zur Farbenlehre' (1810), in Manfred Wenzel, ed., *Goethe Werke* (40 vols, Frankfurt on Main, 1991), XXIII, p. 869. Herder, 'Auch eine Philosophie', p. 680. 'La vie de Voltaire doit être l'histoire ... du pouvoir qu'il a exercé sur les opinions de son siècle'. Marie Jean Antoine Nicolas Caritat, marquis de Condorcet, 'La vie de Voltaire', in *K*, LXX, p. 2. Adam Smith, 'Letter to the Edinburgh Review' (1756), in W. Wightman, ed., *Adam Smith – essays on philosophical subjects* (Indianapolis, 1981), p. 254. 'Traité d'économie politique'. Philippe Steiner, 'J.-B. Say and the political economy of his time: a quantitative approach', *Journal of the History of Economic Thought*, 21 (1999), 349–68, p. 360.
20. Émile Littré, *Dictionnaire de la langue Française* (7 vols, Paris, 1957), IV, p. 935. Venturi, *Utopia*, p. 3. Venturi reminds the reader of an ironic passage by Herder: 'Mit welchem Vergnügen lesen wir einzelne dichterische Erzählungen, vom Ursprung einzelner Dinge, den ersten Schiffer, den ersten Kuß, den ersten Garten, den ersten Todten, das erste Kameel, die erste Schöpfung des Weibes und andre Erdichtungen, in denen die Poeten unserer Sprache noch so sparsam sind'. Johann Gottfried Herder, 'Versuch einer Geschichte der lyrischen Dichtkunst' (1764), Bernhard Suphan, ed., *Sämtliche Werke – Johann Gottfried Herder* (33 vols, Berlin, 1877), XXXII, p. 85. In Venturi's translation the quote ends after 'Kameel'.
21. 'Virgile français'. René Pomeau, 'Introduction', in *OH*, p. 7. René Pomeau, *Voltaire en son temps* (2 vols, Oxford, 1995), I, p. 107. Henri Lagrave, 'Finances', in Jean Goulement *et al.*, eds, *Inventaire Voltaire* (Paris, 1995), p. 548.
22. Gustave Flaubert, 'Dictionnaire des idées reçues', in idem, *Bouvard et Pécuchet* (Paris, 1966), p. 378. 'Il serait intéressant de rechercher dans l'œuvre de Voltaire l'apparition d'industrie dans l'acceptation moderne.' Pomeau, *Voltaire en son temps*, I, p. 937.
23. John Simpson *et al.*, eds, *The Compact Oxford English Dictionary* (Oxford, 1989), p. 899.

1 Industry in Voltaire's Time

1. Michael Sonenscher, *Work and wages, natural law, politics and the eighteenth-century French trades* (Cambridge, 1989), p. 375.
2. Jan de Vries, 'The Industrial Revolution and the Industrious Revolution', *Journal of Economic History*, 54 (1994), 249–70, pp. 254–8, 265. Adam Smith, *An inquiry into the nature and the causes of the wealth of nations* (1776), R.H. Campbell, ed. (2 vols, Indianapolis, 1981), I, p. 421.
3. See the chapter 'Definitions and historiography of retardation', in Patrick O'Brien and Caglar Keyder, *Economic growth in Britain and France 1780–1914* (London, 1978), pp. 15–25. Some of the key contributions to the re-evalution of French industrialisation were by François Crouzet, 'Angleterre et France au XVIIIe siècle: essai d'une analyse comparée de deux croissances économiques', *Annales d'Histoire Économique et Sociale*, 21 (1966), 254–91. Nicholas Crafts, 'Industrial revolution in England and France: some thoughts on the question "Why was England first?" ', *Economic History Review*, 30 (1977), 429–41.
4. O'Brien and Keyder, *Economic growth*, p. 192, 21, 198. The quality of their data is discussed in almost all reviews of O'Brian's and Keyder's work. See the reviews of Malcolm Falkus in *Economic Journal*, 89 (1979), 449–51, p. 451; Charles Freedman in *American Historical Review*, 84 (1979), 1359–60, p. 1360; Paul Hohenberg in *Journal of Economic Literature*, 18 (1980), 135–7, p. 135; Richard Roehl in *Journal of Economic History*, 39 (1979), 778–9, p. 778. Charles Kindleberger, 'Economic growth in Britain and France, 1780–1914 by Patrick O'Brien and Caglar Keyder', *Economic History Review*, 32 (1979), 295–6, p. 296. David Landes, 'Some further thoughts on accident in history: a reply to Professor Crafts', *Economic History Review*, 48 (1995), 599–601, p. 601. Denis Woronoff, *Histoire de l'industrie en France* (Paris, 1998), pp. 177–81. Nicholas Crafts, 'Macroinventions, economic growth, and "industrial revolution" in Britain and France', *Economic History Review*, 48 (1995), 591–8. François Crouzet, 'The historiography of French economic growth in the nineteenth century', *Economic History Review*, 56 (2003), 215–42, p. 234.
5. Woronoff, *Histoire de l'industrie en France*, p. 177. François Crouzet, *De la supériorité de l'Angleterre sur la France* (Paris, 1985), pp. 26–30. Foreign trade is defined here as the sum of imports, exports and re-exports.
6. Woronoff, *Histoire de l'industrie en France*, pp. 627, 33, 69. Tihomir Markovitch, *Les industries lainières de Colbert à la révolution* (Paris, 1976), p. 484.
7. Crouzet, *De la supériorité*, p. 31. Woronoff, *Histoire de l'industrie en France*, p. 176. Line Teisseyre-Sallmann, *L'industrie de la soie en Bas-Languedoc XVIIe–XVIIIe siècles* (Paris, 1995), p. 204. Maurice Garden, *Lyon et les Lyonnais au XVIIIe siècle* (Paris, 1975), p. 276. Teisseyre-Sallmann, *L'industrie de la soie*, p. 223.
8. Crouzet, *De la supériorité*, p. 32. Woronoff, *Histoire de l'industrie en France*, p. 135.
9. Marcovitch, *Les industries lainières*, p. 460. Woronoff, *Histoire de l'industrie en France*, p. 72. O'Brien and Keyder, *Economic growth*, p. 177.
10. Woronoff, *Histoire de l'industrie en France*, pp. 75–6. Patrick O'Brien *et al.*, 'Political components of the Industrial Revolution: Parliament and the English cotton textile industry, 1660–1774', *Economic History Review*, 44 (1991), 395–423, p. 400. Sonenscher, *Work and wages*, p. 210–26.

11. Crouzet, *De la supériorité*, p. 42. David Landes, *The unbound Prometheus* (Cambridge, 1969), p. 41. Crouzet, *De la supériorité*, p. 35.
12. 'Je ne saurais souffrir qu'un homme qui porte un habit de drap Van-Robais ... dise du mal de Jean-Baptiste Colbert'. Voltaire to Marie de Vichy de Chamrond, marquise du Deffant, 1 Nov. 1773, D 18607. Abel Poitrineau, 'Van Robais', in François Bluche, ed., *Dictionnaire du grand siècle* (Paris, 1990), p. 1564. 'Sous nos yeux', 'tous les ouvriers rassemblés sous une même clé'. Josse Van Robais cited in Woronoff, *Histoire de l'industrie en France*, p. 93.
13. Caglar Keyder, 'State and industry in France, 1750–1914', *American Economic Review*, 75 (1985), 308–14, p. 308. 'Que l'on en accepte l'idée ou qu'on la combatte, l'industrie est une affaire d'État.' Woronoff, *Histoire de l'industrie en France*, p. 181. For the mulberry plantations and the dispute about the silk-caps see: Teisseyre-Sallmann, *L'industrie de la soie*, pp. 222, 268. For the export of silk-stockings from Nîmes see: Woronoff, *Histoire de l'industrie en France*, p. 74.
14. Patrick O'Brien, 'The political economy of British taxation, 1660–1815', *Economic History Review*, 41 (1988), 1–32.
15. Terence Hutchison, *Before Adam Smith. The emergence of political economy, 1662–1776* (Oxford, 1988), p. 295. Charles Cole, *Colbert and a century of French mercantilism* (2 vols, New York, 1939), I, p. 335. 'Alliance démagogique'. Crouzet, *De la supériorité*, p. 36. 'Dirigisme d'État'. Jean-Pierre Rioux, *La révolution industrielle* (Paris, 1971), p. 58. Landes, *Prometheus*, p. 134. 'Orphelins de Colbert'. Woronoff, *Histoire de l'industrie en France*, p. 630. Keyder, 'State', p. 308.
16. 'Rompons cette partie'. Voltaire, 'L'indiscret' (1725), in *M*, II, p. 260.
17. 'Dextérité', 'vivre d'industrie', 'vivre de finesse, de filouterie', 'chevalier d'industrie'. Académie Française, *Dictionnaire de l'Académie françoise* (2 vols, Paris, 1694), I, p. 595.
18. 'Adresse', 'vivre d'industrie', 'trouver des moïens de subsister bons ou mauvais'. Pierre Richelet, *Dictionnaire de la langue françoise ancienne et moderne* (2 vols, Paris, 1732), II, p. 41.
19. 'L'agriculture, le commerce, et l'industrie'. Voltaire, 'Remonstrances du Pays de Gex au roi' (1776), in *M*, XXX, p. 342.
20. 'Entreprises de fabrique'. Anne Robert Jacques Turgot, baron de l'Aulne, 'Réflexions sur la formation et la distribution des richesses', in Gustave Schelle, ed. *Œuvres de Turgot* (5 vols, Paris, 1914), II, p. 591.
21. Paul Heinrich Dietrich, Baron von Holbach, *La morale universelle ou les devoirs de l'homme fondés sur sa nature* (5 vols, Paris, An IV de la Republiques Française [1796]), II, p. 9. Abbé Raynal, *Histoire philosophique et politique des établissements et du commerce des Européens dans les deux Indes* (7 vols, Amsterdam, 1770), VI, p. 374. 'Et celui qui éleva le premier l'industrie sur les ruines de l'agriculture.' Denis Diderot, 'Salon de 1767', in Laurent Versini, ed., *Diderot Œuvres* (4 vols, Paris, 1996), II, p. 584. Winfried Schröder finds in his study 'Zum Bedeutungs- und Funktionswandel des Wortes "Industrie" ', (*Lendemains* (1976), 45–62) that the sectoral meaning of industry has become widely used in the period. Earlier studies on the use of the term 'industry' in the French language include: Henri Sée, 'A propos du mot "industrie" ', *Revue Historique*, 149 (1925), 58–61. 'Bulletin historique, histoire économique et sociale', *Revue Historique*, 158 (1928), 297–335, p. 326. Henri Hauser, 'Le mot

"industrie" chez Roland de la Platière', *Revue Historique*, 150 (1925), 189–93, p. 193. Paul Harsin, 'De quand date le mot "industrie" ', *Annales d'Histoire Économique et Sociale*, 2 (1930), 235–42. Kurt Baldinger, 'Einige terminologische Auswirkungen des Aufschwungs der Industrie im 18. Jahrhundert in Frankreich', in Alexander Bergengruen, ed., *Alteuropa und die moderne Gesellschaft – Festschrift für Otto Brunner* (Göttingen, 1963), 318–36. Focko Eulen, *Vom Gewerbefleiß zur Industrie* (Berlin, 1967), pp. 81–143.

22. Voltaire, *Voltaire électronique*, Voltaire Foundation and Chadwyck-Healey, publ., Version 1.0.
23. Mainly, a quantitative approach does not help to understand the sense in which the term is used in the specific context. Even more importantly, it does not indicate how prominent the term's function is in the context of the argument in which it appears. Only if it is taken into consideration in which function the term is used in each case will it be possible to make a statement about a shift of attention. A mere increase in the frequency of the use could, after all, be the result of the term's filtering into the language without reflecting any explicit concern of the author. The findings of the quantitative analysis, therefore, have to be used cautiously. A number of problems arise in the context of a quantitative analysis. In many cases publication dates are not known with precision. Many of Voltaire's writings, for example, were published clandestinely. These editions often contained false indications about the time and place of printing in order to mislead the censor. Moreover, publication dates are often only a very poor approximation for the actual period of writing. The publication dates used for the present quantitative analysis are based on Georges Bengesco's bibliography *Voltaire: bibliographie des ses œuvres* (4 vols, Paris, 1885). It needs also to be pointed out that the frequency of the word 'industry' over a period of time does not reflect the overall writing 'output' of Voltaire in that period. Between the time when he wrote his first text in 1712 and the year 1730 Voltaire used the term 'industry' only three times while he used the word 101 times in the 1750s. The difference is striking. However, his overall writing output in the second period was also significantly higher than in the first. Until 1730 he wrote 184,256 words while he wrote 1,016,663 words in the 1750s. Even considering the differences in output the increase in the use of 'industry' remains noteworthy. The use of the term 'industry' increased almost 34 times while overall output increased less than six times. It would be possible build a calibrated statistical model which takes the fluctuation of overall output into account. Such a model would have to relate the frequency of the term 'industry' to the overall number of words written in a given period. It would also be necessary to take into account the different frequency with which nouns, verbs, and other types of words appear in the language of the time. However, even a complex statistical model would not alter the inherent shortcomings of the quantitative approach. A more refined statistical model would create a misleading impression of precision without offering meaningful information. Rather than trying to refine the quantitative method the present study embeds the quantitative analysis in a thorough qualitative analysis. The limitations of a quantitative approach are even more apparent when a quantitative analysis is applied to a body of texts from more than one author. A good example is the textual base Frantext, one of the largest digital collections of

literary and other works of francophone authors from all periods. The collection is composed of writings of different authors for each year. Therefore changes in frequency of one term from one year or decade to the next can not be taken as an indication of a change of contemporary perception. Such changes are mainly the result of the specific selection of texts that were included by the editors for any specific period. Results from Frantext will therefore only be included as additional illustrations. Continuity and dynamic of the development can only be highlighted by concentrating on the writings of one particular author.

24. The work in question is the ode *La chambre de la justice* of 1716. See Adrien Beuchot's editorial note in *M*, VIII, p. 418.
25. 'Fonds de terre, du commerce et de l'industrie', Sébastien Le Prestre, marquis de Vauban, *Projet d'une dixme royale* (no place, 1707), p. 235.
26. Voltaire, 'Le temple du goût' (1733), in *M*, VIII, p. 558. Voltaire, 'Essai sur la poésie épique' (1732), in *M*, VIII, p. 318.
27. 'Industrie des Altenais'. Voltaire, 'Histoire de Charles XII' (1731), in *OH*, p. 233.
28. 'Ils n'avaient ni abondance, ni industrie, ni goût, ni propreté'. 'Les peuples sont ce que les rois ou les ministres les font être. Le courage, la force, l'industrie, tous les talents restent ensevelis, jusqu'à ce qu'il paraisse un génie qui les ressuscite.' 'La culture des terres, le commerce et l'industrie'. Voltaire, 'Observations sur MM. Jean Lass, Melon et Dutot sur le commerce, le luxe et les impôts' (1738), in *M*, XXII, pp. 362–4, 368.
29. 'Dextérité', 'travail', 'commerce', 'savoir faire'. Académie Française, *Dictionnaire de l'Académie françoise* (2 vols, Paris, 1740), I, p. 926.
30. 'Industrie se dit aussi des arts mécaniques et des manufactures en général'. Académie Française, *Dictionnaire de l'Académie françoise* (2 vols, Paris, 1835), II, p. 30.
31. 'Par raillerie', 'en plaisant'. Académie Française, *Dictionnaire de l'Académie françoise* (1740 edn), I, p. 926.
32. The reader must bear in mind that the findings from this database have to be taken with a grain of salt. The database is composed of texts from different writers for every year and a change in frequency is as much due to the arbitrary selection of the editors as it may be to a change in the use of the term by the contemporaries.
33. Laurent Versini, 'Introduction', in Charles de Secondat, baron de la Brède et de Montesquieu, *De l'Esprit des Lois* (1748) (2 vols, Paris, 1995), I, p. 37. Nicole Ferrier-Caverivière, *Le grand roi à l'aube des lumières, 1715–1751* (Paris, 1985), p. 129.
34. Ibid. 'Progrès de l'esprit humain' 'industrie nouvelle' Voltaire, 'Le siècle de Louis XIV' (1751), in *OH*, pp. 1021, 983, 963–97, 616.
35. 'Le commerce et l'industrie n'ont pu former qu'avec le temps cet état mitoyen qui fait la richesse d'une nation'. Voltaire, 'Essai sur les mœurs' (1753), in *M*, XII, p. 56.

    'L'état est un arbre, les racines sont l'agriculture, le tronc est la population, les branches sont l'industrie, les feuilles sont le commerce'. Victor de Riqueti, marquis de Mirabeau, *L'Ami des hommes ou traité de la population* (7 vols, La Haye, 1758), II, p. 10. Voltaire, 'Essai sur les mœurs' (1753), in *M*, XII, pp. 56, 486. 'Nulle industrie ne secondait ... les présents de la nature'. Ibid., XIII, p. 34; XII, p. 221. 'La raison et l'industrie feront toujours de nouveaux progrès'. Voltaire, 'Conclusion et examen de ce tableau historique' (1763), in *M*, XXIV, p. 475.

36. The distinction between 'industrie' and 'commerce' can be found in many passages. For example: Voltaire, 'Siècle', pp. 983, 1143. Voltaire, 'Essai', in *M*, XII, pp. 22, 56. Voltaire distinguishes the 'produit des terres, du commerce, et de l'industrie' in his 'Des embellissements de Paris' (1749), in *M*, XXIII, p. 301. 'Leur industrie'. Voltaire, 'Siècle', p. 759. 'L'esprit de commerce, d'industrie, d'économie s'est communiqué de proche en proche.' Voltaire, 'Essai', in *M*, XIII, p. 122. 'L'esprit de commerce et d'industrie'. Charles de Secondat, baron de la Brède et de Montesquieu, 'De l'esprit des lois' (1748), in Daniel Oster, ed. *Œuvres complètes Montesquieu* (Paris, 1964), p. 697. 'Le vice-amiral d'Estrées et son lieutenant Martel', writes Voltaire in the *Siècle*, 'firent honneur à l'industrie militaire de la nation française dans trois batailles navales consécutives', 'soins de Colbert'. Voltaire, 'Siècle', p. 725.
37. Harsin, 'Industrie', p. 237.

2 Voltaire, Prussia and Industry

1. 'Picnic spots'. *Berlinische Nachrichten von staats- und gelehrten Sachen*, lxxix (2 July 1750), not paginated. 'Preussische Asiatische Handlungscompagnie'. Ibid., lxxxi (7 July 1750), not paginated. 'Perpetuum mobile'. Ibid., cxlvii (8 Dec. 1750), not paginated. 'Esprit des lois'. Ibid., lxxxxi (30 July 1750), not paginated. 'Den 10ten dieses Monats ist der königl. Französische Cammer Juncker, und Geschichtsschreiber, Herr von Voltaire, aus Paris bey Sr. Majestät dem Könige zu Potsdam angelanget.' Ibid., lxxxv (16 July 1750), not paginated.
2. Martin Fontius, *Voltaire in Berlin* (Berlin, 1966). Hans Jaeck, *Kammerherr und König, Voltaire in Preussen* (Berlin, 1987). Reinhold Koser, *König Friedrich der Große* (2 vols, Stuttgart, 1893), I, pp. 514–27. Christiane Mervaud, *Voltaire et Frederick II* (Oxford, 1985). René Pomeau, *Voltaire en son temps* (2 vols, Paris, 1995 edn), I, pp. 613–748. Theodor Schieder, *Friedrich der Große* (Frankfurt on Main, 1983), pp. 437–65.
3. Frederick called Gabrielle-Émilie Le Tonnelier de Breteuil, marquise du Châtelet-Lomont 'divine Émilie' in a poem of 24 Oct. 1737. The original draft in Frederick's hand is in the Prussian archives. Frederick II, king of Prussia, 'A la divine Émilie', 24 Oct. 1734, Geheimes Staatsarchiv Preußischer Kulturbesitz, Berlin-Dahlem (GStA PK), Brandenburgisch-Preußisches Hausarchiv (BPH), Rep. 47, F I B Spez. 3, 14, not paginated. It has been edited in J.-D.-E. Preuss, ed., *Les œuvres de Frederick le Grand* (10 vols, Berlin, 1849), VIII, pp. 22–4.
4. For the street name see 'Police report on Voltaire', 1751, D app. 112. The editors at Voltaire Foundation chose English titles for the documents in the appendices of the *Les œuvres complètes de Voltaire* (Geneva, 1968–).
5. 'Mme du Châtelet's inventory', part IV, 7 Oct. 1749, D app. 93.
6. 'Salles', 'chambres', 'antichambres', 'vieux parapluye', 'lustre emaillé à six Branches', 'sept différentes figures pagodas de La Chine', 'huit fauteuils de bois doré ... couverts de Damas', 'deux perroquets de verre garnis en cuivre doré', 'verni façon de Chine', 'Venus fouettant l'amour'. Ibid.

7. 'Carrosse', 'nouvelle invention', 'seigneurs', 'riches citoyens'. Denis Diderot, 'Carrosse', in Denis Diderot *et al.*, ed., *Encyclopédie de Diderot et D'Alembert sur CD-ROM (conforme aux 17 volumes de l'édition originale 1751–1765)*, REDON, publ., Version 1.0.0.
8. 'S'il se faisait transporter ... c'était dans une charrette; et moi, je me fais porter dans une carrosse commode et agréable'. 'Il n'a pas fallu plus d'argent dans le royaume pour suspendre sur des cuirs une caisse de bois peinte, il n'a fallu que de l'industrie'. Voltaire, 'Dialogue entre un philosophe et un contrôleur général des finances' (1751), in *M*, XXXIII, p. 503.
9. 'Je suis riche, et même très riche pour un homme de lettres'. Voltaire to Frederick II, king of Prussia, 8 May 1750, D 4139. 'Mme du Châtelet's inventory', part VI ('Etat des Dettes auxquelles M. Le Marquis est obligé soit en son nom, soit solidairement avec Madame'), 7 Oct. 1749, D app. 93.
10. 'Carroissier', 'bourreliers', 'charron', 'serruriers', 'bijoutier', 'dentelle', 'épicier', 'soyerie', 'marchande de mode', 'emailleur', 'ébéniste', 'lapidaire', 'instruments de mathématique', 'parfumeur', 'orloger', 'serinette', 'tabletier', 'sculpteur'.
11. 'Propagation du feu', 'institutions de physique'. Gabrielle-Émilie Le Tonnelier de Breteuil, marquise du Châtelet-Lomont, *Dissertation sur la nature et la propagation du feu* (Paris, 1744). Gabrielle-Émilie Le Tonnelier de Breteuil, marquise du Châtelet-Lomont, *Institutions de physique* (Paris, 1740).
12. 'Une aisance devenüe trop ordinaire pour estre remarquée'. 'L'industrie ... de tout un peuple'. Gabrielle-Émilie Le Tonnelier de Breteuil, marquise du Châtelet-Lomont, 'Préface du traducteur' (1735), Ira Wade, ed., *Studies on Voltaire with some unpublished papers of Mme du Châtelet* (Princeton, 1947), pp. 141–2.
13. 'Honnête homme'. 'Entrez chez lui: la foule des beaux-arts,/Enfants du goût, se montre à vos regards./De mille mains l'éclatante industrie/De ces dehors orna la symétrie'. 'Il leur manquait l'industrie et l'aisance'. Voltaire, 'Le Mondain' (1736), in *M*, X, pp. 85–6, 84.
14. 'Rome sauvée' Pomeau, *Voltaire en son temps*, I, pp. 622–4.
15. 'Romains, j'aime la gloire'. Marie Jean Antoine Nicolas Caritat, marquis de Condorcet, 'Avertissement des éditeurs' in *K*, IV, p. 169.
16. Jan de Vries, 'The Industrial Revolution and the Industrious Revolution', *Journal of Economic History*, 54 (1994), 249–70, pp. 254–8.
17. Michael Sonenscher, *Work and wages, natural law, politics and the eighteenth-century French trades* (Cambridge, 1989), p. 210.
18. Voltaire to Johann Peter von Räsfeld, 8 June 1750, D 4155.
19. Voltaire to Anne Louise Bénédicte de Bourbon-Condé, duchesse Du Maine, 24 June 1750, D 4161.
20. Voltaire to Frederick II, king of Prussia, 26 June 1750, D 4166.
21. 'Roi très chrétien'. Pomeau, *Voltaire en son temps*, I, p. 626.
22. 'Français, Anglais, Germains, aujourd'hui si tranquilles/Fallait il s'égorger pour être si bons amis?' Voltaire to Marie Louise Denis, 9 June 1750, D 4169. It should be noted that after his break with Frederick II Voltaire rewrote some of the letters which he had written to his niece. The originals are lost. However, the manipulated letters principally concern the break with Frederick. They were redrafted largely on the original letter texts and it seems that Voltaire only changed certain points that were relevant to his relationship with Frederick while passages not related to that relationship remained unaltered. See André Magnan, *Dossier Voltaire en Prusse* (Oxford, 1986).

23. 'Il n'y a guerre d'affluence a Clèves'. Voltaire to Marie Louise Denis, 9 July 1750, D 4169.
24. 'Sire, quel chien de pays la Vestphalie'. Voltaire to Frederick II, king of Prussia, 20 July 1750, D 4173.
25. 'J'ai traversé les vastes et tristes et stériles et détestables campagnes de la Westphalie'. 'Animaux qu'on appelle hommes', 'grandes huttes qu'on appelle maisons', 'une certaine pierre dure, noire, et gluante'. Voltaire to Marie Louise Denis, 24 July 1750, D 4175.
26. Voltaire, 'Candide' (1759), in *M*, XXI, p. 138.
27. 'Ces hommes du premier temps sont sains, vigoureux et gais.' Voltaire to Marie Louise Denis, 24 July 1750, D 4175.
28. 'Ce n'est pas que je les envie; / J'aime fort nos lambris dorées, / Je bénis l'heureuse industrie / Par qui nous furent préparés / Cent plaisirs par moi célébrés.' Ibid. The poem is part of the letter to Madame Denis.
29. 'Age d'or', 'age de fer'. Voltaire, 'Le Mondain', p. 84.
30. 'Attendant que je sois assez heureux pour en partir'. Voltaire to Frederick II, king of Prussia, 20 July 1750, D 4173.
31. 'Excellent avec du beurre'. Charles de Secondat, baron de la Brède et de Montesquieu, 'Voyages en Europe – Allemagne' (1729), in Daniel Oster, ed., *Œuvres complètes Montesquieu* (Paris, 1964), pp. 320–1.
32. Frederick, crown prince of Prussia to Voltaire, 24 July 1738, D 1564.
33. Fritz Hartung, 'Der preußische Staat und seine westlichen Provinzen', in Franz Petri, ed., *Westfälische Forschungen 7* (Münster, 1953), 5–13, p. 8.
34. 'Rescript an die Mindensche Cammer zum 20 Janr. wegen Beförderung der Fabriquen in dortigen Provintzien', 1746, GStA PK, II HA, Abt. 17, Titel LXXXV, 2, p. 6.
35. Gustav Schmoller, *Preußische Verfassungs-, Verwaltungs-, und Finanzgeschichte* (Berlin, 1921), pp. 142–4.
36. 'Der Mindener Cammer allerunterthänigster Bericht wegen dem fehlen von Manufacturen und Handwerkern', 21 March 1750, GStA PK, II HA, Titel LXXXV, 2, p. 12.
37. 'Designatio von den Kaufleuten und Fabricanten im Fürstentum Minden', 1765, GStA PK, II HA, Abt. 17, Titel LXXXV, 2, Gen.-Dir. Minden-Ravensberg, p. 119.
38. See the more detailed reports for Ostfriesland. 'Alphabetische General Tabelle von allen in den Städten und Flecken der Fürstenthümer Ostfriesland befindlichen Kaufleuten, Künstler und Handwerkern Pro Anno 1749', 1749, GStA PK, II HA, Abt. 21, LXXXIII, 3, not paginated. For the capital Berlin and Potsdam, 'General Designation', 31 July 1753, GStA PK, I HA, Rep. 96, Nr. 421 B, p. 51.
39. 'Neu revidierter Accise Tarif für die Mindischen und Ravensbergischen Städte', 28 Jan. 1749, GStA PK, II HA, Abt. 24, Gen. Akzise/Zolldept. B XII, Titel XVIII Nr. 2., pp. 7–14.
40. 'Cœmedianten', 'Vieh Handelung', 'Nutz-Holz'. Ibid., p. 31.
41. 'Aufmunterung der Fabriquen und Manufacturen'. 'Extract aus dem Rescript an die Mindensche Cammer vom 4. December', 1764, GStA PK, II HA, Abt. 17, LXXXV, 2, p. 102.
42. 'Wo die Musen nicht gern zu wohnen pflegen'. *Berlinische Nachrichten*, cxxii (18 Oct. 1751), not paginated.

43. Honoré Gabriel Riqueti, comte de Mirabeau, *Histoire secrète de la cour de Berlin ou correspondance d'un voyageur François depuis le mois de Juillet 1786 jusqu'au 19 janvier 1787* (2 vols, London, 1789), I, pp. 88, 94.
44. 'Trop gouverner', 'science du despotisme', 'extraordinairement phlegmatique', 'rudesse', 'ignorance', 'les mœurs y sont réellement bizarres'. Honoré Gabriel Riqueti, comte de Mirabeau, *De la monarchie Prussienne* (4 vols, London, 1788), I, pp. 75, 434.
45. In a very similar vein Montesquieu remarks about industry in Catholic countries: 'Quant aux pays catholiques, non seulement la culture des terres y est abandonnée, mais même l'industrie y est pernicieuse: elle ne consiste qu'à apprendre cinque ou six mots d'une langue morte.' Charles de Secondat, baron de la Brède et de Montesquieu, 'Lettres Persanes' (1748), in Daniel Oster, ed., *Œuvres complètes Montesquieu* (Paris, 1964), p. 124.
46. Jan de Vries, *Economy of Europe in an age of crisis 1600–1750* (Cambridge, 1976), p. 105.
47. 'Genre', 'il faut que Frédérick ait été frappé de l'industrie du petit peuple de Ravensberg.' Ibid., II, p. 136; I, p. 435.
48. Albert Hömberg, *Westfälische Landesgeschichte* (Münster, 1967), pp. 276–82.
49. The commonly used German terms are 'Manufacturen', 'Fabriquen', 'Handwerker', and 'Künstler'.
50. 'J'ay passé par le purgatoire', 'le ciel'. Voltaire to Charles Augustin Feriol, comte d'Argental, 24 July 1750, D 4174.
51. The diary entitled 'Tagebuch aus Friedrichs des Großen Regentenleben' was compiled by Karl Rödenbeck in 1840. About the authorship of the diary, and for later additions to it see Hans Droysen, 'Tageskalender Friedrichs des Großen', *Forschungen zur brandenburgischen und preußischen Geschichte*, 29 (1916), 95–157.
52. 'Heute Voltaire aus Paris in Potsd. an.' Karl Rödenbeck, 'Tagebuch aus Friedrichs des Großen Regentenleben', 1840, GStA PK, BPH, Rep. 47, F III Nr. 5, p. 2.
53. The secondary literature about Voltaire contains descriptions of the city of Berlin at the time of Voltaire's arrival. However, Voltaire's specific experiences with the progress of arts and culture in the first days of his stay are not discussed in detail. See Pomeau's description of Berlin in 1750 in *Voltaire en son temps*, pp. 632–44.
54. Rödenbeck, 'Tagebuch aus Friedrichs des Großen Regentenleben', p. 4.
55. Voltaire to Charles Augustin Feriol, comte d'Argental, 24 July 1750, D 4174.
56. 'Il Conte immaginario'. Voltaire to Marie Louise Denis, 22 Aug. 1750, D 4193.
57. Martin Wörner, *Architekturführer Berlin* (Berlin, 2001), building no. 37.
58. 'Cela ressemble à un temple de la Grèce et on y joue des ouvrages tartares.' Voltaire to Marie Louise Denis, 22 Aug. 1750, D 4193.
59. Le Chaussier to Frederick II, king of Prussia, 15 Oct. 1743, GStA PK, I HA, Rep. 96, Nr. 401 T, p. 8.
60. Voltaire, 'L'homme aux quarante écus' (1768), in *M*, XXI, p. 313.
61. 'Amoureux Mylord Anglois', 'presents considérables'. Lieutnant General Comte de Dohna to Frederick II, king of Prussia, 29 April 1744, GStA PK, I HA, Rep. 96, Nr. 401 T, p. 12.
62. 'Ce bougie ... illume mal', 'je ne fais rien'. Frederick's marginalia on Pöllnitz to Frederick II, king of Prussia, n.d., GStA PK, HA VI, Nl. Pöllnitz, Nr. 6, not paginated.

63. Wörner, *Architekturführer*, building nos. 38, 41.
64. 'Pour les Bâtiments'. 'Disposition générale sur tous les revenus de l'État', 1743, GStA PK, I HA, Rep. 96, Nr. 404 A, not paginated.
65. 'Enfin me voici dans ce séjour autrefois sauvage, et qui est aujourduy aussi embelli par les arts qu'annobli par la gloire'. Voltaire to Charles Auguste de Feriol, comte d'Argental, 24 July 1750, D 4174.
66. Voltaire to Charles Auguste de Feriol, comte d'Argental, 28 Aug. 1750, D 4201. Rödenbeck, 'Tagebuch aus Friedrichs des Großen Regentenleben', p. 3. *Berlinische Nachrichten*, lxxxv (16 July 1750), not paginated. 'Musique guerrière'. Voltaire to Charles Auguste de Feriol, comte d'Argental, 28 Aug. 1750, D 4201.
67. 'C'est le pays des fées.' Ibid. The poem does not seem to feature in any of the editions of Voltaire's works. Therefore one is left with the German translation that the paper printed: 'Niemahls ist zu Athen, und Rohm, so was geschehn,/ Als man beym Caroussel hat in Berlin gesehn,/Indem der Ritter Pracht und That dem Paris gleichte,/Weshalb die Venus auch den guldnen Apfel reichte'. In the poem Voltaire writes that Athens and Rome never witnessed a spectacle similar to that of the 'caroussel' in Berlin. The splendour and the actions of the knights were similar to that of Paris. Therefore, Venus presented them with the golden apple. *Berlinische Nachrichten*, cx (12 Sept. 1750), not paginated. 'C'est le séjour suprême', 'vos beaux yeux'. Ibid., cxi (15 Sept. 1750), not paginated. 'Kammerherr M. de Voltaire', 'geistreich', 'vorsichtig'. Ibid., cxiv (22 Sept. 1750), not paginated.
68. Voltaire to Henri Lamer, d'Herbigny, marquis de Thibouville, 1 Aug. 1750, D 4178. 'Frederic le grand est plus grand que Louis 14.' Voltaire to Charles Auguste de Feriol, comte d'Argental, 28 Aug. 1750, D 4201.
69. Claudia Schröder, *'Siècle de Frédéric' und 'Zeitalter der Aufklärung': Epochenbegriff im geschichtlichen Selbstverständnis der Aufklärung* (Berlin, 2002), pp. 1–17. Cited in: Jochen Schlobach, 'Du siècle de Louis au siècle de Frédéric?' in Christiane Mervaud, ed., *Le siècle de Voltaire – hommage à René Pomeau* (2 vols, Oxford, 1987), II, 831–46, p. 832. Voltaire to Claude Etienne Darget, April 1751, D 4442. Schröder, *'Siècle de Frédéric' und 'Zeitalter der Aufklärung'*, pp. 23–46.
70. Voltaire, 'Essai sur les mœurs' (1753), in *M*, XII, p. 145. The year 1753 is given as the date of publication in the Moland edition. However, the remark about the 'carrouzel' of Catherine II might have been inserted into a later edition. Catherine was crowned only in 1762 but she had moved from Germany to Russia after she had been chosen to become the wife of Peter III in 1744.
71. 'L'art des jardins', 'on établit ... quatre boutiques, remplies de ce que l'industrie des ouvriers de Paris avait produit de plus riche et de plus recherché.' Voltaire, 'Le siècle de Louis XIV' (1751), in *OH*, pp. 931, 1220, 931–2.
72. 'Une espèce de passion', 'comble d'erreur'. Mirabeau, *Monarchie Prussienne*, I, p. 128.
73. 'Plats revendeurs de carottes', 'insupportable engeance', 'exscremens'. Frederick II, king of Prussia, 'Epître contre messieurs de la finance', n.d., GStA PK, BPH, Rep. 47, FI B Spec. 3, 78, p. 4. The poem was later published as 'Épitre contre messieurs les Écornifleurs', in J.-D.-E. Preuss, ed., *Les œuvres de Frederick le Grand* (10 vols, Berlin, 1849), VIII, pp. 22–4.

74. 'Frederick II a tout tenté pour encourager l'industrie; ce fut un des principaux des son administration.' Mirabeau, *Monarchie Prussienne*, I, p. 116. 'La puissance de la Prusse n'est point fondée sur une force intrinsèque, mais uniquement sur l'industrie.' Frederick II, king of Prussia, 'Testament politique' (1752), in Gustav Volz, ed., *Die politischen Testamente Friedrich's des Grossen* (sic) (Berlin, 1920), p. 4.
75. Voltaire mentions that he was reading Frederick's *Mémoires pour servir à l'histoire de Brandenbourg* in several letters. Voltaire to Louis Armand François Du Plessis, duc de Richelieu, 31 Aug. 1750, D 4206. According to Magnan the letter dates from 1751. Magnan, *Dossier*, p. 154. Voltaire to Marie Louise Denis, 28 Oct. 1750, D 4251. Voltaire to Frederick II, king of Prussia, June/July 1751, D 4510. 'Des mœurs, des coutumes, de l'industrie, des progrès de l'esprit humain dans les arts et dans les sciences', 'la naissance de l'industrie', 'les causes qui l'ont développé', 'une connoissance parfaite d'un état', 'les politiques & les philosophes'. Frederick II, king of Prussia, *Mémoires pour servir à l'histoire de Brandenbourg* (Berlin, 1750), pp. 201–3. Voltaire to Louis Armand François Du Plessis, duc de Richelieu, 31 Aug. 1750, D 4206. 'J'aime un peu ce grand-père parce qu'il était magnifique et qu'il a laissé de beaux monuments.' Voltaire to Marie Louise Denis, 28 Oct. 1750, D 4251. 'Cela est net, élégant, précis, et surtout philosophique!' 'Mœurs', 'gouvernement', 'religion'. Voltaire to Frederick II, king of Prussia, June/July 1751, D 4510.
76. R. Harris, *Absolutism and enlightenment* (London, 1964), pp. 1–9, 174. Wilhelm Treue, *Wirtschafts- und Technikgeschichte Preussens* (Berlin, 1984), pp. 51–6.
77. Stefi Jersch-Wenzel, *Juden und 'Franzosen' in der Wirtschaft des Raumes Berlin/Brandenburg* (Berlin, 1978), p. 89. Hans-Ulrich Wehler, *Deutsche Gesellschaftsgeschichte* (3 vols, Munich, 1987), I, p. 84.
78. Treue, *Wirtschafts- und Technikgeschichte Preussens*, p. 67.
79. Hermann Kellenbenz, *Deutsche Wirtschaftsgeschichte* (2 vols, Munich, 1977), pp. 340, 306–8.
80. Harris, *Absolutism and enlightenment*, pp. 182–4. Wolfram Fischer and Adelheid Simsch, 'Industrialisierung in Preussen. Eine staatliche Veranstaltung?', in Werner Süß, ed., *Übergänge – Zeitgeschichte zwischen Utopie und Machbarkeit* (Berlin, 1989), pp. 107, 114.
81. Notably the German historical school around Gustav Schmoller emphasised the benign role of the Prussian state. Gustav Schmoller, *Umrisse und Untersuchungen zur Verfassungs-, Verwaltungs-, und Wirtschaftsgeschichte* (Leipzig, 1898), pp. 56–9, 557–61. See also Gustav Schmoller, *The Mercantile system*, W.J. Ashley, ed. (New York, 1896), pp. 87–90. Also later scholars, most prominently William Henderson, agreed with this view of Prussian economic development. William Henderson, *Studies in the economic policy of Frederick the Great* (London, 1963), pp. 159–65. Against this perspective, Richard Tilly argued in 1980 that the involvement of the Prussian state mainly hampered economic development by interfering with private initiative. Richard Tilly, *Kapital, Staat und sozialer Protest in der deutschen Industrialisierung* (Göttingen, 1980), pp. 15–77.
82. Fischer and Simsch, 'Industrialisierung in Preussen. Eine staatliche Veranstaltung?', pp. 109–13.

83. 'Ajoutez à cela que nous allons avoir une compagnie des Indes.' Voltaire to Charles Auguste de Feriol, comte d'Argental, 28 Aug. 1750, D 4201. 'Tributaire de l'industrie hollandaise'. Voltaire, 'Siècle', p. 965. 'Industrie des négociants'. Voltaire, 'Essai', in *M*, XI, p. 181. 'Ces marchandises de l'Inde, devenues nécessaires'. Voltaire, 'Siècle', p. 965.
84. 'Acta betr. die Asiatische Handelscompagnie in Emden', 1753, GStA PK, I HA, Rep. 96, Nr. 423 D, p. 13. 'Nécessaire a la consommation du peuple du nord'. 'Mémoire', n.d. but clearly of 1750, GStA PK, I HA, Rep. 68, E Nr. 16 J 1, p. 74.
85. Sébastien Longchamp, 'Mémoires', in Sébastien Longchamp *et al.*, ed., *Mémoires sur Voltaire* (2 vols, Paris, 1826), II, pp. 334–6. 'Voltaire in account with Laleu', 1754, D app. 137.
86. Schmoller, *The Mercantile System*, p. 87. 'Louis XIV, qui allait à la gloire et à l'avantage de sa nation par toutes les routes fonda, en 1664, par les soins de l'immortel Colbert, une compagnie des Indes puissante.' Voltaire, 'Fragments sur quelques révolutions dans l'Inde' (1773), in *M*, XXIX, p. 89. 'Partisans de l'ancienne économie timide, ignorante, et resserrée'. Voltaire, 'Siècle', S. 965. Note that 'économie' was at the time used in the sense of 'thriftiness'.
87. 'Les projets les plus vastes'. Hop, Dutch envoy to Hanover, to anonymous, 25 Aug. 1750, London, Public Records Office (PRO), Secretaries of State: State papers foreign, France, 1577–1780, SP78/237, p. 22–5. Newcastle to Albermarle, 3/14 Sept. 1750, PRO, Secretaries of State: State papers foreign, France, 1577–1780, SP78/237, p. 20–2. 'Staats- und gelehrte Zeitung des hamburgischen unpatheyischen Correspondenten, no. 1777 (Nov. 1750)', Geheimes Staatsarchiv Preußischer Kulturbesitz (GStA PK), Berlin-Dahlem, I HA, Rep. 68, E Nr. 16 J 1, p. 116. Voltaire to Charles Auguste de Feriol, comte d'Argental, 28 Aug. 1750, in *Les œuvres complètes de Voltaire*, Voltaire Foundation, ed. (135 vols, Geneva, 1968–), Letter no. D 4201.
88. Klaus Weber, *Deutsche Kaufleute im Atlantikhandel 1680–1830: Unternehmen und Familien in Hamburg Cadiz und Bordeaux* (Munich, 2004).
89. Bernard Bailyn 'The idea of Atlantic History', *Itinerario*, 1 (1996), pp. 19–44, p. 33. David Hancock, 'The British Atlantic World co-ordination, complexity, and the emergence of an Atlantic market economy, 1651–1815', *Itinerario*, 2 (1999), pp 107–26, p. 118.
90. William O'Reilly, 'Genealogies of Atlantic history', *Atlantic Studies*, I, 1 (2004), pp. 66–84, p. 81.
91. 'Les secrets les plus cachés du commerce'. 'Avis des conseillers commissaires de l'Amirauté concernant quelques considérations sur ce qui a été traité pour rétablir la décadence du commerce des Païs bas', 9 Aug. 1751, GStA PK, I HA, Rep. 96, Friedrich II Politic, Fach 76, Lit. B, not paginated. Concession granted by the King of Prussia to La Touche, for establishing a trading company at Emden, 1 Sept. 1750, PRO, Secretaries of State: State papers foreign, France, 1577–1780, S78/237. Hop to anonymous, 25 Aug. 1750, PRO, Secretaries of State: State papers foreign, France, 1577–1780, SP78/237, pp. 22–3.
92. Johannes-Hendrik Sonntag, *Die preußische Wirtschaftspolitik in Ostfriesland 1744–1806/1813–1815 unter besonderer Berücksichtigung der Stadt Emden und des Emsverkehrs* (Aurich, 1987), pp. 20–6.
93. Ammon to Frederick II, king of Prussia, 16 Jan. 1748, GStA PK, I HA, Rep. 68, E Nr. 16 J 1, p. 32. Ammon to Frederick II, king of Prussia, 23 Jan. 1748, I HA, Rep. 68, E Nr. 16 J 1, p. 35. Frederick II, king of Prussia, to Ammon, 1 Feb.

1748, I HA, Rep. 68, E Nr. 16 J 1, p. 38. Ammon to Frederick II, king of Prussia, 23 Jan 1748, I HA, Rep. 68, E Nr. 16 J 1, p. 35. Proposals by the following merchants are contained in 'Acta betr. die Einrichtung einer Asiatischen Compagnie in Embden', GStA PK, I HA, Rep. 68, E Nr. 16 J 1: Pedro Slayer from Antwerp (18 April 1744, pp. 4–7), Borgers from Emden and Berlin (27 Nov. 1744, p. 10), Abbé Mercenati (19 Oct. 1746, p. 18), Hieronimus Jogues (15 Dec. 1747, pp. 25–42), Heinrich Thomas Stuart (6 Aug.1750, pp. 58–62), Chevalier de la Touche (30 Aug. 1750, pp. 84–104), Capitaine de Ruvyuer (20 Nov. 1750, p. 135). A proposal of 21 Nov. 1753 by a certain Harris is contained in 'Acta Auswärtiges Departement', GStA PK, I HA, Rep. 68, E Nr. 16 J 2, p. 10. A proposal of a merchant Buzaglo of 28 Dec. 1756 is in 'Vorschläge des Burzaglo und des d'Andibert Caillé betr. Handel mit Marocco 1756–1794', I HA, Rep. 11 Nr. 179, 4, pp. 2–22.

94. Heinrich Thomas Stuart received a privilege for the trade with Canton on 4 Aug. 1750. 'Octroi', 4 Aug. 1750, GStA PK, I HA, Rep. 68, E Nr. 16 J 1, p. 61. Keith to Manstein, 17 Jan. 1752, I HA, Rep. 96, Nr. 423 F, p. 19. 'En fin englouti par les Indes', 'peu capable de se défendre', 'exactement', 'cent millions d'écus'. 'Mémoire touchant une expedition à Bengal', n.d. but probably part of Keith's letter of 17 Jan. 1752, I HA, Rep. 96, Nr. 423 F, pp. 21–7. 'J'avoue que je tombois de mon haut quand il vint a m'expliquer le moien de les avoir.' Keith to Manstein, 17 Jan. 1752, I HA, Rep. 96, Nr. 423 F, p. 19. 'Un rien', 'ce ne sont que des chimères toutes pures'. 'Vorschläge des Burzaglo und des d'Andibert Caillé betr. Handel mit Marocco 1756–1794', I HA, Rep. 11 Nr. 179, 4, pp. 2–22. Frederick II, king of Prussia to Hertzberg, 4 Feb. 1764, I HA, Rep. 11 Nr. 179, 4, p. 22.

95. Albermarle to Newcastle, 22/23 Oct. 1750, PRO, Secretaries of State: State papers foreign, France, 1577–1780, SP78/237, p. 105.

96. 'Mémoire', n.d. but probably of 1750, GStA PK, I HA, Rep. 68, E Nr. 16 J 1, p. 72–9.

97. 'Sur le tapis'. Hop to anonymous, 25 Aug. 1750, PRO, Secretaries of State: State papers foreign, France, 1577–1780, SP78/237, p. 22.

98. Newcastle to Albermarle, 3/14 Sept. 1750, PRO, Secretaries of State: State papers foreign, France, 1577–1780, SP78/237, p. 20.

99. Albermarle to Bedford, 10/21 Sept. 1750; Albermarle to Bedford, 5/16 Sept. 1750, Albermarle to Newcastle, 13/24 Sept. 1750, PRO, Secretaries of State: State papers foreign, France, 1577–1780, SP78/237.

100. Newcastle to Harrington, 19 July 1745, PRO, Secretaries of State: state papers domestic, George II, SP36/66, not paginated. Bedford to York, 20 March 1748/49, PRO, Secretaries of State: State papers foreign, France, 1577–1780, SP78/232, not paginated.

101. Frederick also gave a charter to a Bengalische Handelkompangie but its operations never fully developed. Sonntag, *Die preußische Wirtschaftspolitik*, pp. 274–93.

102. 'Preußische Asiatische Kompagnie in Emden nach Canton in China'. Hop to anonymous, 25 Aug. 1750, PRO, Secretaries of State: State papers foreign, France, 1577–1780, SP78/237, p. 22.

103. 'Ausführliche Nachricht von der octroyrten königlichen Preußischen Asiatischen Kompagnie in Emden nach Canton in China', GStA PK, I HA, Rep. 96, 423 B, p. 104.

104. 'Das erste Schiff: die König von Preußen' and 'Burg von Emden', GStA PK, I HA, Rep. 96, 423 B, pp. 100–2.
105. 'Quelque compagnie étrangère'. For the participation of Dutch merchant capital in other trade companies see Emmer and Klooster, 'The Dutch Atlantic', p. 64.
106. 'Gagnant leur subsitence par quelque fabrique, trafic ou metier', 'la felicité de nôtre Republique', 'c'est a nous principalement qu'on en veut'.
107. Harris to Forbes, 3/14 March 1752, GStA PK, I HA, Rep. 96, Nr. 423 F, p. 28. 'Ausführliche Nachricht von der octroyrten königlichen Preußischen Asiatischen Kompagnie in Emden nach Canton in China', GStA PK, I HA, Rep. 96, 423 B, p. 110. *Berlinische Nachrichten*, xliv (11 April 1752), not paginated.
108. 'Les voisins sont interessés à veiller avec soin aux nouvautés qu'on pourroit entreprendre'. Hop to anonymous, 25 Aug. 1750, PRO, Secretaries of State: State papers foreign, France, 1577–1780, SP78/237, p. 22.
109. 'Lebens-Strafe', 'ehe man sie öffnet'. 'Publicandum wegen der zu Rouon in Frankreich grassierenden Pest' (sic), 30 Jan. 1754, GStA PK, II HA, Abt. 21, Ostfr. LXI, Nr. 1, not paginated.
110. Frederick II, king of Prussia, to the magistrate of Emden, 30 Jan. 1754; 'Antwort auf des Rescriptum vom 24 Januar wegen Pest in Rouen', 24 Feb. 1754; 'Extrait de la depeche de Sr Michel à Londres', 22 Jan. 1754; GStA PK, II HA, Abt. 21, Ostfr. LXI, Nr. 1, not paginated.
111. There had been previous attempts to establish overseas trading companies in Prussia by the Great Elector. However, the projects did not result in the establishment of a sustainable oceanic trade. Viktor Ring, *Die asiatischen handelscompagnien Friederichs des Großen* (Berlin, 1890), pp. 1–44.
112. 'Ce projet peut devenir très important, s'il se réalise.' Frederick II, king of Prussia, 'Testament politique' (1752), in Gustav Volz, ed., *Die politischen Testamente Friedrich's des Grossen* (sic) (Berlin, 1920), p. 25. Sonntag, *Die preußische Wirtschaftspolitik*, p. 286.
113. Ring, Die Handelskompagnien, pp. 45–57. 'Ce grand commerce [n'est] pas à nôtre portée'. Frederick II, king of Prussia, 'Testament politique' (1768), in Volz, ed., *Die politischen Testamente*, p. 123. 'Avis des conseillers commissaires de l'Amirauté concernant quelques considérations sur ce qui a été traité pour rétablir la décadence du commerce des Païs bas', 9 Aug. 1751, GStA PK, I HA, Rep. 96, Friedrich II Politic, Fach 76, Lit. B, not paginated. 'Tous les memoires et eclaircissemens necessaire pour cet effet'. Hop to anonymous, 25 Aug. 1750, PRO, Secretaries of State: State papers foreign, France, 1577–1780, SP78/237, p. 23.
114. 'Au moindre choc', 'le pavillon de nôtre Province paroisse souvent dans le Mediterranée'. 'Avis des conseillers commissaires de l'Amirauté concernant quelques considerations sur ce qui a été traité pour retablir la décadence des Païs bas', 9 Aug. 1751, GStA PK, I HA, Rep. 96, Friedrich II Politic, Fach 76, Lit B, not paginated. 'Le Roy a voulu faire voir qu'il étoit en Etat de soutenir le commerce aussi bien que les anglois qui pretendent que la France n'a plus de vaisseaux', 'le principal sujet de notre mission [est] de se faire voir aux cotes etrangers'. 'Copie d'une lettre de Lisbonne d'un officier de l'Escadron de France', July 1750; 'Copie d'une lettre d'un officier François de l'Escadron de M Macnamara à Alicante', 14 Sept. 1750, PRO, Secretaries of State: State

papers foreign, France, 1577–1780, SP78/237. 'La Prusse est une puissance de terre ferme il lui faut une bonne armée et point de flotte.' Frederick II, 'Testament politique' (1768), p. 123. Ibid., p. 126.

115. 'Ces drogues des Indes'. Frederick II, 'Testament politique' (1752), p. 19–20. Hans-Ulrich Wehler, *Deutsche Gesellschaftsgeschichte* (3 vols, Munich, 1987), I, p. 84.
116. 'Cette compagnie sera utile pour faciliter et augmenter nos exportations en draps, étoffes de laine, ambre, toile et porcelaine.' Frederick II, 'Testament politique' (1768), pp. 125–6. 'Manufactures et fabriques'. 'Avis des conseillers commissaires de l'Amirauté concernant quelques considérations sur ce qui a été traité pour rétablir la décadence du commerce des Païs bas', 9 Aug. 1751, GStA PK, I HA, Rep. 96, Friedrich II Politic, Fach 76, Lit. B, not paginated.
117. 'Nous avons à Berlin des vers à soye et des beaux esprits transplantez.' Voltaire to Jacques Bagieu, 19 Dec. 1753, D 5117.
118. Francesco Algarotti, *Il newtonianismo per le dame* (Milan, 1739).
119. 'Une industrie nouvelle'. Voltaire, 'Siècle', p. 968. 'Pierre de Barry inspecteur des pépinières & plantages des Meuriers en Languedoc pour le Roi Louis XIV.' C. de Mareschall to Frederick II, king of Prussia, 18 Nov. 1747, GStA PK, I HA, Rep. 9, JJ 12c, Packet 1, 1690–1765, not paginated. Henderson, *Studies on the economic policy of Frederick the Great*, p. 23. Jersch-Wenzel, *Juden und 'Franzosen' in der Wirtschaft des Raumes Berlin/Brandenburg*, p. 261.
120. 'Edict wegen Anlegung der Plantagen von Maulbeer Bäumen', 12 Nov. 1742, GStA PK, I HA, Rep. 9, JJ 12c, Packet 1, 1690–1765, not paginated. 'Edict daß niemand sich unterstehen soll, die Maulbeer-Bäume zu beschädigen', 15 Dec. 1746, GStA PK, I HA, Rep. 9, JJ 12c, Packet 1, 1690–1765, not paginated.
121. Voltaire, 'Siècle', p. 967. Mirabeau, *De la monarchie Prussienne*, III, pp. 114–45. Schmoller, *The Mercantile System*, p. 86.
122. The elector Frederick III was the later Frederick I, king *in* Prussia. It was only under Frederick II that the Hohenzollerns became kings *of* Prussia. 'Toutes les personnes éclairées et informées de ce qui se passe, conviennent que les pays sont fleurissans, lorsqu'outre les productions de la nature il y a du travail et de l'industrie'. Leibniz Archiv Hannover (LA), Leibniz Handschriften (LH), untitled, n.d., LXXXIV, p. 197. The content suggests that it was written before the academy had been founded in 1700. For this dissertation, the microfilm of the manuscript has been consulted in the Leibniz Archive. The text has been edited in Onno Klopp, ed., *Die Werke Leibniz* (11 vols, Hannover, 1877) X, p. 21.
123. 'Se sont évertué', 'rendre les jeunes gens laborieux et industrieux', 'ce qui regarde les manufactures et le commerce', 'enfin on auroit encore pour objet les arts, les sciences, les experiences et les etudes', 'les commodités et les ornemens de la vie commune'. LA, LH, untitled, n.d., LXXXIV, pp. 197–8.
124. 'Die Praxis mit der Theorie zu verbinden und neben den Künsten und Wissenschaften und durch sie alles, was das Land und Volk interessiert, Ackerbau, Industrie, Handel, Lebensmittel zu verbessern'. Dietrich Hilger, 'Industrie, Gewerbe – III. Die Freisetzung des Industriebegriffs aus dem Bezugsfeld von traditioneller Ökonomik und praktischer Philosophie', in Reinhart Koselleck *et al.*, eds, *Geschichtliche Grundbegriffe* (8 vols, Stuttgart,

1982), III, p. 251. Focko Eulen, *Vom Gewerbefleiß zur Industrie* (Berlin, 1967), p. 29.
125. Christian Bartholmèss, *Histoire philosophique de l'Académie de Prusse* (2 vols, Paris, 1850). Anonymous, *Denkschrift der königlichen Akademie gemeinnütziger Wissenschaften in Erfurt* (Erfurt, 1854). Anonymous, *Denkschrift*, p. lxxxvi.
126. Bartholmèss, *Histoire*, I, p. 22. Gottfried Wilhelm Leibniz, 'Denkschrift über die Errichtung einer Churfürstlichen Societät der Wissenschaften', G. Guhrauer, ed., *Leibniz deutsche Schriften* (2 vols, Berlin, 1840), II, p. 268.
127. See the privilege granted by queen Sophie Charlotte and related documents. Sophie Charlotte, queen in Prussia, to Leibniz, 8 Jan. 1703, LA, LH, XIX, p. 111.
128. 'Cabanes de bois et de plâtre', 'palais somptueux'. Voltaire, 'Essai', in *M*, XII, p. 244.
129. 'Ertötender Druck'. Friedrich Engels, 'Die Lage der arbeitenden Klasse in England' (1845), in Institut für Marxismus-Leninismus der SED, ed., *Marx Engels Werke*, II, p. 647. Oscar Wilde, *Phrases and philosophies for the use of the young* (London, 1894), p. 7.
130. Henderson, *Studies in the economic policy of Frederick the Great*, p. 36.
131. Marie Jean Antoine Nicolas Caritat, marquis de Condorcet, 'La vie de Voltaire', in *K*, LXX, p. 77.
132. 'Siècle le plus éclairé qui fut jamais'. Voltaire, 'Siècle', p. 616. Voltaire, 'Lettre à Milord Hervey' (1740), in *OH*, p. 611.

3 A European Debate about Colbert

1. Adam Smith, *An inquiry into the nature and the causes of the wealth of nations* (1776), R.H. Campbell, ed., (2 vols, Indianapolis, 1981), I, p. 467.
2. For the history of the phrase 'laissez-faire' see Oncken, *Die Maxime laissez-faire et laissez passer*.
3. R. Harris, *Absolutism and enlightenment* (London, 1964), p. 80. Lionel Rothkrug, *Opposition to Louis XIV* (Princeton, NJ: 1965), pp. 86–111, 175–211. 'Peuple insensé'. Voltaire, 'Le siècle de Louis XIV' (1751), in *OH*, p. 983. 'Réformateurs'. Joseph Spengler, 'Boisguilbert's economic views vis-à-vis those of contemporary réformateurs', in Marc Blaug, ed., *Pre-classical economists* (Aldershot, 1991), 88–107, p. 88.
4. 'J'ai porté la vue sur ce que [Colbert] a fait de mémorable ... non sur la manière dont il mettait son rabat'. Voltaire, 'Supplément au Siècle de Louis XIV' (1753), in *OH*, p. 1256. The only character trait of Colbert that the reader is told about by Voltaire is, in fact, a negative one. Colbert is criticised for his behaviour vis-à-vis his rival Nicolas Fouquet. Voltaire, 'Siècle', p. 900. Fouquet was minister of finance until 1661. The splendour of his castle which offended the king, together with the denunciations of Colbert led to his imprisonment for life in 1664.
5. 'Homme au masque de fer', 'Colbert ... fit naître l'industrie en France'. Voltaire to Pierre Joseph Laurent, 6 Dec. 1771, D 17496.
6. 'Cet homme qui fit naître tant d'abondance en ranimant tant d'industries'. Voltaire, 'Éloge funèbre des officiers qui sont morts dans la guerre de 1741' (1748), in *M*, XXIII, p. 250.

7. Nicole Ferrier-Caverivière, *Le grand roi à l'aube des lumières, 1715–1751* (Paris, 1985), pp. 98–104. Letter cited in Georges Bengesco, *Voltaire, bibliographie de ses œuvres* (4 vols, Paris, 1882), I, p. 341.
8. René Pomeau, *Voltaire en son temps* (2 vols, Paris, 1995 edn), I, p. 660. Voltaire to Marie Louise Denis, 28 Oct. 1750, D 4251. Voltaire to Marie Louise Denis, 26 Dec. 1750, D 4307.

   Marc Serge Rivière, 'Contemporary reactions to the early editions of Le siècle de Louis XIV', *Studies on Voltaire and the eighteenth century*, 266 (1989), 225–52, pp. 226–30.

   'Encouragement', 'example'. Voltaire, 'Fragment sur l'histoire générale' (1773), in *M*, XXIX, p. 258. Voltaire, 'Siècle', p. 616.
9. 'Cabale pour rabaisser tout ce qui a fait la gloire de ces temps mémorables'. Voltaire to Baron de Faugères, 3 May 1776, D 20103.
10. 'Objet bien dégoûtant'. Voltaire, 'Les cabales' (1772), in *M*, X, p. 180. Voltaire, 'Diatribe à l'auteur des Éphémérides' (1775), in *M*, XXIX, p. 386.
11. Bengesco, *Voltaire, bibliographie de ses œuvres*, I, pp. 340–7. Frederick II, king of Prussia to Voltaire, 25 Feb. 1752, D 4819. Adam Smith, 'Letter to the Edinburgh Review' (1756), in W. Wightman, ed., *Adam Smith – Essays on philosophical subjects* (Indianapolis, IN: 1981), p. 247. Mornet points out that this finding is all the more significant since the owners of private libraries in this period tended to be biased against Voltaire. Daniel Mornet, 'Les enseignements des bibliothèques privées (1750–1780)', *Revue d'histoire littéraire de la France*, 17 (1910), 448–96, pp. 460, 466.
12. Frederick II, king of Prussia to Voltaire, 25 Feb. 1752, D 4819.
13. 'Un Bois-Guillebert'. Voltaire, 'Siècle', p. 983.
14. Pierre le Pesant de Boisguilbert, *La France ruinée sous le règne de Louis XIV. Par qui et comment* (Cologne, 1696). The text of this tract is largely identical to Boisguilbert's *Détail de la France*.
15. 'Brûlé à petit feu'. Pierre le Pesant de Boisguilbert, 'Factum de la France' (1707), in Eugène Daire, ed., *Économistes-Financiers du XVIIIe siècle* (Paris, 1843), p. 315.
16. 'J'ai la clef de toute sorte d'industrie'. Pierre le Pesant de Boisguilbert to Nicolas Desmaretz, 16 Feb. 1713, in Jacqueline Hecht, ed., *Boisguilbert ou la naissance de l'économie politique (correspondance, œuvres imprimés et manuscrits)* (2 vols, Paris, 1966), I, p. 473. In an attempt at a psychological approach to Boisguilbert, Jacqueline Hecht sees the overly self-confident expressions of Boisguilbert as a symptom of his 'névrose'. Jacqueline Hecht, 'Pour une interprétation psychanalytique de Boisguilbert', in Jacqueline Hecht, ed., *Boisguilbert parmi nous* (Paris, 1989), 331–45, pp. 344–5.
17. Pierre le Pesant de Boisguilbert, 'Factum de la France' (1707), Hecht, ed., *Boisguilbert ou la naissance*, II, p. 881. For Boisguilbert's family relation to Pierre Corneille see the genealogy included in Hecht's *Boisguilbert parmi nous*, not paginated. René Pomeau, 'Introduction', in *OH*, p. 7.
18. 'Rien n'était ... plus faux', 'c'était précisément le contraire'. Voltaire, 'Siècle', p. 983.
19. 'Vigueur', 'corps de l'État', 'langueur'. Ibid. 'Ce Bois-Guillebert avait une grande connaissance des finances du royaume'. Voltaire, 'Dictionnaire philosophique' (1764), in *M*, XVII, p. 82. It does not seem necessary to reproduce the great number of less favourable comments of Voltaire. One example

from the poem *Les Cabales* may suffice: 'Assez de grands esprits, dans leur troisième étage,/N'ayant pu gouverner leur femme et leur ménage,/Se sont mis, par plaisir, à régir l'univers./Sans quitter leur grenier, ils traversent les mers;/Ils raniment l'État, le peuplent, l'enrichissent:/Leurs marchands de papiers sont les seuls qui gémissent'. That Boisguilbert is targeted here, is made clear in a footnote by Voltaire. Voltaire, 'Les cabales', p. 180.

20. 'La passion de critiquer toutes les opérations du grand Colbert l'emporta trop loin.' Voltaire, 'Dictionnaire', in *M*, XVII, p. 82.
21. Voltaire blames the policies of the post-Colbert era for the economic crisis: 'depuis la guerre de 1689 jusqu'à la fin de 1769, où nous écrivons, on a fait presque sans discontinuation tout ce qu'on a pu pour ruiner la France. ... C'est un bon corps qui a eu la fièvre pendant quatre-vingts ans ... et qui a été entre les mains des charlatans, mais qui vivra'. Voltaire, 'Dictionnaire', in *M*, XVII, p. 358. The other reason for the economic problems of France were, according to Voltaire, the wars of Louis XIV. He blames the powerful minister of war and enemy of Colbert, François Michel Le Tellier, marquis de Louvois for the wars: '[Colbert] fut jeté hors de toutes ses measures par les guerres de Louis XIV'. Voltaire to Etienne Noël Damilaville, 21 Feb. 1766, D 13181. See also: Voltaire, 'Défense de Louis XIV contre l'auteur des Éphémérides' (1769) in *OH*, p. 1291. 'Les Français lui doivent certainement leur industrie et leur commerce'. Voltaire, 'Siècle', p. 983.
22. 'Depuis l'an 1663 jusqu'en 1672 chaque année de ce ministère fut marquée par l'établissement de quelque manufacture', 'ranima l'industrie', 'il travaillait pour des ingrats'. Ibid., pp. 967, 1048, 966.
23. Boisguilbert's thought will only be presented here as far as necessary to show the differences to Voltaire. There are several good analyses of Boisguilbert's views: Gilbert Faccarello, *Aux origines de l'économie politique libérale: Pierre de Boisguilbert* (Paris, 1986). Hecht, ed., *Boisguilbert ou la naissance* and *Boisguilbert parmi nous*. Hazel Roberts, *Boisguilbert, economist of the reign of Louis XIV* (New York, 1935). Joseph Schumpeter, *History of economic analysis* (London, 1954), pp. 215–18. 'Ingratitude'. Pierre le Pesant de Boisguilbert, 'Traité de la nature' (1707), in Hecht, ed., *Boisguilbert ou la naissance*, II, pp. 870–1.
24. 'La nature même, jalouse de ses opérations se venge aussitôt par un déconcertement général, du moment qu'elle voit que par un mélange étranger on se défie de ses lumières et de la sagesse de ses opérations.' Pierre le Pesant de Boisguilbert, 'Dissertation de la nature des richesses' (1707), in Hecht, ed., *Boisguilbert ou la naissance*, II, p. 992.
25. For the attribution of the phrase 'laissez-faire' to Le Gendre see August Oncken, *Die Maxime laissez-faire et laissez passer* (Bern, 1886). Boisguilbert does not mention that Le Gendre used the phrase 'laissez-faire'. Since, at Boisguilbert's time, the phrase did not have the prominence that it acquired later, he may not have paid special attention to the wording used by Le Gendre. At the same time it is possible that the phrase is wrongly attributed to Le Gendre. While Oncken's argument is plausible, it remains difficult to show the origin of the phrase conclusively. 'Et ses semblables', 'ardeur de gagner', 'intérêt personnel', 'tout irait parfaitement bien', 'intérêts indirects', 'intérêt personnel'. Boisguilbert, 'Factum' (1966 edn), p. 795.

26. Boisguilbert's condemnation of Colbert's policies are unequivocal and ubiquitous. He advertises, however, the conviction that the minister's erroneous policies did not spring from a genuinely bad character but rather from his ignorance. In a letter to the minister of finance Michel Chamillart, Boisguilbert writes: 'M. de Vaubourg ... déclara hautement que, si M. Colbert m'aurait connu, il m'aurait acheté à quelque prix que ce fût, par la grande pratique que j'avais du commerce et du labourage'. Pierre le Pesant de Boisguilbert to Michel Chamillart, 27 Oct. 1703, in Hecht, ed., *Boisguilbert ou la naissance*, I, p. 295. Vaubourg was a nephew of Colbert.
27. 'L'intérêt particulier fascine les yeux et rétrécit l'esprit', 'vous avez trouvé la voiture renversée d'un côté, et vous l'avez renversée de l'autre', 'grossier', 'bien général', 'esprit philosophique'. Voltaire, 'Siècle', pp. 966–7.
28. Abraham Nicolas Amelot de la Hossaie, *Mémoires historiques, politiques, critiques, et littéraires* (2 vols, Amsterdam, 1722), II, pp. 99–104.
29. B.H. Latrobe, *Characteristic anecdotes and miscellaneous authentic papers tending to illustrate the character of Frederic II* (London, 1788), p. 129. Ernst Pfeiffer, *Die Revuereisen Friedrich des Großen besonders die schlesischen nach 1763* (Berlin, 1904), pp. 169–71. 'Pour la facilité du commerce'. Frederick II, king of Prussia to Voltaire, 24 Oct. 1773, D 18597. Note that Voltaire regarded the 'canal du Languedoc' as the greatest achievement of Colbert. Voltaire, 'Siècle', p. 971.
30. William Henderson, *Studies in the economic policy of Frederick the Great* (London, 1963), p. xi.
31. 'Ce n'est qu'à la pointe de l'épée que la justice se maintient dans ces rencontres; c'est néanmoins de quoi la nature et la Providence se sont chargées', 'opulence', 'pourvue qu'on laisse faire la nature'. Boisguilbert, 'Factum' (1966 edn), p. 891. Boisguilbert uses the terms 'nature' and 'Providence' interchangeably: 'la nature, ... n'est autre chose que la Providence'. Boisguilbert, 'Traité', p. 869.
32. 'Il n'y a point de nature, ... tout est art', 'Y a-t-il un Théos?', 'fabricateur', 'ouvrier', 'un assemblage de choses qui existent', 'un mot inventé pour signifier l'universalité des choses'. Voltaire, 'Dialogues d'Évhémère' (1777), in *M*, XXX, p. 471. The statement is made by the dialogue character Évhémère who represents Voltaire's views in this piece.
33. 'Absurde'. Voltaire, 'Lettres de Memmius a Cicéron' (1771), in *M*, XXVIII, p. 448.
34. 'Administrateur des finances'. Jacques Necker, *Éloge de Jean-Baptiste Colbert* (Paris, 1773), p. 6. Voltaire, 'Lettre à Milord Hervey' (1740), in *OH*, p. 611. 'Félicité publique'. Necker, *Éloge*, p. 6.

    'Le gouvernement de Dieu', 'administration de J.-B. Colbert'. Voltaire to Suzanne Necker, 3 Sept. 1773, D 18537.
35. 'Il réglerait', 'il dirigerait'. Frederick II, king of Prussia, 'Essai sur l'amour-propre envisagé comme principe de morale', in J.-D.-E. Preuss, ed., *Œuvres de Frédéric le Grand* (10 vols, Berlin, 1849), IX, p. 90. 'L'amour-propre bien dirigé', 'vertu', 'bonheur'. Voltaire to Frederick II, king of Prussia, 25 Jan. 1770, D 16114. Albert Hirschmann, *The passions and the interests* (Princeton, 1977), pp. 14–9.

    Voltaire, 'Remarques sur les pensées de Pascal' (1728), in *M*, XXII, p. 36. Smith, *Wealth of nations*, I, p. 27.

36. 'Industriezweige'. Karl Marx, 'Zur Kritik der politischen Ökonomie' (1859), in Institut für Marxismus-Leninismus der SED, ed., *Marx Engels Werke* (41 vols, Berlin, 1964), XIII, p. 40.
37. Smith, *Wealth of nations*, I, pp. 75–7.
38. Adam Smith, 'Letter to the Edinburgh Review', p. 247. Adam Smith, *The theory of moral sentiments* (1759), A. Macfie, ed., (Oxford, 1976), p. 54. Smith, *Wealth of nations*, II, p. 664.
39. 'Esprit qui dirige le travail', 'savez-vous qu'un ministre des finances peut faire beaucoup de bien', 'le grand Colbert'. Voltaire, 'Dialogue entre un philosophe et un contrôleur général des finances' (1751), in *M*, XXIII, p. 500.
40. 'Etre riche, c'est jouir', 'jouissance', 'réellement'. Ibid. Diderot's article 'Carrosse' in the *Encyclopédie* gives a sense of how the number of coaches was seen as an indicator of progress. In the article Diderot traces the technical development of coaches and the increase in number as an indicator of general material progress throughout French history. In a similar way Frederick II uses the diffusion of coaches as an indicator of progress in his *Mémoires pour servir a l'histoire de la maison de Brandenbourg*. 'Chênes pourrissaient autrefois dans les forêts', 'le sable restait inutile sur la terre', 'hommes laborieux', 'esprit qui dirige le travail'. Voltaire, 'Dialogue entre un philosophe et un contrôleur général des finances', p. 503. Voltaire, 'Siècle', pp. 967–8.
41. 'Il n'est pas question entre nous de politesse'. Angliviel de La Beaumelle, *Réponse au supplément au siècle de Louis XIV* (Colmar, 1754), p. 13.
42. 'Autorité souveraine'. Voltaire, 'Siècle', p. 618.
43. Angliviel de La Beaumelle, 'Footnote l', in Voltaire, *Le siècle de Louis XIV (Augmenté d'un très grand nombre de Remarques par M. de la B***)* (3 vols, Frankfurt on Main, 1753), I, p. 7. Subsequent references to La Beaumelle's edition of the *Siècle* will indicate the full title in order to differentiate this edition from the one in *OH*.
44. 'Derniers des écrivains'. Voltaire, 'Supplément', p. 1244.
45. Voltaire, 'Les honnêtetés littéraires' (1767), in *M*, XXVI, p. 133. The biographical information about La Beaumelle is based on Claude Lauriol's fundamental study *La Beaumelle – un protestant cévenol entre Montesquieu et Voltaire* (Geneva, 1978).
46. 'Apprenti ministre'. Marie Jean Antoine Nicolas Caritat, marquis de Condorcet, 'La vie de Voltaire', in *K*, LXX, p. 72.
47. Robert Shackleton, *Montesquieu – a critical biography* (Oxford, 1961), p. 365.
48. 'Magicien'. Charles de Secondat, baron de la Brède et de Montesquieu, *Lettres Persanes* (1721) (Geneva, 1954), pp. 64–9, 97–9.
49. 'Persan'. Angliviel de La Beaumelle, *Lettre de monsieur de la Beaumelle à M. de Voltaire* (London, 1763), p. 35.
50. Voltaire, 'Dictionnaire', in *M*, XVIII, p. 254.
51. Voltaire, 'Siècle', p. 611. Voltaire, 'Commentaire sur l'esprit des lois' (1777), in *M*, XXX, p. 420. While Voltaire's comments contain often stinging criticism of Montesquieu's work, it should not be forgotten that Voltaire always went to great length in order to emphasise that 'malgré ses défauts, cet ouvrage doit être toujours cher aux hommes'. Voltaire, 'L'A, B, C' (1768), in *M*, XXVII, p. 321. Voltaire's principal defence of Montesquieu is the *Remerciement sincère a un homme charitable* of 1750. In the Kehl edition,

Condorcet introduces this opuscule as follows: 'M. de Voltaire a eu constamment la générosité et le courage de défendre contre les fanatiques ceux même des philosophes ou des hommes de lettres qui s'étaient déclarés ses ennemies.' Marie Jean Antoine Nicolas Caritat, marquis de Condorcet, 'Footnote', in *K*, XXXXVI, p. 6. 'Plaidoyer'. Antoine Adam, 'Introduction', in Voltaire, *Le siècle de Louis XIV* (1751) (Paris, 1962), p. 18. 'Tableau fidèle du progrès de l'esprit humain chez les Français'. Voltaire, 'Siècle', p. 1021. '*L'Esprit des Lois* de Voltaire'. Laurent Versini, 'Introduction', in Charles de Secondat, baron de la Brède et de Montesquieu, *De l'esprit des lois* (1748) (2 vols, Paris, 1995), I, p. 37. 'Louis le Grand étoit le plus grand de tous les princes'. Montesquieu, *Lettres Persanes*, p. 330.

52. Angliviel de La Beaumelle, 'Introduction', in Voltaire, *Le siècle de Louis XIV (Augmenté d'un très grand nombre de Remarques par M. de la B***)*, I, p. xx.
53. 'Incapable de offenser personne'. Angliviel de La Beaumelle, *Mes pensées* (Paris, 1753), p. ii. That La Beaumelle's work has the same title as the 1899 edition of Montesquieu's notes seems to be a coincidence.
54. 'Peu de connoissances', 'point de goût', 'ses premiers pas furent des faux pas, ses premières choix furent ridicules, ses premières entreprises furent des fautes, & ses dernières des vexations', 'pensée CCCCXXV', 'il y eut de plus grands poètes que Voltaire; il n'y en eut jamais de si bien récompensés', 'bouffon'. Ibid., pp. 132, 269. There are, however, excellent accounts of the events in René Pomeau's Voltaire biography and in Claude Lauriol's biography of La Beaumelle. Pomeau, *Voltaire en son temps*, I, pp. 665–83. Lauriol, *La Beaumelle*, pp. 259–314.
55. Reinhold Koser discussed the authorship of the pamphlet in his 1893 article. He suggested that despite the contemporary view according to which La Beaumelle was the author of the pamphlet, Voltaire could be that author. It remains difficult to determine conclusively who the author was. The two handwritten copies of the pamphlet which were used for this study were unknown to Koser. Reinhold Koser, 'Voltaire und die "Idée de la cour de Prusse" ', *Forschungen zur brandenburgischen und preußischen Geschichte*, 6 (1893), 141–80. Anonymous, 'Kurzer Begriff von der Person und Lebensart des Königs in Preussen angefertigt von Monsieur de la Beaumelle 1752', GStA PK, BPH, Rep. 47, 164. The French version was among Voltaire's papers seized in Frankfurt by a Prussian official in 1753. The French text is dated 1752 but does not indicate the author. Anonymous, 'Idée de la Personne, de la manière de vivre, et de la cour du R. de P.', GStA PK, BPH, Rep. 47, FII.
56. Angliviel de La Beaumelle, *L'Asiatique tolérant, traité à l'usage de Zéokinizul* [Louis quinze], *roi des Kofirans* [Français] *surnommé le chéri; ouvrage traduit de l'arabe du voyageur Bekrinoll par M. de **** (Amsterdam, 1748).
57. 'Autorité souveraine', 'âge heureux', 'ultramontaines', 'barbares'. Voltaire, 'Siècle', p. 618.
58. 'Liberté fondée sur les lois', 'autorité souveraine ... affermie sans contradiction'. Ibid. La Beaumelle, 'Footnote l', p. 7. 'Puissance royale', 'le génie des Français', 'gouvernement gothique', 'sans industrie'. Voltaire, 'Siècle', pp. 618–20. It should be added that La Beaumelle found Voltaire's use of the term 'gouvernement gothic' in the sense of a backward and weak form of government quite unacceptable. He echoes Montesquieu's sympathy for the rule of the Frankish aristocracy when he commented: 'On n'entend point ce mot;

gouvernement gothique; Ce n'est sans doute ce gouvernement établi par les Goths, ce gouvernement si bien fait pour l'Europe, si propre à entendre le génie'. La Beaumelle, 'Footnote o', in Voltaire, *Le siècle de Louis XIV (Augmenté d'un très grand nombre de Remarques par M. de la B***)*, I, p. 9.

59. 'Découvertes', 'inventions'. Voltaire, 'Siècle', p. 619. 'Nations inventrices', 'constitution de ces peuples'. La Beaumelle, 'Footnote q', in Voltaire, *Le siècle de Louis XIV (Augmenté d'un très grand nombre de Remarques par M. de la B***)*, I, p. 9.
60. Voltaire, 'Siècle', p. 969.
61. 'Quatre à cinq laquais'. Christiaan Huygens, Fragment of a letter by Huygens of 1686, in Société Hollandaise des Sciences, ed., *Œuvres complètes de Christiaan Huygens* (22 vols, La Haye, 1950), IX, p. 79. Huygen's letter to his brother Lodewijk of 1673 contains not only remarks about the weather in Paris ('fort beau') but also a detailed description of the pump ('fort bien'). Christiaan Huygens to Lodewijk Huygens, 22 Sept. 1673, in Société Hollandaise des Sciences, ed., *Œuvres complètes de Christiaan Huygens*, VII, pp. 356–61. For Huygen's role in the context of the construction of Versailles and its gardens see Huygen's biography in the *Œuvres complètes de Christiaan Huygens*, XXII, pp. 266–8, 711–2.
62. Wilhelm Treue, *Wirtschafts- und Technikgeschichte Preussens* (Berlin, 1984), pp. 85–91. See also Otto Büsch, *Militärsystem und Sozialleben im alten Preussen (1713–1807)* (Berlin, 1962), pp. 51–67.
63. 'Toutes sortes de commodités','peu de besoins', 'beaucoup de besoins', 'peu de commodités', 'paresse', 'industrie et l'activité'. Charles de Secondat, baron de la Brède et de Montesquieu, 'De l'esprit des lois' (1748), in Daniel Oster, ed., *Œuvres complètes Montesquieu* (Paris, 1964), p. 659.
64. Ibid.
65. 'Industrieux et docile, savant et aimable'. Voltaire, 'Commentaire', p. 455.
66. 'Le climat fait les hommes blonds ou bruns, c'est le gouvernement qui fait leurs vertus et leurs vices.' Ibid. 'Les peuples sont ce que les rois ou les ministres les font être', 'courage', 'force', 'industrie'. Voltaire, 'Observations sur MM. Jean Lass, Melon et Dutot sur le commerce, le luxe et les impôts' (1738), in *M*, XXII, p. 362.
67. Pomeau, *Voltaire en son temps*, I, p. 703. For Schmid's position in the company see among others 'Ausführliche Nachricht von der Octroyrten königlich Preussischen Asiatischen Compagnie', 1 July 1751, GStA PK, I HA, Rep. 96, Nr. 423 B, p. 111. For his role in Voltaire's arrest: 'Ordre an Freytag und Schmid', 19 April 1753, GStA PK, BPH, Rep. 47, FII Voltairiana 8, p. 3. See also Pomeau, *Voltaire en son temps*, I, p. 727. René Pomeau, 'Présentation', in René Pomeau, ed., *La Politique de Voltaire* (Paris, 1963), p. 36.

4 How Much Industry Does a Nation Need?

1. Denis Diderot, 'Salon de 1767', in Laurent Versini, ed., *Diderot Œuvres* (4 vols., Paris, 1996), II, p. 584.
2. 'Arts mécaniques'. Jean Le Rond d'Alembert, *Discours préliminaire de l'Encyclopédie* (1751), Louis Ducros, ed. (Paris, 1893), p. 62. 'Faculté d'âme', 'productions & operations mécaniques'. Louis de Jaucourt, 'Industrie', in Denis Diderot *et al.*, ed., *Encyclopédie de Diderot et D'Alembert sur CD-ROM*

(conforme aux 17 volumes de l'édition originale 1751–1765), REDON, publ., Version 1.0.0.

3. Joseph Drouet, *L'Abbé de Saint-Pierre* (Paris, 1912), p. 41. Gustave de Molinari, *L'Abbé de Saint-Pierre* (Paris, 1857), pp. 26–9. Saint-Pierre's most prominent project was the *Projet pour rendre la paix perpétuelle en Europe*, a league of European nations for the preservation of peace. Charles Irénée de Castel, Abbé de Saint-Pierre, *Projet pour rendre la paix perpétuelle en Europe* (2 vols, Utrecht, 1713). For a discussion of the evolution of contemporary and modern perceptions of the Abbé's projects see my own: ' "Halb Philosoph und halb Verrückter" – Die Projekte des Abbés de Saint-Pierre', in Markus Krajewski, ed., *Projektemacher* (Berlin, 2004), 95–107. Louis Moréri, *Le grand dictionnaire historique* (Paris, 1759), p. 56. 'Écrivait d'une manière à ne rendre personne jaloux'. Voltaire, 'Lettres à mgr. le prince de ***' (1767), in *M*, XXVI, p. 501.
4. Voltaire, 'Le siècle de Louis XIV' (1751), p. 1203. Voltaire, 'Ce qu'on ne fait pas et ce qu'on pourrait faire' (1745), in *M*, XXIII, p. 185. Voltaire even agreed to some extent with Saint-Pierre's critique of the power hungry ministers of Louis XIV. This is probably due to the fact that the Abbé's main target was the minister of war and not Colbert. Charles Irénée de Castel, Abbé de Saint-Pierre, *Annales politiques (1658–1740)* (2 vols, London, 1758), I, p. 400. Voltaire, 'Dictionnaire philosophique' (1764), in *M*, XVIII, p. 254. The *Académie Française* did not forgive Saint-Pierre. After his death the customary 'éloge' was not read. Voltaire commented: 'Ces vaines fleurs qu'on jette sur le tombeau d'un académicien n'ajoutent rien ni à sa réputation ni à son mérite; mais le refus fut un outrage, et les services que l'abbé de Saint-Pierre avait rendus, sa probité, et sa douceur, méritaient un autre traitement'. Voltaire, 'Siècle', p. 1204. Saint-Pierre was rehabilitated by the academy in 1775.
5. 'Moitié fou et moitié filosofe'. Voltaire to Charles Augustin Feriol, comte d'Argental, 8 Sept. 1752, D 5011. Voltaire, 'Épigramme' (n.d.), in *M*, X, p. 484.
6. Jean de la Bruyère, *Les caractères* (1688) (Paris, 1999), p. 200. 'Heilige Einfalt'. Johann Gottfried Herder, 'Briefe zur Beförderung der Humanität' (1793–7), in Hans Dietrich Irmscher *et al.*, ed., *Johann Gottfried Herder Werke* (10 vols, Frankfurt on Main, 1991), VII, p. 297. Christoph Wieland, 'Geschichte des Agathon' (1766), Klaus Manger, ed., *Wieland Werke* (12 vols, Frankfurt on Main, 1986), III, p. 450.
7. Maxine Berg and Helen Clifford, 'Introduction', in idem, eds, *Consumers and luxury, consumer culture in Europe 1650–1850* (Manchester, 1999), p. 13. 'Fauteuil de poste', 'mélancolie', 'vapeurs', 'glandes du bas ventre', 'obstructions des petits canaux des glandes', 'gens d'Étude', 'Communautez Religieuses', 'ministres'. Charles Irénée de Castel, Abbé de Saint-Pierre, 'Fauteuil de poste', *Mercure de France* (Dec. 1734), pp. 2879–82, 2884. On the authorship of the article in the *Mercure* see Drouet, *L'Abbé Saint-Pierre*, pp. 96–7. Those who are seeing in the Abbé's invention an early precursor of modern gyms will be delighted by the further development of the Abbé's project. As ownership of a 'Trémoussoir' was limited to the wealthy (note that it required not only a large space but also a 'trémousseur' to operate it) Saint-Pierre made the suggestion that 'les Apothicaires et les Chirurgiens' should offer machines for public use. Ibid., p. 2881. In fact, 'Trémoussoirs' for public use were soon available. In the *Mercure* of April 1735 an 'avertissement' announced that a certain M. Duguet offered the machine for trial. For a charge of 25 *sols* per day – plus an initial

fee of three *livres* – the machine could also be rented. Anonymous, 'Avertissement', *Mercure de France,* (April 1735), p. 688. Gustave Flaubert, *Bouvard et Pécuchet* (Paris, 1966), p. 215.

8. 'Ses idées politiques n'ont pas toujours été des rêves'. Voltaire, 'Siècle', p. 1203. Voltaire to Charles Auguste Feriol, comte d'Argental, 8 Sept. 1752, D 5011. Gustav Droysen, 'Über die Schrift Anti-St Pierre und deren Verfasser', *Monatsberichte der königlichen Preussischen Akademie der Wissenschaften zu Berlin* (1878), 711–46, p. 712. 'Arbitrage Europeane'. 'Les quatre plus importantes projets politiques de M. l'Abbé de St. Pierre', n.d., Geheimes Staatsarchiv Preußischer Kulturbesitz, Berlin-Dahlem (GStA PK), Brandenburgisch-Preußisches Hausarchiv (BPH), Rep. 47, F II, Spec. 4, pp. 2–4. Gustav Droysen, 'Über die Schrift Anti-St Pierre und deren Verfasser', pp. 711–15.
9. 'Il proposait presque toujours des choses impossibles', 'rêves d'un bon citoyen', 'vues philosophiques', 'praticables'. Voltaire, 'Siècle', pp. 1203, 952. 'Il s'est rendu un peu ridicule en France par l'excès de ses bonnes intentions.' Voltaire, 'Discours en vers sur l'homme' (1734), in *M*, IX, p. 424.
10. Voltaire mentions that he was reading Saint-Pierre's work in a letter to Nicolas Claude Thieriot of 20 August 1756, D 6976. To one of the footnotes about the *Annales* Voltaire added: 'Cette note a été écrite au mois d'août 1756'. Voltaire, 'Siècle', p. 966. Voltaire does not state the date of the other footnotes. They are, however, absent in the first editions of the *Siècle* and since they equally refer to the *Annales* it is plausible that they were also added in 1756. Voltaire said about his last visit to Saint-Pierre: 'Je lui demandai, quelques jours avant sa mort comment il regardait ce passage. Il me répondit: "Comme un voyage à la campagne" '. Voltaire, 'Siècle', p. 1204. 'Fou sérieux'. Voltaire to Nicolas Claude Thieriot, 20 Aug. 1756, D 6976.
11. 'Espèce de fainéants', 'misérables successeurs de ces Romains si estimables', 'Colbert en négligeant les compagnies de commerce maritime pour avoir plus de soin des sciences curieuses et des beaux-arts, prit l'ombre pour le corps'. Saint-Pierre, *Annales*, I, pp. 184–7.
12. 'Tributaire de l'industrie hollandaise'. Voltaire, 'Siècle', pp. 965–6.
13. 'La plus opulente de républiques'. Ibid., p. 970.
14. 'Ceux qui attribuaient l'affaiblissement des sources de l'abondance aux profusions de Louis XIV dans ses bâtiments, dans les arts et dans les plaisirs, ne savaient pas qu'au contraire les dépenses qui encouragent l'industrie enrichissent un État.' Ibid., pp. 989, 968.
15. 'Une vérité palpable'. Voltaire, 'Des embellissements de Paris' (1749), in *M*, XXIII, p. 302.
16. 'Pour encourager de tous côtés l'industrie'. Voltaire to Jean Baptiste Machault d'Arnouville, 16 May 1749, D 3927. The letter was also published as a pamphlet. Voltaire, 'Lettre à l'occasion de l'impôt du vingtième' (1749), in *M*, XXXIII, pp. 305–12. 'Étouffer toute industrie'. Voltaire, 'Idées républicaines' (1762), in *M*, XXIV, p. 417.
17. 'Oisifs', 'florissant'. Voltaire, 'Ce qu'on ne fait pas et ce qu'on pourrait faire' (1742), in *M*, XXIII, pp. 185–7.
18. 'Grandeur', 'magnanimité', 'abondance', 'superflu'. Voltaire, 'Des embellissements de Paris', pp. 299–300.

19. Voltaire, 'Siècle', p. 1019. 'Mauvais usage du superflu', 'augmentation du travail'. Charles Irénée de Castel, Abbé de Saint-Pierre, *Les rêves d'un homme de bien* (Paris, 1775), p. 225.
20. Saint-Pierre, *Projet pour rendre la paix perpétuelle en Europe*, I, p. 226. 'Il [est] impossible d'avoir chez soi le superflu que par la surabondance des arts de la première nécessité'. Voltaire, 'Siècle', p. 1007.
21. 'Industrie humaine'. Ibid., p. 1220.
22. Saint-Pierre, *Annales*, I, p. 186. Charles de Secondat, baron de la Brède et de Montesquieu, 'Considérations sur les causes de la grandeur des Romains et de leur décadence' (1734), in Daniel Oster, ed., *Œuvres complètes Montesquieu* (Paris, 1964), pp. 453–4. Voltaire, 'Siècle', p. 970.
23. 'Les Sciences contribuent le plus à polir les hommes, qui les rendent plus doux, plus justes', 'citoyiens', 'raisonable', 'cete magniere de pensér'. The notes are in Frederick's own hand. The spelling is his. Frederick II, king of Prussia, untitled, 10 Aug. 1739, GStA PK, BPH, Rep. 47, FIB Spec. 3.34, p. 2. A different version of the text can be found in J.-D.-E. Preuss, ed., *Les œuvres de Frederick le Grand* (10 vols, Berlin, 1849), VIII, p. 56. The passages quoted here are only in the version in GStA PK. 'Pour les avilir'. 'Revolution générale', 'esprit', 'mœurs', 'gouvernement'. Voltaire, 'Siècle', pp. 617, 1204.
24. Voltaire, 'Dictionnaire', in *M*, XVII, p. 53.
25. 'Cultivateurs', 'manufacturiers', 'industrie', 'élévation d'âme', 'amour du bien public'. Voltaire, 'De l'horrible danger de la lecture' (1765), in *M*, XXV, p. 336. 'Culture du travail'. René Pomeau, 'Introduction', in Voltaire, *Essai sur les mœurs* (1753) (2 vols, Paris, 1963), I, p. xlviii.
26. 'Fils imperceptibles', 'industrie Françoise', esprit national', 'ouvrages d'industrie'. Jacques Necker, *Éloge de Jean-Baptiste Colbert* (Paris, 1773), p. 56.
27. 'La musique la plus savante'. Voltaire, 'Dialogue entre un philosophe et un contrôleur général des finances' (1751), in *M*, XXIII, p. 502.
28. Gareth Stedman Jones, *'Industrie', Pauperism and the Hanoverian State: the genesis and political context of the original debate about the 'Industrial Revolution' in England and France, 1815–1840*, Working paper of the Centre for History and Economics (Cambridge, 1997), p. 7.
29. Note that many of the controversies between Saint-Pierre and Voltaire informed the quarrels between Jean Jacques Rousseau and Voltaire. Saint-Pierre's views exercised a considerable influence on Rousseau. However, the exchanges between Voltaire and Rousseau will not be discussed in the present enquiry because they were not directly related to the debates about Colbert and 'industrie'.
30. Cited in Jeanne-Lydie Goré, 'Introduction', in Fenélon, *Les aventures de Télémaque* (1699) (Paris, 1987), p. 91. Gustave Flaubert, *Bouvard et Pécuchet* (1966, Paris), p. 297.
31. Fenélon, *Télémaque*, p. 521, 'Bonne mère' 195, 524, 324, 'arts nécessaires' 263.
32. 'Contagion', ibid., p. 524; 'des fournaises ardentes', 'tourbillons de fumée' 342; 'arts pernicieux' 339; 'artisans superflus' 343, 531, 355.
33. Ibid., p. 339.
34. Roger Charbonnaud, *Les idées économiques de Voltaire* (Angoulême, 1907). Simone Dailey, 'Voltaire et les physiocrates' (unpublished PhD thesis, University of Massachusetts, 1972). A. Hartig, *Großbürgerliche Aufklärung als*

Klassenversöhnung: Voltaire (West Berlin, 1972). Nuçi Kotta, *L'homme aux quarante écus: a study of Voltairean themes* (The Hague, 1966). Alicia Morris, 'A new interpretation of Voltaire's tale 'L'homme aux quarante écus' (unpublished PhD thesis, University of Massachusetts, 1978). Edward Ousselin, 'L'homme aux quarante écus: Voltaire économiste', *French Review*, 22 (1999), 493–502. Concerning the regulation of the grain trade under Colbert, Voltaire writes: 'C'est la seule tache de son ministère'. Despite Voltaire's advocacy of a less regulated grain trade, he hardly ever spoke out for a complete liberalisation. He favoured a regime 'avec des restrictions à peu près semblables à celles dont on use en Angleterre'. Voltaire, 'Siècle', p. 987. See also the article *Blé ou Bled* of 1770 in the *Dictionnaire Philosophique*. Besides certain remarks about English beer ('aussi nourrissante que dégoûtante') the article contains a description of the English system of flexible restriction and encouragement as a model for the grain trade. Voltaire, 'Dictionnaire', in *M*, XVIII, pp. 12–13. Marie Jean Antoine Nicolas Caritat, marquis de Condorcet, 'Avertissement & c.', in *K*, LV, p. 6.

35. 'Solidité des connoissances', 'vérité des inductions', 'utilité des vues', 'très digne de l'impression'. Louis (Censeur Royal), 'Approbation', *Éphémérides du citoyen*, 7 (1769), not paginated.
36. 'Garçon épicier'. *Supplément à la gazette d'Utrecht*, LXXXIII (14 Oct. 1768), not paginated.
37. 'Les productions naturelles en elles mêmes, des assortimens, des mélanges, des façons & décorations qu'elles ont reçues de l'art ou de l'industrie', 'vous sentez, Madame, en ouvrant un pâté chaud, qu'il ne faut pas confondre le Pâtissier avec le Laboureur'. Abbé Baudeau, *Explication du tableau économique à madame de *** (Extrait des Éphémérides de 1767 & 1768)* (Paris, 1776), p. 87. 'Industrie', 'objet dispendieux'. Pierre Samuel Du Pont de Nemours, 'Notes sur les Maximes', in Pierre Samuel Du Pont de Nemours, ed., *Physiocratie ou constitution naturelle du gouvernement le plus avantageux au genre humain* (Leyde, 1768), p. 136. See Georges Weulersse's chapter on 'Stérilité de l'industrie' in his *Le mouvement Physiocratique en France (de 1756 à 1770)* (2 vols, Paris, 1910), I, pp. 280–305.
38. 'Vraiment, efficacement, directement & immédiatement productif'. Baudeau, *Explication*, p. 114. Du Pont, 'Notes', p. 136. 'Les vraies richesses sont chez nous, elles sont dans notre industrie.' Voltaire to Pierre Samuel Du Pont de Nemours, 16 July 1770, D 16525.
39. 'Taxe unique'. Voltaire to François de Fargès, 25 Feb. 1776, D 19952. Bruno Racle, 'Voltaire et ses montriers', in Cercle d'études Ferneysiennes, ed., *Ferney-Voltaire* (Annecy, 1990), 207–28, pp. 210–12. Bruno Racle *et al.*, 'Voltaire entrepreneur d'horlogerie', *Bulletin de l'association nationale des collectionneurs et amateurs d'horlogerie et d'art*, 74 (1995), 5–28, pp. 6–11.
40. 'Le superflu, chose très nécessaire'. Anonymous, 'Théorie du Luxe', *Éphémérides du citoyen*, 9 (1770), 181–206, p. 196.
41. 'Dépenses stériles', 'dépenses productives'. Ibid., p. 199. 'La sureté des la propriété est le fondement essential de l'ordre économique de la societé.' François Quesnay, 'Maximes générales du gouvernement économique d'un royaume agricole', in Du Pont, ed., *Physiocratie*, p. 108.
42. 'Jouissance', 'l'injustice par essence', 'autre chose', bienfaisance'. Anonymous, 'Théorie du luxe', pp. 192–6.

43. 'Riz économique'. Anonymous, 'Riz économique', *Éphémérides du citoyen*, 3 (1769), 205–20, p. 207. In order to maximize the savings that can be realised by changing one's diet to the 'riz économique', the author gives strict instructions for the peeling of potatoes. If peeled in the wrong way 'il y auroit beaucoup de perte, comme on l'a éprouvé'. Ibid., p. 212. Fenélon, *Télémaque*, p. 339. 'Un dindon aux truffes de Ferney, tendre comme un pigeonneau, et gros comme l'évêque de Genève'. From a letter of Voltaire, cited in Christiane Mervaud, *Voltaire à table* (Paris, 1998), p. 62.
44. Weulersse, *Le mouvement Physiocratique en France (de 1756 à 1770)*, I, p. 3.
45. Quesnay, 'Maximes', p. 111. For the Physiocratic perspective on 'industrie' see also: Mr B, 'Sur la stabilité de l'ordre legal – rapports des dépenses avec l'industrie', *Éphémérides du citoyen*, 3 (1769), 3–26. François Quesnay, 'Lettre de M. N. – La productibilité du commerce et de l'industrie' (1766), in Auguste Oncken, ed., *Œuvres économiques et philosophiques de François Quesnay* (Frankfurt on Main, 1888), 444–94. 'Un ordre à la rivière de couler'. Anonymous, 'Suite & conclusion du petit traité du commerce & de la Compagnie des Indes', *Éphémérides du citoyen*, 10 (1769), 173–209, p. 178. Anonymous, 'Du commerce & de la Compagnie des Indes', in *Éphémérides du citoyen*, 8 (1769), 169–284, p. 229. Anonymous, 'Suite & conclusion', p. 180.
46. 'Sans industrie, croupissant dans leur misère', 'croupissaient dans le besoin de tous les arts, ... qui étouffait toute industrie', 'la face de son pays'. Voltaire, 'Siècle', p. 619. Voltaire, 'Histoire de Charles XII' (1732), in *OH*, pp. 69, 75.
47. 'Bonhomme Guillebert', 'notre précurseur', 'le beau siècle de la France', 'historiens'. Victor de Riqueti, marquis de Mirabeau, 'Notes inédites sur Boisguilbert par le Marquis de Mirabeau', Georges Weulersse, ed., *Revue d'histoire des doctrines économiques et sociales* (1910), 115–51, p. 118. If this remark targeted Voltaire, the dislike was mutual. Voltaire characterised 'Mr. Myrabaud' as a 'fou, qui a de beaux accès de raison'. Voltaire to Germain Gilles Richard de Ruffey, 16 Jan. 1761, D 9555. Nicole Ferrier-Caverivière, *Le grand roi à l'aube des lumières*, 1715–51 (Paris, 1985).
48. Adam Smith, *An inquiry into the nature and the causes of the wealth of nations* (1776), R.H. Campbell, ed., (2 vols, Indianapolis, 1981), I, p. 467. 'Quelques personnes ne cessent depuis plusieurs années de critiquer l'administration du célèbre Colbert'. Voltaire, 'Défense de Louis XIV contre l'auteur des Éphémérides' (1769), in *OH*, p. 1288. M.P. Alekseev *et al.*, *Bibliothèque de Voltaire: catalogue des livres* (Moscow, 1961), catalogue entry no. 2841. 'On ne oubliera jamais qu'un Ministre du dernier siècle, ébloui du commerce des Hollandois & de l'éclat des Manufactures de luxe, a jeté sa patrie dans un ... délire', 'travail des doigts'. Du Pont, 'Notes', p. 137.
49. Voltaire, 'Siècle', pp. 984, 1289.
50. 'La gloire de ce grand siècle, si cher à nos beaux esprits, était passée comme les étoupes qu'on brûle devant le pape à son exaltation.' Anonymous, 'Du commerce & de la Compagnie des Indes', p. 236.
51. 'Un esprit faux et bas, sans culture, sans goût'. Voltaire, 'Défense', pp. 1284, 1220.
52. 'Ex natura, jus, ordo & leges. Ex homine, arbitrium, regimen & coercitio.' Frontispiece of Du Pont, ed., *Physiocratie*. 'Quel usage nous devons nécessairement faire de nos facultés ... pour être aussi heureux qu'il nous est

possible'. Pierre Samuel Du Pont de Nemours, 'Discours de l'éditeur', in Du Pont, ed., *Physiocratie*, p. xiv.

53. Voltaire, 'Siècle', p. 1186. 'Molière & ses comédies si plaisantes doivent être comptés parmi les fléaux qui ont appauvri la Nation.' Pierre Samuel Du Pont de Nemours, 'Les saisons: poëme', *Éphémérides du citoyen*, 3 (1769), 133–58, p. 137. 'Laboureur', 'cabanes du pauvre'. Jean François, marquis de Saint-Lambert, *Les saisons* (Amsterdam, 1769), p. 52. 'Poësie vulgaire'. Du Pont, 'Les saisons', pp. 101, 99. Another passage that did not meet with the approval of Du Pont was Saint-Lambert's remark that 'il y a des siècles que tout ce que la saine raison pouvoit dire à l'avantage de l'Agriculture a été dit, & qu'on répète trop aujourd'hui'. Only slightly offended Du Pont replied: 'Nous croyons quant a nous, qu'il s'en faut beaucoup que *tout* ait été dit *il y a des siècles*'. Ibid., p. 91.
54. Voltaire to Pierre Samuel Du Pont de Nemours, 7 June 1769, D 15679. Voltaire's reaction is also mentioned by Weulersse. However, he does not discuss Du Pont's critique of Saint-Lambert or the disagreement between Voltaire and Du Pont. Weulersse, *Le mouvement Physiocratique en France (de 1756 à 1770)*, I, p. 197. For a more general presentation of the Physiocratic perspective on art see: Anonymous, 'Du principe commun à tous les beaux arts, & de leurs rapports avec l'utilité publique', *Éphémérides du citoyen*, 6 (1771), 42–55. René Pomeau, *Voltaire en son temps* (2 vols, Paris, 1995 edn), I, pp. 540–55.
55. 'Ces guerres, dis-je, en apparence si fatales aux arrangements économiques de Colbert, furent néanmoins son ouvrage, et la suite de sa cupidité'. Mirabeau, 'Notes inédites', p. 123. Charles Cole, *Colbert and a century of French mercantilism* (2 vols, New York, 1939), II, p. 551. Voltaire, 'Siècle', p. 771; 'Défense', p. 1291. Charles Irénée de Castel, Saint-Pierre, *Annales*, I, p. 400. Voltaire, 'Dictionnaire philosophique' (1764), in *M*, XX, p. 604. 'Honnête opulence', 'séjour de la paix et de l'industrie' 'honnête industrie', 'louable industrie', 'industrie paisible'. Voltaire, 'La guerre civile de Genève' (1768), in *M*, IX, p. 548. Voltaire, 'Lettre d'un membre du conseil de Zurich' (1767), in *M*, XXVI, p. 105. Voltaire, 'Traité sur la tolérance' (1763), in *M*, XXV, p. 108. Albert Hirschmann, *The passions and the interests* (Princeton, NJ: 1977), pp. 56–62. Gareth Stedman Jones, *'Industrie', Pauperism and the Hanoverian State: the genesis and political context of the original debate about the 'Industrial Revolution' in England and France, 1815–1840*, Working paper of the Centre for History and Economics (Cambridge, 1997), p. 8. 'L'or, l'argent, l'industrie, les talents ne sont d'aucune religion'. Voltaire, 'Idées républicaines' (1762), in *M*, XXIV, p. 418. Voltaire, 'Essai', in *M*, XII, p. 53.
56. 'Tyrannie exercé sur les âmes'. Voltaire, 'Traité sur la tolérance' (1763), in *M*, XXV, p. 108. In a similar sense, Voltaire saw 'industrie' also as a phenomenon that was able to tame even the most savage nations. If the Scots were bellicose and always ready for a raid that promised even minimal haul that was, according to Voltaire, mainly due to the lack of 'industrie' in their lands Voltaire, 'Précis du siècle de Louis XIV' (1769), in *OH*, p. 1425.
57. After several unsuccessful French attempts to create a trading company on the model of the English and Dutch companies (founded in 1600 and 1602, respectively), Colbert created the *Compagnie des Indes Orientales* in 1664. The success of the company did not meet with the minister's expectations.

In 1681 he lifted its monopoly on the East India trade and opened the trade to some extent for private merchants. However, the liberalisation did not last. His successor re-established the monopoly in 1685. The company's operation continued to be unsuccessful and it had run up ten million *livres* of debts by 1712. In 1719 the company was merged with the *Compagnie d'Occident* in order to form John Law's *Compagnie des Indes*. After the collapse of Law's system, a new *Compagnie des Indes* was founded in 1722. This company was the subject of the debates of the 1760s. Christian Huetz de Lemps, 'Compagnie des Indes Orientales', in François Bluche, ed., *Dictionnaire du grand siècle* (Paris, 1990), pp. 372–3. For a full account of the history of the Compagnie see Henry Weber, *La compagnie française des Indes (1604–1875)* (Paris, 1904). 'L'industrie raffinée du négociant'. Voltaire, 'L'homme aux quarante écus' (1768), in *M*, XXI, p. 319. 'Universe'. Voltaire, 'Défense', p. 1293.

58. 'Rentes sur la compagnie des Indes'. 'Voltaire in account with Laleu', 1754, D app. 137. Sébastien Longchamp, 'Mémoires', in Sébastien Longchamp *et al.*, eds, *Mémoires sur Voltaire* (2 vols, Paris, 1826), II, pp. 332–3.
59. 'On se doute bien avec quelle éloquence victorieuse il soutient une pareille cause'. Louis Bachaumont, *Mémoires secrètes pour servir à l'histoire de la république des lettres en France* (36 vols, London, 1788), XIX, p. 149.
60. 'Commerce des indes', 'dans ces *Éphémérides*'. Voltaire, 'Défense', pp. 1283–4. Gustave Schelle, *Du Pont de Nemours et l'école Physiocratique* (Paris, 1888), pp. 99–137. The article about the East India commerce is also listed in Schelle's bibliography of Du Pont's writings. Ibid. p. 405.
61. 'Une Puissance civile & militaire, pour administrer & défendre [ces] établissements', 'dépenses de guerre & de souveraineté', 'commerçante & souveraine'. Anonymous, 'Du commerce & de la Compagnie des Indes', pp. 184, 267, 283. See Emma Rothschild, *La mondialisation en perspective historique: l'Amérique hyper-puissance*, Working paper of the Centre for History and Economics (Cambridge, 2001) and 'Global commerce and the question of sovereignty in the eighteenth-century provinces', *Modern Intellectual History*, 1 (2004), 3–25.
62. 'Industrie du négociant', 'tributaire', 'industrie hollandaise'. Voltaire, 'Siècle', p. 965.
63. Ibid., p. 1292. 'Cadavre a deux têtes', 'conseil', 'tête', 'pouvoir souverain'. Voltaire, 'Fragments sur quelques révolutions dans l'Inde' (1773), in *M*, XXIX, pp. 126, 161–2, 157.
64. 'Je doute fort que ce commerce puisse jamais être florissant entre les mains des particuliers.' Voltaire to Pierre Samuel Du Pont de Nemours, 16 July 1770, D 16525. 'Une grande puissance souveraine'. 'Dépenses de souveraineté'. Voltaire, 'Défense', p. 1293.
65. For the history of the family and their commercial undertakings see Maurice Bérard, *Les Bérard* (Paris, 1937). Herbert Lüthy, *La banque protestante en France* (2 vols, Paris, 1961), II, pp. 439–41, 677–8. Lüthy mentions Voltaire's involvement in the venture of the *Hercule* without going into details. The enterprise is also briefly mentioned in Pomeau, *Voltaire en son temps*, II, p. 538. Voltaire to Gaspard Henry Schérer, 8 Jan. 1772, D 17546. Voltaire to François Tronchin, 15 March 1774, D 18855. 'Florian and the Hercule', May 1772, D app. 358. It may be helpful to give some references in order to understand the size of Voltaire's investment. The total cost of the expedition of the *Hercule* was of 800,000 *livres*. Lüthy, *La banque protestante*, II, p. 440.

Voltaire's share of 40,000 *livres* was thus 5 per cent of the whole investment. Voltaire's annual income at the time has been estimated at 200,000 *livres*. Henri Lagrave, 'Finances' in André Magnan *et al.*, eds, *Inventaire Voltaire* (Paris, 1995), p. 549. Consequently, his investment in the *Hercule* represented 20 per cent of his annual income.

66. Voltaire to Gaspard Henry Schérer, 16 March 1772, D 17642. Christian Huetz de Camps, 'Lorient', in François Bluche, ed., *Dictionnaire du grand siècle* (Paris, 1990), p. 892.
67. Thomas-Simon Bérard, 'Journal de voyage aux Indes', Maurice Bérard, ed., *Bulletin de la société de l'histoire du Protestantisme français*, 90 (1941), 239–62. I have tried to consult the originals of Thomas-Simon Bérard's papers. Some of his possessions have been given to the Musée de la Compagnie des Indes in Lorient by his family. However, his private papers are still in possession of the family. At the moment, however, it is not possible to consult the material. Voltaire to Suzanne Necker, 3 Sept. 1773, D 18537.
68. 'Que 5 nœuds', 'un ignorant incapable de faire du pain', 'trêve de sauces', 'une ample progéniture'. Th.-S. Bérard, 'Journal', pp. 243–5.
69. Anjouan (Nzwani) is one of the Comoro Islands. 'Mal assoisonné', 'grotesque', 'une dizaine de bouteilles vuides', 'baril de farine gâtée'. Th.-S. Bérard, 'Journal', p. 254.
70. 'On a partagé la proye. Je ne souffrirai pas cette injustice'. Voltaire to Gaspard Henry Schérer, 14 March 1774, D 18853.
71. 'Arrangement'. Voltaire to Augustin de Candolle, 16 March 1774, D 18856. Voltaire to François Tronchin, 18 March 1774, D 18861.
72. Voltaire to Henry Gaspard Schérer, 16 March 1774, D 18858. Voltaire to Jean Le Rond d'Alembert, 6 Nov. 1775, D 19729. Voltaire to Jean Baptiste Nicolas de Lisle, 27 May 1774, D 18959.
73. Voltaire to Philippe Antoine de Claris, marquis de Florian, 6 Jan. 1777. D 20505. It seems that Bérard was in reality on his way to China. Maurice Bérard, 'Introduction', in Th.-S. Bérard, 'Journal', p. 241. Voltaire to Gaspard Henry Schérer, 17 June 1777, D 20700. Voltaire to Philippe Antoine de Claris, marquis de Florian, 6 Jan. 1777, D 20505.
74. M. Bérard, *Les Bérard*, p. 26. 'Complots liberticides du tyran Capet'. M. Bérard, 'Introduction', p. 243.
75. 'Que je m'occupe en Suisse de ce qui se passe dans l'Inde'. Voltaire to Jean Baptiste Nicolas de Lisle, 13 Oct. 1773. D 18583.
76. 'Prix d'éloquence', 'éloge de Colbert'. Eugène Asse, *L'Académie Française* (Paris, 1890), pp. 134–6. 'Toutes les idées, ni toutes les expressions'. Note in Necker, *Éloge*, p. 3.
77. Voltaire to Suzanne Necker, 3 Sept. 1773, D 18537. Voltaire to Jean François de la Harpe, 2 Sept. 1773, D 18535.
78. 'Arithmétique'. Voltaire to Marie de Vichy de Chamrond, marquise du Deffant, 1 Nov. 1773, D 18607. 'Répondez aux questions que je vous fais', 'il y a [in the *Éloge de Jean-Baptiste Colbert*] autant de mauvais que de bon, autant de phrases obscures que de claires, autant de mots impropres que d'expressions justes, autant d'exagérations que de vérités'. Voltaire to Marie de Vichy de Chamrond, marquise du Deffant, 16 Nov. 1773, D 18629.
79. 'Nouveaux objets d'industrie', 'c'etoient des institutions d'un père tendre, qui, connoiss[ait] l'industrie de ses enfants', 'esprit d'ordre'. Necker, *Éloge*, pp. 30–4, 14.

80. Ibid., pp. 6, 53–8. Voltaire to Suzanne Necker, 3 Sept. 1773, D 18537.
81. 'L'importance des matières ne doit point faire oublier le style.' Voltaire, 'Observations sur MM. Lass, Melon et Dutot sur le commerce, le luxe et les impôts' (1738), in *M*, XXII, p. 361. Voltaire, 'Épître à Mme Necker' (1776), in *M*, X, p. 453.
82. Jan de Vries, 'The Industrial Revolution and the Industrious Revolution', *Journal of Economic History*, 54 (1994), 249–70, p. 257.

5 A Political Campaign for Industry

1. The most detailed study on the campaign for the serfs of Saint-Claude is Roger Bergeret's and Jean Maurel's *L'avocat Christin collaborateur de Voltaire (1741–1799)*, (Saint-Claude, 2002). The affair is also mentioned in most biographies of Voltaire. René Pomeau writes about it in a number of instances. René Pomeau, *Voltaire en son temps* (2 vols, Paris, 1995 edn), II, pp. 361–2, 459–61, 470. However, the role of the concept of 'industrie' in the debate is not discussed in the literature.
2. Claude Courtepée, 'Saint-Claude', in Charles-Joseph Panckoucke *et al.*, ed., *Supplément à l'Encyclopédie* (4 vols, Amsterdam, 1776), IV, p. 697.
3. Anne Soprani, 'Florian, Philippe Antoine de Claris, marquis de', in André Magnan *et al.*, eds, *Inventaire Voltaire* (Paris, 1995), pp. 555–6. Jean-Pierre de Claris, marquis de Florian, 'Voltaire et le serf du Jura', in *Collection des œuvres de M. de Florian* (5 vols, Neuchâtel, 1789), IV, pp. 277–84. The academy proposed the topic 'abolition de la servitude dans les domaines du roi' on this occasion. The prize was not awarded until 1782 because of the unsatisfactory entries in the competition. Jean-Pierre de Claris, marquis de Florian, 'Avant-propos', in *Collection des œuvres de M. de Florian*, IV, p. 273.
4. Marcel Marion, *Dictionnaire des institutions de la France aux XVIIe et XVIIIe siècles* (Paris, 1923), p. 509. Voltaire, 'Nouvelle requête au roi en son conseil' (1770), in *M*, XXVIII, p. 369.
5. J. Mackrell, *The attack on 'feudalism' in eighteenth-century France* (London, 1973), p. 2.
6. The question, as given in the *Gazette de France* in January 1767, was: 'Est-il plus avantageux & plus utile au bien public que le Paysan possède des terres en propre, ou seulement des biens mobiliers? & jusqu'où doit s'étendre le droit du Paysan sur cette propriété afin qu'il en résulte le plus grand avantage pour le bien public?' Cited in V.A. Somov, 'Volter na konkurse volnogo ekonomicheskogo obschestva (dve rukopisi, prislannye iz Shveytsarii v 1767g)' ('Voltaire at the competition of the free economic society (two manuscripts sent from Switzerland in 1767)'), in anonymous, ed., *Russko-Frantsuzkie kulturnye svyazi v epokhu Prosvescheniya (Russo-French cultural relations in the epoch of the enlightenment)* (Moscow, 2001), 37–99, p. 40. The article is in Russian, and Voltaire's texts are reproduced in French and Latin. I am grateful to V.A. Somov who made the article available to me and to Nikolay Belkov who translated the Russian parts of the text for me. 'L'industrie', 'les arts', 'pour son amusement'. Jacob Friedrich Bielfeld to Frederick II, king of Prussia, 22 Aug. 1760, Geheimes Staatsarchiv Preußischer Kulturbesitz, Berlin-Dahlem (GStA PK), I HA, Rep. 96, Nr. 36 T, p. 41. Edited in *M*, X, pp. 119–31. The complex relationship of Catherine, Frederick, Voltaire has been discussed in a

recent study by Claus Scharf, *Katharina II, Deutschland und die Deutschen* (Mainz, 1995), p. 423.

7. Pierre Samuel Du Pont de Nemours, 'Discours de l'éditeur', in Pierre Samuel Du Pont de Nemours, ed., *Physiocratie ou constitution naturelle du gouvernement le plus avantageux au genre humain* (Leyde, 1768), p. xcix. 'Ce pauvre Solon nommé La Rivière'. Voltaire to Catherine II, empress of Russia, 16 Dec. 1774, D 19239. 'L'occident n'est parvenu à être quelque chose qu'à force d'industrie'. Voltaire to Andrei Petrovich Shouvalov, 30 Sept. 1767, D 14450.
8. Somov, 'Voltaire at the competition of the free economic society (two manuscripts sent from Switzerland in 1767)', pp. 40, 45, 48.
9. Ibid., pp. 55, 41.
10. Bergeret and Maurel, *L'avocat Christin collaborateur de Voltaire,* pp. 22–9. 'Propriété'. Ibid., pp. 41, 50. Note that the article *Propriété* of the *Questions sur l'Encyclopédie* became part of the *Dictionnaire Philosophique* in many later editions. Voltaire, *Dissertation sur l'établissement de l'abbaye de Saint-Claude* (Neuchâtel, 1772), p. 149. Cited in Bergeret and Maurel, *L'avocat Christin collaborateur de Voltaire,* p. 49. Somov, 'Voltaire at the competition of the free economic society (two manuscripts sent from Switzerland in 1767)', p. 42.
11. Ibid., pp. 42–4.
12. 'Âme abrutie', 'bien général', 'étouffé'. Voltaire, 'Discours sur le sujet proposé par la société œconomique', V.A Somov, ed., 'Voltaire at the competition of the free economic society (two manuscripts sent from Switzerland in 1767)', 65–70, p. 68.
13. 'L'excédent des cultivateurs nécessaires se répand dans les villes, dans les ports des mers, dans les ateliers des artistes, dans les armées', 'progrès de l'industrie et du commerce.' Ibid., pp. 65–7.
14. 'Cette liberté leur tiendra lieu de propriété', 'leurs bras et de la bonne volonté.' Ibid., p. 68. 'Le manœuvre, l'ouvrier, doit être réduit au nécessaire pour travailler.' Voltaire, 'Siècle' (1751), in *OH*, p. 996. In the same passage Voltaire adds: 'Il faut que ce grand nombre d'hommes soit pauvre, mais il ne faut pas qu'il soit misérable'.
15. Karl Marx, *Capital* (1867), Ernest Mandel, ed., (3 vols, London, 1990), I, p. 272.
16. 'Cette classe d'hommes si méprisables aux yeux des puissants'. Voltaire, 'Discours', p. 69.
17. 'Par son industrie', 'terres nôbles'. Ibid., pp. 69, 70.
18. 'Messire François Marie Arouet de Voltaire, chevalier, gentilhomme ordinaire de la Chambre du roi, comte de Tourney, Prégny et Chambésy, seigneur de Ferney'. Pomeau, *Voltaire en son temps,* II, p. 56.
19. 'Moyen ordre', 'par l'industrie, 'ministres et courtisans'. Voltaire, 'Siècle', p. 996.
20. Voltaire, 'Essai historique et critique sur les dissensions des églises de Pologne' (1767), in *M*, XXVI, p. 466.
21. 'Mon très cher petit philosophe'. Voltaire to Charles Frédéric Christin, 16 Nov. 1770, D 16766. 'Mon nom est fatal en matières ecclésiastiques'. Voltaire to Marie de Vichy de Chamrond, marquise du Deffant, 1 June 1770, D 16372.
22. 'Gênes', 'leur cœur, leur industrie, et leur postérité'. Voltaire, 'Coutume de Franche-Comté' (1771), in *M*, XXVIII, p. 377.
23. Voltaire, 'L'homme aux quarante écus' (1768), in *M*, XXI, p. 307.
24. 'Établissement', 'fonction', 'lèpre de l'esclavage', 'hommes-plantes'. Ibid., pp. 372–7.

25. Voltaire, 'La voix du curé sur les procès des serfs du Mont-Jura' (1772), in *M*, XXVIII, p. 569.
26. 'Un débiteur suffisant et de bonne foi'. Voltaire, 'Coutume', p. 375.
27. Adam Smith, *An inquiry into the nature and the causes of the wealth of nations* (1776), R.H. Campbell, ed. (2 vols, Indianapolis, 1981), I, p. 25. 'Hypothèque'. Voltaire, 'Coutume', p. 375. Voltaire, 'Nouvelle requête au roi en son conseil', p. 370.
28. 'Avec la liberté [les souverains] firent présent de l'industrie et de la prospérité aux sujets de leurs domaines. La France entière, dont le nom, l'aspect, l'industrie et le bonheur excitent la jalousie des nations, ne jouit de ces avantages que depuis les jours de sa liberté.' Voltaire, 'Coutume', pp. 377, 378.
29. Voltaire to Charles Frédéric Gabriel Christin, 16 Nov. 1770, D 16766. 'Plus sage et le plus heureux'. Voltaire to Adam, count Lewenhaupt, 15 Dec. 1774, D 19235.
30. 'Le Dégoût, l'Ennui, le Repentir', 'deux baisers en passant', 'guide fidèle', 'ange'. Voltaire, 'Sésostris' (1776), in *M*, X, pp. 69–70.
31. Voltaire to Charles Augustin Feriol, comte d'Argental, 5 Sept. 1774, D 19110. Voltaire to Charles Augustin Feriol, comte d'Argental, 23 Sept. 1774, D 19125. Voltaire to Adam, count Lewenhaupt, 15 Dec. 1774, D 19235. 'Siècle de Louis XVI'. Voltaire to Louise Florence Pétronille de Tardieu d'Esclavelles d'Epinay, 8 July 1774, D 19017. At the same time, Voltaire successfully pursued the project of changing the tax regime of the Pays de Gex where Ferney is located. Many of the letters and memoranda to Turgot regard this matter which will not be discussed here.
32. Emma Rothschild, *Economic sentiments* (Cambridge, MA., 2001), p. 22.
33. Voltaire to Joseph Vasselier, 15 March 1776, D 19989.
34. 'Bizarres, tyranniques, contraires aux bonnes mœurs', 'goût', 'nécessité', 'citoyen', 'préjudice immense ... à l'industrie'. Anne Robert Jacques Turgot, baron de l'Aulne, 'Édit du roi, portant suppression des jurandes (Février 1776)', in Eugène Daire, ed., *Œuvres de Turgot* (2 vols, Paris, 1844), II, pp. 305, 303, 306.
35. 'Sans intelligence'. Anne Robert Jacques Turgot, baron de l'Aulne, 'Édit du roi qui supprime les corvées, et ordonne la confection des grandes routes à prix d'argent (Février 1776)', in Daire, ed., *Œuvres de Turgot*, II, pp. 288, 291.
36. 'Auberge', 'l'industrie sera plus gênée', writes the author, 'plus tyrannisée par la liberté même qu'elle n'auroit jamais pu l'être par les règlemens', 'perfection des arts'. 'Développement de l'industrie'. Anonymous, *Réflexions des six corps de la ville de Paris, sur la suppression des jurandes* (Paris, 1776), pp. 10, 4, 3.
37. 'Asyles de l'industrie', 'barrière qui effraye leur imagination', 'consommation des ... productions de l'industrie', 'honteuses distractions', 'une premiere police', 'independence anarchique', 'balançoit tout'. Ibid., pp. 13–4, 15–6.
38. Edgar Faure, *La disgrâce de Turgot* (Paris, 1961), p. 442.
39. 'Guerre de farine'. Voltaire, 'Diatribe à l'auteur des *Éphémérides*' (1775), in *M*, XXIX, pp. 359–70.
40. 'Au pied du grand éscalier du Palais'. Antoine-Louis Séguier, 'Arrêt de la cour de parlement', in Pierre François de Boncerf, *Les invonvéniens des droits féodaux* (Paris, 1776), p. 65.
41. 'Tyrannie féodale', 'myriade', 'créance hypothécaire', 'mille embarras & difficultés', 'temps, industrie & activité', 'industrie', 'arts', 'agriculture',

'économie', 'manufactures', 'commerçants' and 'industrieux'. Boncerf, *Les invonvéniens*, pp. 45, 7, 23, 47, 54–6.

42. Ibid., p. 42. Voltaire to André Morellet, 29 Dec. 1775, D 19826.
43. 'Multitude ... echauffée', 'l'anarchie la plus cruelle'. Séguier, 'Arrêt de la cour de parlement', pp. 68, 70.
44. 'Frénésie', 'parti secret', 'agent caché'. Ibid., p. 66. 'Que ce morceau est sublime!' Voltaire, 'Lettre du père révérend Polycarpe, prieur des Barnardins de Chézery à M. l'avocat général Séguier' (1776), in *M*, XXX, p. 336.
45. Marie Jean Antoine Nicolas de Caritat, marquis de Condorcet to Voltaire, 7 March 1776, D 19973. Voltaire to Pierre François de Boncerf, 8 March 1776, D 19974. Faure, *Turgot*, p. 444. Jérôme Vercruysse, 'Turgot et Vergennes contre la lettre de Voltaire à Boncerf', *Studies on Voltaire and the eighteenth century*, 67 (1969), 65–71. 'Révérend Père Polycarpe, prieur des Bernardins de Chézery', 'abominable et détestable brochure'. Voltaire, 'Lettre du père révérend Polycarpe', p. 333.
46. Cited in Voltaire, 'Lettre d'un Bénédictin de Franche-Comté à M. l'avocat général Séguier' (1776), in *M*, XXX, p. 340. The edict reads: 'Dieu, en donnant à l'homme des besoins, en lui rendant nécessaire la ressource du travail, a fait du droit de travailler la propriété de tout homme, et cette propriété est la première, la plus sacrée et la plus imprescriptible de toutes'. Turgot, 'Édit du roi, portant suppression des jurandes', p. 306.
47. 'Liberté à l'industrie'. Voltaire, 'Lettre d'un Bénédictin', p. 340.
48. 'Nous devons surtout cette protection à cette classe d'hommes qui, n'ayant de propriété que leur travail et leur industrie.' Turgot, 'Édit du roi, portant suppression des jurandes', p. 302.
49. Ibid., p. 303.
50. See the discussion of eighteenth-century critiques of the institution of apprenticeship in Rothschild, *Economic sentiments*, pp. 87–113.
51. Marie Jean Antoine Nicolas Caritat, marquis de Condorcet, 'La vie de Voltaire', in *K*, LXX, p. 147. Turgot, 'Édit du roi, portant suppression des jurandes', pp. 306–7.
52. Voltaire, 'Coutume', p. 378.
53. 'Cette seconde opération sera pour l'industrie ce que la première sera pour l'agriculture', 'richesses de l'État'. Anne Robert Jacques Turgot, baron de l'Aulne, 'Mémoire au roi sur six projets d'édits', in Daire, ed., *Œuvres de Turgot*, II, p. 248.
54. 'Un peuple aimable et vain', he wrote, 'Clabaude le matin contre un édit du roi,/Le soir s'en va siffler quelque moderne, ou moi'. Voltaire, 'Épître à un homme' (1776), in *M*, X, p. 452. Condorcet, 'La vie de Voltaire', pp. 144–6. As has been mentioned, the serfs on the royal estates were freed during the ministry of Necker in 1779. The edict expressed the king's regret that respect for the lord's property rights prevented him from abolishing serfdom altogether.
55. 'Objet propre'. Alexis de Tocqueville, *L'ancien régime et la révolution* (1856) (Paris, 1967), p. 85. 'Il combattit les athées et les fanatiques, il inspira la tolérance, il réclama les droits de l'homme contre la servitude de la féodalité.' Bergeret and Maurel, *L'avocat Christin collaborateur de Voltaire*, p. XVI. 'Chacun s'était trouvé ébranlé dans sa condition, troublé dans ses habitudes ou gêné dans son industrie'. Tocqueville, *L'ancien régime et la révolution*, pp. 274, 311, 274, 94.

56. 'Tout ouvrage qui exige quelque instruction, quelque industrie particulière, est impossible à exécuter par corvée.' Turgot, 'Édit du roi qui supprime les corvées', p. 290.
57. 'La Societé des arts consiste en échanges d'industrie'. Jean-Jacques Rousseau, 'Émile ou de l'éducation' in Michel Launay, ed., *Œuvres* de Rousseau (3 vols, Paris, 1971), III, p. 134.

Conclusion

1. François Varlet, *Déclaration des droits de l'homme dans l'état social* (Paris, 1793), pp. 18–19.
2. Jan de Vries, 'The Industrial Revolution and the Industrious Revolution', *Journal of Economic History*, 54 (1994), 249–70, pp. 262, 257.
3. Ibid., pp. 256–8.
4. See for example Voltaire, 'Les édits de sa majesté Louis XVI pendant l'administration de M. Turgot' (1775), in *M*, XXIX, p. 414. Voltaire to Charles Augustin Feriol, comte d'Argental, 22 Sept 1775, D 19670. Voltaire to Nicolas Baudeau, March/April 1775, D 19396.
5. 'Bien général'. Voltaire, 'Le siècle de Louis XIV' (1751), in *OH*, p. 966.
6. 'Intérêt particulier', 'comme les autres aiment leurs intérêts'. Voltaire to Marie de Vichy de Chamrond marquise du Deffant, 12 Aug. 1774, D 19075.
7. Voltaire, 'Diatribe à l'auteur des *Éphémérides*' (1775), in *M*, XXIX, p. 378.
8. Voltaire to Dominique Audibert, 19 Feb. 1774, D 19242.
9. 'Toutes les parties du monde entier, sont réunies depuis environ deux siècles et demi par l'industrie de nos pères.' Voltaire, 'Remarques sur l'histoire' (1742), in *OH*, p. 44.

Bibliography

Abbreviations

D	Voltaire's correspondence in Voltaire, *Les œuvres complètes de Voltaire,* Voltaire Foundation, ed., (135 vols, Geneva, 1968–).
D app.	Appendices with edited documents in Voltaire, *Les œuvres complètes de Voltaire,* Voltaire Foundation, ed., (135 vols, Geneva, 1968–).
GStA PK	Geheimes Staatsarchiv Preußischer Kulturbesitz, Berlin-Dahlem.
K	Voltaire, *Œuvres complètes de Voltaire,* Marie Jean Antoine Nicolas Caritat, marquis de Condorcet, *et al.*, ed., (70 vols, Kehl, 1785–89).
LA	Leibniz Archiv, Hannover.
M	Voltaire, *Œuvres complètes de Voltaire,* Louis Moland, ed., (52 vols, Paris, 1877–85).
OH	Voltaire, *Œuvres historiques,* René Pomeau, ed., (Paris, 1957).
PRO	Public Records Office, National Archives, Kew.

French and German citations have been translated by the author unless stated otherwise. The citations in the original language are given in the endnotes. References to Voltaire's works are given in the form: author, title of individual work, date of first publication, edition (abbreviated *M, OH* or *K*), volume in roman numerals, page number. References to Voltaire's correspondence are to Theodore Besterman's edition [Voltaire, *Les œuvres complètes de Voltaire,* Voltaire Foundation, ed., (135 vols, Geneva, 1968–)]. They are given in the form: sender, addressee, date, number of the letter (e.g. D 4711). The Besterman edition also contains appendices of documents concerning Voltaire. References to the appendices are in the form: title of the document (document-titles in this edition are in English), date, number of the document (e.g. D app. 8).

Archival sources

Geheimes Staatsarchiv Preußischer Kulturbesitz (GStA PK), Berlin-Dahlem

Files from the following holdings of GStA PK have been used:

Brandenburgisch-Preußisches Hausarchiv
GstA PK, BPH, Rep. 47 König Friedrich II

I Hauptabteilung

GstA PK, I HA Geheimer Rat, Rep. 9 Allgemeine Verwaltung
GstA PK, I HA Geheimer Rat, Rep. 11 Auswärtige Beziehungen
GstA PK, I HA Geheimer Rat, Rep. 68 Ostfriesland
GstA PK, I HA Geheimer Rat, Rep. 96 Geheimes Zivilkabinett, ältere Periode (bis 1797)

II Hauptabteilung

GstA PK, II HA Generaldirektorium, Abt. 17 Minden und Ravensberg
GstA PK, II HA Generaldirektorium, Abt. 21 Ostfriesland
GstA PK, II HA Generaldirektorium, Abt. 24 Generalakzise- und Zolldepartement

VI Hauptabteilung

GstA PK, VI HA Nachlaß Pöllnitz

Leibniz Archiv (LA), Hannover
Files from the following holdings of LA have been used:

Leibniz Handschriften (LH), Microfilms XIX and LXXXIV

Public Records Office, National Archives (PRO), Kew
Files from the following holding of PRO have been used:

Secretaries of state: State papers foreign, France, 1577–1780, SP78/237

Edited sources

Thomas-Simon Bérard, 'Journal de voyage aux Indes' (1772), Maurice Bérard, ed., *Bulletin de la société de l'histoire du Protestantisme français*, 90 (1941), 239–62.

Gabrielle-Émilie Le Tonnelier de Breteuil, marquise du Châtelet-Lomont, 'Préface du traducteur' (1735), Ira Wade, ed., *Studies on Voltaire with some unpublished papers of Mme du Châtelet* (Princeton, NJ: 1947), 131–87.

Victor Riqueti, marquis de Mirabeau, 'Notes inédites sur Boisguilbert par le Marquis de Mirabeau' (between 1757 and 1760), Georges Weulersse, ed., *Revue d'histoire des doctrines économiques et sociales* (1910), 115–51.

Voltaire, 'Discours sur le sujet proposé par la société œconomique' (1766/7), V.A.Somov, ed., 'Volter na konkurse volnogo ekonomicheskogo obschestva (dve rukopisi, prislannye iz Shveytsarii v 1767g.)' ('Voltaire at the competition of the free economic society (two manuscripts sent from Switzerland in 1767)'), in anonymous, ed., *Russko-Frantsuzkie kulturnye svyazi v epokhu Prosvescheniya* (*Russo-French cultural Relations in the epoch of the enlightenment*) (Moscow, 2001), 37–99, pp. 65–70.

Voltaire, *Les œuvres complètes de Voltaire*, Voltaire Foundation, ed., (135 vols, Geneva, 1968–). Volumes 85–135 of the edition contain Voltaire's correspondence. The appendices contain the following relevant documents:

'Police report on Voltaire' (1751) in appendix 112,
'Mme du Châtelet's inventory' (7 Oct. 1749) in appendix 93,
'Florian and the Hercule' (May 1772) in appendix 358,
'Voltaire in accounts with Laleu' (1754) in appendix 137.

Contemporary and nineteenth-century printed material

Books

When modern editions of contemporary texts are used the original date of publication is given in brackets.

Anonymous, *Réflexions des six corps de la ville de Paris, sur la suppression des jurandes* (Paris, 1776).

Anonymous, *Denkschrift der königlichen Akademie gemeinnütziger Wissenschaften in Erfurt* (Erfurt, 1854).

Académie Française, *Dictionnaire de l'Académie françoise* (2 vols, Paris, 1694).

Académie Française, *Dictionnaire de l'Académie françoise* (2 vols, Paris, 1740).

Académie Française, *Dictionnaire de l'Académie françoise* (2 vols, Paris, 1835).

Jean Le Rond d'Alembert, *Discours préliminaire de l'Encyclopédie* (1751), Louis Ducros, ed., (Paris, 1893).

Francesco Algarotti, *Il newtonianismo per le dame* (Milan, 1739).

Abraham Nicolas Amelot de la Hossaie, *Mémoires historiques, politiques, critiques, et littéraires* (2 vols, Amsterdam, 1722).

Louis Bachaumont, *Mémoires secrètes pour servir à l'histoire de la république des lettres en France* (36 vols, London, 1788).

Francis Bacon, 'In praise of knowledge', in *The works of Francis Bacon*, Basil Montagu, ed., (16 vols, London, 1825).

Christian Bartholmèss, *Histoire philosophique de l'Académie de Prusse* (2 vols, Paris, 1850).

Abbé Baudeau, *Explication du tableau économique à madame de *** (Extrait des Éphémérides de 1767 et 1768)* (Paris, 1776).

Pierre le Pesant de Boisguilbert, *La France ruinée sous le règne de Louis XIV. Par qui et comment* (Cologne, 1696).
Pierre le Pesant de Boisguilbert, 'Factum de la France' (1707), in Eugène Daire, ed., *Économistes-Financiers du XVIIIe siècle* (Paris, 1843).
Pierre le Pesant de Boisguilbert, *Boisguilbert ou la naissance de l'économie politique (correspondance, œuvres imprimés et manuscrits)*, Jacqueline Hecht, ed., (2 vols, Paris, 1966).
Pierre François de Boncerf, *Les invonvéniens des droits féodaux* (sic) (Paris, 1776).
Jean de la Bruyère, *Les caractères* (1688) (Paris, 1999).
Gabrielle-Émilie Le Tonnelier de Breteuil, marquise du Châtelet-Lomont, *Institutions de physique* (Paris, 1740).
Gabrielle-Émilie Le Tonnelier de Breteuil, marquise du Châtelet-Lomont, *Dissertation sur la nature et la propagation du feu* (Paris, 1744).
Denis Diderot, *Diderot Œuvres*, Laurent Versini, ed., (4 vols, Paris, 1996).
Henri-Gabriel Duchesne, *Dictionnaire de l'industrie* (6 vols, Paris, 1795).
Pierre Samuel Du Pont de Nemours, ed., *Physiocratie ou constitution naturelle du gouvernement le plus avantageux au genre humain* (Leyde, 1768).
Jean-Pierre de Claris, marquis de Florian, *Collection des œuvres de M. de Florian* (5 vols, Neuchâtel, 1789).
Gustave Flaubert, *Bouvard et Pécuchet* (Paris, 1966).
Frederick II, king of Prussia, *Mémoires pour servir à l'histoire de Brandenbourg* (Berlin, 1750).
Frederick II, king of Prussia, *Les œuvres de Frederick le Grand*, J.-D.-E. Preuss, ed., (10 vols, Berlin, 1849).
Frederick II, king of Prussia, *Die politischen Testamente Friedrich's des Grossen* (sic), Gustav Volz, ed., (Berlin, 1920).
Frederick II, king of Prussia and Voltaire, *L'Anti-Machiavel* (1740), Charles Fleischauer, ed., (Geneva, 1958).
Johann Wolfgang von Goethe, *Goethe Werke*, Manfred Wenzel, ed., (40 vols, Frankfurt on Main, 1991).
Georg Wilhelm Friedrich Hegel, *Phaenomenologie des Geistes* (Leiden, 1907).
Georg Wilhelm Friedrich Hegel, *Phenomenology of spirit*, A.V. Miller, transl. (Oxford, 1977).
Johann Gottfried Herder, *Sämtliche Werke – Johann Gottfried Herder*, Bernhard Suphan, ed., (33 vols, Berlin, 1877).
Johann Gottfried Herder, *Herder Werke*, Wolfgang Pross, ed., (2 vols, Munich, 1984).
Johann Gottfried Herder, *Johann Gottfried Herder Werke*, Hans Dietrich Irmscher *et al.*, eds, (10 vols, Frankfurt on Main, 1991).
Paul Heinrich Dietrich, Baron von Holbach, *La morale universelle ou les devoirs de l'homme fondés sur sa nature* (5 vols, Paris, An IV de la Republiques Française [1796]) II, p. 9.
Christiaan Huygens, *Œuvres complètes de Christiaan Huygens*, Société Hollandaise des Sciences, ed., (22 vols, La Haye, 1950).
Immanuel Kant, *Foundations of the metaphysics of moral, What is enlightenment*, Lewis White Beck, transl. (Chicago, IL: 1949).
Immanuel Kant, 'Beantwortung der Frage: Was ist Aufklärung', in Horst Brandt, ed., *Was ist Aufklärung* (Hamburg, 1999).
Angliviel de La Beaumelle, *L'Asiatique tolérant, traité à l'usage de Zéokinizul, roi des Kofirans surnommé le chéri; ouvrage traduit de l'arabe du voyageur Bekrinoll par M. de* *** (Amsterdam, 1748).

Angliviel de La Beaumelle, *Mes pensées* (Paris, 1753).
Angliviel de La Beaumelle, *Réponse au supplément au siècle de Louis XIV* (Colmar, 1754).
Angliviel de La Beaumelle, *Lettre de monsieur de la Beaumelle à M. de Voltaire* (London, 1763).
B.H. Latrobe, *Characteristic anecdotes and miscellaneous authentic papers tending to illustrate the character of Frederic II* (London, 1788).
Gottfried Wilhelm Leibniz, *Leibniz deutsche Schriften*, G. Guhrauer, ed., (2 vols, Berlin, 1840).
Gottfried Wilhelm Leibniz, *Die Werke Leibniz*, Onno Klopp, ed., (11 vols, Hannover, 1877).
Gotthold Ephraim Lessing, *Lessing Werke*, Karl Eibl, ed., (8 vols, Munich, 1973).
Sébastien Longchamp *et al.*, ed., *Mémoires sur Voltaire* (2 vols, Paris, 1826).
Jean-François Marmontel, *Mémoires* (1804) (2 vols, Clermont-Ferrand, 1972).
Karl Marx and Friedrich Engels, *Marx Engels Werke*, Institut für Marxismus-Leninismus der SED, ed., (41 vols, Berlin, 1964).
Karl Marx, *Capital*, Ernest Mandel, ed., (3 vols, London, 1990).
Victor de Riqueti, marquis de Mirabeau, *L'Ami des hommes ou traité de la population* (7 vols, La Haye, 1758).
Honoré Gabriel Riqueti, comte de Mirabeau, *De la monarchie Prussienne* (4 vols, London, 1788).
Honoré Gabriel Riqueti, comte de Mirabeau, *Histoire secrète de la cour de Berlin ou correspondance d'un voyageur François depuis le mois de Juillet 1786 jusqu'au 19 janvier 1787* (2 vols, London, 1789).
Charles de Secondat, baron de la Brède et de Montesquieu, *Lettres Persanes* (1721) (Geneva, 1954).
Charles de Secondat, baron de la Brède et de Montesquieu, *Œuvres complètes Montesquieu*, Daniel Oster, ed., (Paris, 1964).
Louis Moréri, *Le grand dictionnaire historique* (Paris, 1759).
Jacques Necker, *Éloge de Jean-Baptiste Colbert* (Paris, 1773).
Charles-Joseph Panckoucke *et al.*, ed., *Supplément à l'Encyclopédie* (4 vols, Amsterdam, 1776).
François Quesnay, *Œuvres économiques et philosophiques de François Quesnay*, Auguste Oncken, ed., (Frankfurt on Main, 1888).
Abbé Raynal, *Histoire philosophique et politique des établissements et du commerce des Européens dans les deux Indes* (7 vols, Amsterdam, 1770).
Jean-Jacques Rousseau, *Les Rêveries du promeneur solitaire*, Henri Roddier, ed., (Paris, 1960).
Jean-Jacques Rousseau, *Œuvres* de Rousseau, Michel Launay, ed., (3 vols, Paris, 1971).
Pierre Richelet, *Dictionnaire de la langue françoise ancienne et moderne* (2 vols, Paris, 1732).
Jean François, marquis de Saint-Lambert, *Les saisons* (Amsterdam, 1769).
Charles Irénée de Castel, Abbé de Saint-Pierre, *Projet pour rendre la paix perpétuelle en Europe* (2 vols, Utrecht, 1713).
Charles Irénée de Castel, Abbé de Saint-Pierre, *Annales politiques (1658–1740)* (2 vols, London, 1758).
Charles Irénée de Castel, Abbé de Saint-Pierre, *Les rêves d'un homme de bien* (Paris, 1775).
Adam Smith, *The theory of moral sentiments* (1759), A. Macfie, ed., (Oxford, 1976).

Adam Smith, *Adam Smith – essays on philosophical subjects*, W. Wightman, ed., (Indianapolis, 1981).

Adam Smith, *An inquiry into the nature and the causes of the wealth of nations* (1776), R.H. Campbell, ed., (2 vols, Indianapolis, IN: 1981).

Alexis de Tocqueville, *L'ancien régime et la révolution* (1856) (Paris, 1967).

Anne Robert Jacques Turgot, *Œuvres de Turgot*, Eugène Daire, ed., (2 vols, Paris, 1844).

Anne Robert Jacques Turgot, baron de l'Aulne, *Œuvres de Turgot*, Gustave Schelle, ed., (5 vols, Paris, 1914).

François Varlet, *Déclaration des droits de l'homme dans l'état social* (Paris, 1793).

Voltaire, *Le siècle de Louis XIV (Augmenté d'un très grand nombre de Remarques par M. de la B***)*, Angliviel de La Beaumelle, ed., (3 vols, Frankfurt on Main, 1753).

Sébastien Le Prestre, marquis de Vauban, *Projet d'une dixme royale* (no place, 1707).

Voltaire, *Œuvres complètes de Voltaire*, Marie Jean Antoine Nicolas, marquis de Condorcet *et al.*, ed., (70 vols, Kehl, 1785–89). This edition is abbreviated *K.*

Voltaire, *Œuvres complètes de Voltaire*, Louis Moland, ed., (52 vols, Paris, 1877–85). This edition is abbreviated *M.*

Voltaire, *Œuvres historiques*, René Pomeau, ed., (Paris, 1957) This edition is abbreviated *OH.*

Christoph Wieland, *Wieland Werke*, Klaus Manger, ed., (12 vols, Frankfurt on Main, 1986).

Oscar Wilde, *Phrases and philosophies for the use of the young* (London, 1894).

Periodicals

Berlinische Nachrichten von staats- und gelehrten Sachen (1750–53)

Éphémérides du citoyen (1769–76)

Mercure de France (1734–35)

Supplément à la gazette d'Utrecht (1768)

Secondary literature

Books

Antoine Adam, 'Introduction', in Voltaire, *Le Siècle de Louis XIV* (1751) (Paris, 1962).

Theodor Wiesengrund Adorno and Max Horkheimer, *Dialectic of enlightenment*, Edmund Jephcott, transl. (Stanford, 2002).

Theodor Wiesengrund Adorno and Max Horkheimer, *Dialektik der Aufklärung* (Frankfurt, 2004).

M.P. Alekseev *et al.*, *Bibliothèque de Voltaire: catalogue des livres* (Moscow, 1961).

Eugène Asse, *L'Académie Française* (Paris, 1890).

Kurt Baldinger, 'Einige terminologische Auswirkungen des Aufschwungs der Industrie im 18. Jahrhundert in Frankreich', in Alexander Bergengruen, ed., *Alteuropa und die moderne Gesellschaft – Festschrift für Otto Brunner* (Göttingen, 1963), 318–36.

Georges Bengesco, *Voltaire: bibliographie des ses œuvres* (4 vols, Paris, 1885).

Maurice Bérard, *Les Bérard* (Paris, 1937).

Maxine Berg and Helen Clifford, eds, *Consumers and luxury: consumer culture in Europe 1650–1850* (Manchester, 1999).
Maxine Berg and Elizabeth Eger, eds, *Luxury in the eighteenth-century: debates desires and delectable goods* (Basingstoke, 2003).
Roger Bergeret and Jean Maurel, *L'avocat Christin collaborateur de Voltaire (1741–1799)* (Saint-Claude, 2002).
François Bluche, ed., *Dictionnaire du grand siècle* (Paris, 1990).
Otto Büsch, *Militärsystem und Sozialleben im alten Preussen (1713–1807)* (Berlin, 1962).
Roger Charbonnaud, *Les idées économiques de Voltaire* (Angoulême, 1907).
Charles Cole, *Colbert and a century of French mercantilism* (2 vols, New York, 1939).
François Crouzet, *De la supériorité de l'Angleterre sur la France* (Paris, 1985).
Lorraine Daston, *Eine kurze Geschichte der wissenschaftlichen Aufmerksamkeit* (Munich, 2001).
Jan De Vries, *Economy of Europe in an age of crisis 1600–1750* (Cambridge, 1976).
Joseph Drouet, *L'Abbé de Saint-Pierre* (Paris, 1912).
Focko Eulen, *Vom Gewerbefleiß zur Industrie* (Berlin, 1967).
Gilbert Faccarello, *Aux origines de l'économie politique libérale: Pierre de Boisguilbert* (Paris, 1986).
Edgar Faure, *La disgrâce de Turgot* (Paris, 1961).
Nicole Ferrier-Caverivière, *Le grand roi à l'aube des lumières, 1715–1751* (Paris, 1985).
Wolfram Fischer and Adelheid Simsch, 'Industrialisierung in Preussen. Eine staatliche Veranstaltung?', in Werner Süß, ed., *Übergänge – Zeitgeschichte zwischen Utopie und Machbarkeit* (Berlin, 1989).
Martin Fontius, *Voltaire in Berlin. Zur Geschichte der bei G.C. Walther veröffentlichten Werke Voltaires* (Berlin, 1966).
John Galbraith, *A history of economics* (London, 1987).
Maurice Garden, *Lyon et les Lyonnais au XVIIIe siècle* (Paris, 1975).
Peter Gay, *Voltaire's politics* (Princeton, NJ: 1959).
Charles Gide and Charles Rist, *Histoire des doctrines économiques* (Paris, 1909).
R. Harris, *Absolutism and enlightenment* (London, 1964).
A. Hartig, *Großbürgerliche Aufklärung als Klassenversöhnung: Voltaire* (West Berlin, 1972).
Fritz Hartung, 'Der preußische Staat und seine westlichen Provinzen', in Franz Petri, ed., *Westfälische Forschungen 7* (Münster, 1953), pp. 5–13.
Jacqueline Hecht, 'Pour une interprétation psychanalytique de Boisguilbert', in Jacqueline Hecht, ed., *Boisguilbert parmi nous* (Paris, 1989), pp. 331–45.
Robert Heilbroner, *The worldly philosophers* (London, 1967).
William Henderson, *Studies in the economic policy of Frederick the Great* (London, 1963).
Dietrich Hilger *et al.*, 'Industrie', in Reinhart Koselleck *et al.*, eds, *Geschichtliche Grundbegriffe* (8 vols, Stuttgart, 1982), III, pp. 237–304.
Albert Hirschmann, *The passions and the interests* (Princeton, NJ: 1977).
Eric Hobsbawm, *Industry and empire* (London, 1999).
Albert Hömberg, *Westfälische Landesgeschichte* (Münster, 1967).
Terence Hutchison, *Before Adam Smith. The emergence of political economy, 1662–1776* (Oxford, 1988).
Nannerl Keohane, *Philosophie and the state in France: the Renaissance to the Enlightenment* (Princeton, NJ: 1980).

Hans Jaeck, *Kammerherr und König, Voltaire in Preussen* (Berlin, 1987).
Stefi Jersch-Wenzel, *Juden und "Franzosen" in der Wirtschaft des Raumes Berlin/Brandenburg* (Berlin, 1978).
Colin Jones, *The great nation* (London, 2002).
Hermann Kellenbenz, *Deutsche Wirtschaftsgeschichte* (2 vols, Munich, 1977).
Reinhold Koser, *König Friedrich der Große* (2 vols, Stuttgart, 1893).
Nuçi Kotta, *L'homme aux quarante écus: a study of Voltairean themes* (The Hague, 1966).
David Landes, *The unbound Prometheus* (Cambridge, 1969).
Catherine Larrère, *L'invention de l'économie au XVIIIe siècle* (Paris, 1992).
Claude Lauriol, *La Beaumelle – un protestant cévenol entre Montesquieu et Voltaire* (Geneva, 1978).
Émile Littré, *Dictionnaire de la langue Française* (7 vols, Paris, 1957 edn).
Herbert Lüthy, *La banque protestante en France* (2 vols, Paris, 1961).
J. Mackrell, *The attack on 'feudalism' in eighteenth-century France* (London, 1973).
André Magnan, *Dossier Voltaire en Prusse* (Oxford, 1986).
André Magnan *et al.*, ed., *Inventaire Voltaire* (Paris, 1995).
Marcel Marion, *Dictionnaire des institutions de la France aux XVIIe et XVIIIe siècles* (Paris, 1923).
Tihomir Markovitch, *Les industries lainières de Colbert à la révolution* (Paris, 1976).
Francine Markovits, *L'ordre des échanges* (Paris, 1986).
Christine Mervaud, *Voltaire et Frédéric II: une dramaturgie des Lumières, 1736–1778* (Oxford, 1985).
Christine Mervaud, *Voltaire à table* (Paris, 1998).
Joel Mokyr, ed., *The economics of the industrial revolution* (London, 1985).
Gustave de Molinari, *L'Abbé de Saint-Pierre* (Paris, 1857).
Patrick O'Brien and Caglar Keyder, *Economic growth in Britain and France 1780–1914* (London, 1978).
August Oncken, *Die Maxime laissez-faire et laissez passer* (Bern, 1886).
Jean-Claude Perrot, *Une histoire intellectuelle de l'économie politique (XVIIe–XVIIIe siècle)* (Paris, 1992).
Ernst Pfeiffer, *Die Revuereisen Friedrich des Großen besonders die schlesischen nach 1763* (Berlin, 1904).
René Pomeau, 'Présentation', in René Pomeau, ed., *La Politique de Voltaire* (Paris, 1963).
René Pomeau, 'Introduction', in Voltaire, *Essai sur les mœurs* (1753) (2 vols, Paris, 1963).
René Pomeau, *Voltaire en son temps* (2 vols, Paris, 1995 edn).
Bruno Racle, 'Voltaire et ses montriers', in Cercle d'études Ferneysiennes, ed., *Ferney-Voltaire* (Annecy, 1990), pp. 207–28.
Victor Ring, *Die asiatischen Handelscompagnien Friedrichs des Großen* (Berlin, 1890).
Jean-Pierre Rioux, *La révolution industrielle* (Paris, 1971).
Hazel Roberts, *Boisguilbert, economist of the reign of Louis XIV* (New York, 1935).
Lionel Rothkrug, *Opposition to Louis XIV* (Princeton, NJ: 1965).
Emma Rothschild, *Economic sentiments* (Cambridge, MA: 2001).
Emma Rothschild, *La mondialisation en perspective historique: l'Amérique hyper-puissance*, Working paper of the Centre for History and Economics (Cambridge, 2001).
Constance Rowe, *Voltaire and the State* (New York, 1955).
Claus Scharf, *Katharina II, Deutschland und die Deutschen* (Mainz, 1995).

Gustave Schelle, *Du Pont de Nemours et l'école Physiocratique* (Paris, 1888).
Theodor Schieder, *Friedrich der Große* (Frankfurt on Main, 1983).
Jochen Schlobach, 'Du siècle de Louis au siècle de Frédéric?' in Christiane Mervaud, ed., *Le siècle de Voltaire – hommage à René Pomeau* (2 vols, Oxford, 1987), II, pp. 831–46.
Gustav Schmoller, *The Mercantile System*, W.J. Ashley, ed., (New York, 1896).
Gustav Schmoller, *Umrisse und Untersuchungen zur Verfassungs-, Verwaltungs-, und Wirtschaftsgeschichte* (Leipzig, 1898).
Gustav Schmoller, *Preußische Verfassungs-, Verwaltungs-, und Finanzgeschichte* (Berlin, 1921).
Claudia Schröder, *'Siècle de Frédéric II' und 'Zeitalter der Aufklärung'* (Berlin, 2002).
Florian Schui, ' "Halb Philosoph und halb Verrückter" – Die Projekte des Abbés de Saint-Pierre', in Markus Krajewski, ed., *Projektemacher* (Berlin, 2004), pp. 95–107.
Joseph Schumpeter, *The history of economic analysis* (London, 1954).
Robert Shackleton, *Montesquieu – a critical biography* (Oxford, 1961).
John Simpson *et al.*, ed., *The Compact Oxford English Dictionary* (Oxford, 1989).
V.A. Somov, 'Volter na konkurse volnogo ekonomicheskogo obschestva (dve rukopisi, prislannye iz Shveytsarii v 1767g.)' ('Voltaire at the competition of the free economic society (two manuscripts sent from Switzerland in 1767)'), in anonymous, ed., *Russko-Frantsuzkie kulturnye svyazi v epokhu Prosvescheniya* (*Russo-French cultural Relations in the epoch of the enlightenment*) (Moscow, 2001), pp. 37–99.
Joseph Spengler, 'Boisguilbert's economic views vis-à-vis those of contemporary réformateurs', in Marc Blaug, ed., *Pre-classical economists* (Aldershot, 1991), pp. 88–107.
Michael Sonenscher, *Work and wages: natural law, politics, and the eighteenth-century French trades* (Cambridge, 1989).
Gareth Stedman Jones, *'Industrie', pauperism and the Hanoverian State: the genesis and political context of the original debate about the 'Industrial Revolution' in England and France, 1815–1840*, Working paper of the Centre for History and Economics (Cambridge, 1997).
Gareth Stedman Jones, *An end to poverty* (London, 2004).
Line Teisseyre-Sallmann, *L'industrie de la soie en Bas-Languedoc XVIIe–XVIIIe siècles* (Paris, 1995).
Richard Tilly, *Kapital, Staat und sozialer Protest in der deutschen Industrialisierung* (Göttingen, 1980).
Wilhelm Treue, *Wirtschafts- und Technikgeschichte Preussens* (Berlin, 1984).
Franco Venturi, *Utopia and reform in the Enlightenment* (Cambridge, 1971).
André Versaille, ed., *Dictionnaire de la pensée de Voltaire par lui-même* (Paris, 1994).
Laurent Versini, 'Introduction', in Charles de Secondat, baron de la Brède et de Montesquieu, *De l'Esprit des Lois* (1748) (2 vols, Paris, 1995).
Henry Weber, *La compagnie française des Indes (1604–1875)* (Paris, 1904).
Klaus Weber, *Deutsche Kaufleute im Atlantikhandel 1680–1830: Unternehmen und Familien in Hamburg Cadiz und Bordeaux* (Munich, 2004).
Hans-Ulrich Wehler, *Deutsche Gesellschaftsgeschichte* (3 vols, Munich, 1987).
George Weulersse, *Le mouvement Physiocratique en France (de 1756 à 1770)* (2 vols, Paris, 1910).
Raymond Williams, *Keywords* (London, 1988 edn).

Martin Wörner, *Architekturführer Berlin* (Berlin, 2001).
Denis Woronoff, *Histoire de l'industrie en France* (Paris, 1998).

Periodicals

Bernard Bailyn 'The idea of Atlantic History', *Itinerario*, 1 (1996), pp. 19–44.
Nicholas Crafts, 'Industrial revolution in England and France: some thoughts on the question "Why was England first?" ', *Economic History Review*, 30 (1977), 429–41.
Nicholas Crafts, 'Macroinventions, economic growth, and "industrial revolution" in Britain and France', *Economic History Review*, 48 (1995), 591–8.
François Crouzet, 'Angleterre et France au XVIIIe siècle: essai d'une analyse comparée de deux croissances économiques', *Annales d'Histoire Économique et Sociale*, 21 (1966), 254–91.
François Crouzet, 'The historiography of French economic growth in the nineteenth century', *Economic History Review*, 56 (2003), 215–42.
Gavin De Beer, 'Voltaire's British visitors', *Studies on Voltaire and the eighteenth century*, 4 (1957), 7–137.
Jan de Vries, 'The Industrial Revolution and the Industrious Revolution', *Journal of Economic History*, 54 (1994), 249–70.
Gustav Droysen, 'Über die Schrift Anti-St. Pierre und deren Verfasser', *Monatsberichte der königlichen Preussischen Akademie der Wissenschaften zu Berlin* (1878), 711–46.
Gustav Droysen, 'Tageskalender Friedrichs des Großen', *Forschungen zur brandenburgischen und preußischen Geschichte*, 29 (1916), 95–157.
Malcolm Falkus, 'Economic growth in Britain and France, 1780–1914 by Patrick O'Brien and Caglar Keyder', *Economic Journal*, 89 (1979), 449–51.
Charles Freedman, 'Economic growth in Britain and France, 1780–1914 by Patrick O'Brien and Caglar Keyder', *American Historical Review*, 84 (1979), 1359–60.
David Hancock, 'The British Atlantic World co-ordination, complexity, and the emergence of an Atlantic market economy, 1651–1815', *Itinerario*, 2 (1999), pp. 107–26.
Paul Harsin, 'De quand date le mot "industrie" ', *Annales d'Histoire Économique et Sociale*, 2 (1930), 235–42.
Henri Hauser, 'Le mot "industrie" chez Roland de la Platière', *Revue Historique*, 150 (1925), 189–93.
Paul Hohenberg, 'Economic growth in Britain and France, 1780–1914 by Patrick O'Brien and Caglar Keyder', *Journal of Economic Literature*, 18 (1980), 135–7.
Peter Jones, 'Living the enlightenment and the French Revolution: James Watt, Matthew Boulton, and their sons', *Historical Journal*, 1 (1999), 157–82.
Caglar Keyder, 'State and industry in France, 1750–1914', *American Economic Review*, 75 (1985), 308–14.
Charles Kindleberger, 'Economic growth in Britain and France, 1780–1914 by Patrick O'Brien and Caglar Keyder', *Economic History Review*, 32 (1979), 295–6.
Reinhold Koser, 'Voltaire und die "Idée de la cour de Prusse" ', *Forschungen zur brandenburgischen und preußischen Geschichte*, 6 (1893), 141–80.
David Landes, 'Some further thoughts on accident in history: a reply to Professor Crafts', *Economic History Review*, 48 (1995), 599–601.
Icob Mârza, 'Une liste de livres interdits en Transylvanie (seconde moitié du XVIII siècle)', *Revue des Études Sud-Est Européennes*, 21 (1983), 177–81.

Daniel Mornet, 'Les enseignements des bibliothèques privées (1750–1780)', *Revue d'histoire littéraire de la France*, 17 (1910), 448–96.

Patrick O'Brien, 'The political economy of British taxation, 1660–1815', *Economic History Review*, 41 (1988), 1–32.

Patrick O'Brien *et al.*, 'Political components of the Industrial Revolution: Parliament and the English cotton textile industry, 1660–1774', *Economic History Review*, 44 (1991), 395–423.

William O'Reilly, 'Genealogies of Atlantic history', *Atlantic Studies*, I, 1 (2004), pp. 66–84.

Edward Ousselin, 'L'homme aux quarante écus: Voltaire économiste', *French Review*, 22 (1999), 493–502.

Bruno Racle *et al.*, 'Voltaire entrepreneur d'horlogerie', *Bulletin de l'association nationale des collectionneurs et amateurs d'horlogerie et d'art*, 74 (1995), 5–28.

Marc Serge Rivière, 'Contemporary reactions to the early editions of *Le Siècle de Louis XIV*', *Studies on Voltaire and the eighteenth century*, 266 (1989), 225–52.

Richard Roehl, 'Economic growth in Britain and France, 1780–1914 by Patrick O'Brien and Caglar Keyder', *Journal of Economic History*, 39 (1979), 778–9.

Emma Rothschild, 'An alarming commercial crisis in eighteenth-century Angoulême: sentiments in economic history', *Economic History Review*, 51 (1998), 268–93.

Emma Rotschild, 'Global commerce and the question of sovereignty in the eighteenth-century provinces', *Modern Intellectual History*, 1 (2004), 3–25.

Winfried Schröder, 'Zum Bedeutungs- und Funktionswandel des Wortes "Industrie" ', *Lendemains* (1976), 45–62.

Henri Sée, 'A propos du mot "industrie" ', *Revue Historique*, 149 (1925), 58–61.

Henri Sée, 'Bulletin historique, histoire économique et sociale', *Revue Historique*, 158 (1928), 297–335.

Philippe Steiner, 'J.-B. Say and the political economy of his time: a quantitative approach', *Journal of the History of Economic Thought*, 21 (1999), 349–68.

Jérôme Vercruysse, 'Turgot et Vergennes contre la lettre de Voltaire à Boncerf', *Studies on Voltaire and the eighteenth century*, 67 (1969), 65–71.

CD ROM

Denis Diderot *et al.*, eds, *Encyclopédie de Diderot et D'Alembert sur CD-ROM (conforme aux 17 volumes de l'édition originale 1751–1765)*, REDON, publ., Version 1.0.0.

Voltaire, *Voltaire électronique*, Voltaire Foundation and Chadwyck-Healey, publ., Version 1.0.

Unpublished PhD dissertations

Simone Dailey, 'Voltaire et les physiocrates' (unpublished PhD thesis, University of Massachusetts, 1972).

Michael Fodor, 'De l'ancien régime à la nouvelle économie. Lettres françaises et économie au dix-huitième siècle' (unpublished PhD thesis, Harvard University, 1999).

Alicia Morris, 'A new interpretation of Voltaire's tale "L'homme aux quarante écus" ' (unpublished PhD thesis, University of Massachusetts, 1978).

Jane Tucker-Vasiliou, 'The reflection of money in eighteenth-century French literature' (unpublished PhD thesis, CUNY, 1998).

Index